NO SINGLE THREAD
Psychological Health in Family Systems

No Single Thread

Psychological Health in Family Systems

by

JERRY M. LEWIS, M.D.
W. ROBERT BEAVERS, M.D.
JOHN T. GOSSETT, PH.D.
VIRGINIA AUSTIN PHILLIPS

Timberlawn Foundation
Dallas, Texas

BRUNNER/MAZEL, *Publishers*   New York

SECOND PRINTING

Copyright © 1976 by BRUNNER/MAZEL, INC.

Published by
BRUNNER/MAZEL, INC.
19 Union Square West, New York, New York 10003

MANUFACTURED IN THE UNITED STATES OF AMERICA

Library of Congress Cataloging in Publication Data
Main entry under title:
No single thread: psychological health in family systems.
    Includes bibliographies.
    1. Mental hygiene.   2. Family.   I.   Lewis, Jerry M.,
1924-   [DNLM: 1. Family   2. Mental health.
3. Interpersonal relations.   HQ728 N739]
RA790.5.N6   613   75-25777
ISBN 0-87630-111-1

This book is dedicated to the memory of
WILLIAM H. DICKINSON, JR., B.D., D.D.
without whose belief and support the study
might not have evolved.

"Once the realization is accepted that even between the closest human beings infinite distances continue to exist, a wonderful living side by side can grow up, if they succeed in loving the distance between them which makes it possible for each to see the other whole against the sky."

RAINER MARIA RILKE

PREFACE

TODAY—WORKERS in the fields of psychiatry and psychology and all other fields interested in the study of man have come home to a deeper comprehension of the function of the family in the ongoing development and life-style of each individual family member.

Today—we are not only able *to listen to individuals talk about* their early life and relationships to and with the members of their family network in order to gain insight—we are also able to interview and *record their verbal and nonverbal interactions with each other on videotape.* By utilizing the achievements of modern technological science which have made high quality television equipment available at low cost for use in our field, the authors have recorded, for repeated review, study and research, family interactions and systems which have allowed them to conduct a large-scale pioneering study of how families function. Their research is based largely on the study of family systems which has been a widely accepted outgrowth and practical application of general systems theory. In accord with scientific tradition, the authors present as background for their work:

1) The data from sociopsychological studies of healthy families, based on the study of individuals and followed by the creation of a composite picture of their family;

2) The clues from control groups used in interactional studies of dysfunctional families; and

3) The growing body of theoretical writings about optimally functioning family systems.

The authors are modest in their conclusions and are well aware that the socio-economic-religious background of the families studied in their project is narrow. Nevertheless, I believe that the microscopic analysis of the family systems, focused on in their videotapes, has enough basis to allow for the significant generalizations made about optimally functioning or "healthy" families, as well as about those families which function less optimally.

As workers in psychiatry have learned to modify their excessive goals for patients and families, there has been an increasing interest in and willingness to risk examination of the parameters of emotional and mental health in individuals and families.

Although their initial study involved patient-containing families, as well as families without patients, the authors gradually moved towards focusing their attention on healthy or competent families. They did not discard their earlier data which offered clear evidence that there is a significant correlation between the degree of family dysfunctioning and the severity of individual adolescent patient psychopathology. That research finding is in accord with clinical evidence reported by many workers.

Chapter IX is invaluable in its presentation of an overview of the findings. I found it of major interest to learn that the "adequate families resembled patently dysfunctional or midrange families in their oppositional attitudes, only modest respect for subjective world views, use of distancing communication mechanisms, less than firm parental coalitions, reliance upon simple explanations of human behavior, reduced spontaneity, and a tendency toward blandness in individual characteristics. The strengths of these adequate families which have militated against the development of individual symptomatology or family system dissolution included *high initiative* resulting in multiple family involvements with neighborhood and community, predictability of structure and function, high levels of self-esteem (often based upon favorable contrast of one's family to less fortunate others), and a firm belief in the value of family."

The authors of this book are to be commended for designing and successfully executing their research project. They have given psychiatrists, psychologists, social workers, nurses, educators, sociologists and all others interested in how families function significant facts and concepts useful in primary prevention, as well as in treatment intervention.

I predict that their findings will profoundly influence and alter our approach to understanding and working with individuals and families no matter what the setting or theoretical framework for our work. Perhaps even more important is the fact that they have delineated systems for examination by every family interested in its own competency and impact on all of its members.

MILTON M. BERGER, M.D.
Director, Education and Training,
South Beach Psychiatric Center
Clinical Associate Professor of Psychiatry
Down State Medical Center (S.U.N.Y.)

CONTENTS

Appendices

ACKNOWLEDGMENTS

THIS STUDY, CONSUMING SEVEN YEARS, involved the input of many individuals. We dedicate this book to the memory of William H. Dickinson, the late pastor of the Highland Park Methodist Church in Dallas. Doctor Dickinson, "Bill," was committed to the concept of research which offered the possibility of data to be used in primary prevention. His commitment led to a sizeable grant from his church, which enabled us to inaugurate the project. In addition, he played a crucial role in encouraging families to participate in the time-and-energy-consuming business of family research. He was assisted by other members of the church staff, in particular Rev. Kenneth Dickson, Associate Pastor, whose belief in the value of this research helped in many ways.

The Board of Trustees of Timberlawn Foundation not only encouraged the research staff in regard to this project, but developed additional funding. In particular, the authors would like to thank the following members of the Board: R. Vernon Coe, Trammell Crow, R. Percy Goyne, John R: Hill, Jr., Leo Patterson, Jr., and Charles E. Seay.

A number of other individuals or agencies supported the project at critical phases. We wish to acknowledge the support of the Jonsson Foundation, Doctor and Mrs. Floyd Norman, Mr. and Mrs. Philip Stewart, and the Timberlawn Psychiatric Hospital.

Many other individuals gave their time to this study. Raters included Jeanette Spier Beavers, M.S.S.W., Margie Buell, M.S.S.W., Roy H. Fanoni, M.D., Anne Gossett, Kay Hagebak, Madeline Hartford, M.D., Keith H. Johansen, M.D., Pat Lewis, R.N., Susan

Lewis, M.A., David H. Lipsher, Ph.D., Charles G. Markward, M.D., Stanley L. Seaton, M.D., Robert P. Stewart, M.S.S.W., David Switzer, Th.D., Larry E. Tripp, M.D., and Kathy Woods, M.S.S.W. Two experienced family therapists, Carroll David, M.S.S.W., and Bill Turnage, M.S.S.W., interviewed the families. Several graduate students were involved in various aspects of the project. Included in this group were Barbara Neill, R.N., M.S., and Stephen J. Oatis, Th.D. The research group was fortunate to enlist the services of several dedicated research volunteers. These included Frances McElvaney, Jean Stewart, R.N., and Gayle Morgan.

We wish also to acknowledge the assistance of F. David Barnhart, M.A., on conceptual and statistical issues.

During the years of this study, a number of devoted secretaries have worked on numerous drafts of the manuscript. In particular, we wish to emphasize our debt to Nannette Bruchey and Virginia Zinchak.

INTRODUCTION

THIS BOOK DESCRIBES an ongoing research project which searches for certain characteristics of optimally functioning or "healthy" families. Our research group was particularly interested in family variables which are interactional rather than based solely on individual observations. We have been significantly involved in the search for the quantifiable interactional variables necessary for healthy family functioning. This book reports our research efforts with 44 research volunteer families, which represent only a relatively small portion of the families studied thus far. The remainder are dysfunctional families with identified patients, who serve as extensions and controls for the study of capable families.

There is considerable literature regarding the pathological family types, but this book's specific focus is on the healthy family, regarding which there is a scarcity of data. To observe family functioning, we presented family members with a series of tasks for them as a family and videotaped their responses. Our interest was in the process of the interaction rather than the substances of their exchange. The videotapes of families interacting together are analyzed from three different levels: the "clinical eye," rating scales, and a microanalytic or "counting" method.

Our work originated with the hope that if the qualities of families which produce capable, adaptive, and healthy individuals can be known and understood, we may be able to teach those involved in helping roles: parents, teachers, mental health professionals. Thus, this research is aimed at finding facts and concepts useful in primary prevention as well as treatment intervention.

The following outline is a brief resume of the flow of this presentation:

Chapter I

Here we explore our reasons for research involvement with healthy families, particularly examining the value of the family in this culture and the relative absence of normative data. Our primary methodological approach to the study of families was largely based on family systems research, itself an outgrowth of general systems theory. However, we review traditional sociopsychological studies of healthy families (that is, those based upon interviewing or studying individuals and putting together a composite of the family), the clues from control groups used in interactional studies of dysfunctional families, and the growing body of theoretical writings about optimally functioning systems. We also describe a representative work from each of these perspectives.

It is in this initial chapter that we also attempt to deal with a variety of issues which perplex any research effort in the area of normality or health. We strongly believe that health cannot be studied independently of time, place, and values.

We also share with the reader historical and evolutional aspects of the project which, in the beginning, were based upon purely clinical concerns and gradually assumed a basic research orientation.

Chapter II

In this chapter we describe the evolution of our initial research effort involving a small group of 11 volunteer families and 12 patient-containing families. We describe our methodology in detail and discuss the initial and fundamental questions regarding the reliability and validity of observations about level of health in the family. A number of other issues, for example the correlation between the quality of the parental marriage and the degree of health in the whole family, are approached in this chapter.

Chapter III

At this stage of the evolution of the research project, W. Robert Beavers joined the research team, bringing with him prior experience in family research with dysfunctional families and an evolving theoretical framework for the study of families. This is the only chapter in the book which carries individual credit. This chapter presents a comprehensive, coherent framework for family system characteristics that produce healthy children, as well as those associated with a variety of disturbed children. A theoretical framework is presented and central system characteristics are elaborated, including the power structure of the family, the tolerance of the family for individuation and autonomous functioning, the affect or feeling tone of the family, the family's perception of reality, and the family's capacity for acceptance of loss.

Chapter IV

In this chapter we move to the replication study and consider data analysis at the level of rating scales which we have developed and with which we now have considerable experience. These rating scales, each of which attempts to quantify interactional or family system characteristics, have now been used to rate 120 families, including the 33 healthy families in the replication study. These 13 rating scales are firmly based in the theory presented in Chapter III.

Chapter V

This chapter concerns itself with clinical observations of the final group of 12 families; six of these were seen as "optimally" functioning, and six were "adequate" in their functioning but represented a group quite distinct from the optimal families. Each of these 12 families underwent six hours of videotaped exploratory family interviews—three hours by each of two experienced family therapists. One of the authors (WRB) intensively reviewed the 72 hours of family interviews, and we present his clinical overview of these 12 families.

Chapter VI

Chapter VI presents the microanalytic or "counting" approach to data analysis, which was applied to communication sequences from the six optimal and six adequate families. This finely focused method, derived by family research investigators in another setting, allowed a reliability check on the more global observations described in Chapter V.

Chapter VII

In addition to our primary commitment to an interactional or family systems approach, we also were interested in individual characteristics of the family members. Each of the 55 individuals in the 12 families selected for intensive study underwent exploratory psychiatric interviews, and 43 of the individuals also were administered psychological tests. In this chapter we look at the view one gets of a family from studying the individuals and developing a composite of the family, contrasting that view with the data one gets from studying the family together as a system.

Chapter VIII

Part of our research interest was in the physical as well as the emotional health of the families, especially in whether or not we could find clues to suggest that there are ways of being a family which are associated with greater or lesser vulnerability to all physical illnesses. This chapter reviews the psychophysiologic literature relating to general susceptibility to illness in individuals, as well as those few studies which have had as their focus the family as the unit of illness. Our findings in this chapter must be considered tentative and need to be incorporated in a predictive design. Nevertheless, because of their provocativeness we have included these data and interpretations.

Chapter IX

In this chapter we summarize and discuss our findings in regard to healthy families and articulate as clearly as possible those threads which emerge from the various levels of data analysis. In addition, we relate our findings to other relevant studies.

Chapter X

The final chapter explores implications of the findings for mental health clinicians. The research data should have implications for both the family therapist and, at a greater level of inference, the clinician who does individual or group psychotherapy.

Above all, this volume is a collaborative effort of the four authors, who hopefully have functioned as a healthy family in attempting to produce what we believe is the most intensive study of the ingredients of the healthy family in our society.

NO SINGLE THREAD
Psychological Health in Family Systems

CHAPTER I

ISSUES AND EVOLUTION
OF THE STUDY

AT A TIME WHEN there are multiple pressures to use all available energies in the treatment of individuals and families who present themselves as troubled, we believe there are compelling reasons to study healthy families. This belief constitutes a significant initial impetus to report this phase of our research.

Early in our use of research methodologies in the exploration of family systems, it became apparent that these methods had not been focused specifically on healthy families. In the past decade there has been a growing literature reporting the results of systems research with disturbed families. Lidz, Fleck, and Cornelison (17, 18) studied in detail, over a period of 12 years, 17 families with a schizophrenic offspring and an asymptomatic sibling. They employed multiple techniques, individual and interactional, to explore the intrafamilial environment in which the schizophrenic patients grew up. Stabeneau, Tupin, Werner, and Pollin (30) described the transactional characteristics which differentiated groups of families who produced a schizophrenic, a delinquent, or a normal child. Wynne and Singer (36), focusing on structure rather than content, described the relationship between differing patterns of family transactions and types of schizophrenic thought disorders in the offspring. These provocative studies suggested that families containing an identified psychiatric patient demonstrated different interactional patterns than did families selected on the basis

1

of absence of individual patienthood. In spite of the various interpretations which can be made regarding such findings, we were
impressed that such interactional measures were not only predictors of considerable strength, but also quantifiable methods of
comparing and contrasting a wide spectrum of families. Both the
availability of these techniques and the fact that they had not
been used in healthy family studies played a role in stimulating
our efforts.

Another factor which lured us to this project was our commitment to the family as a social system crucial to the continuation
of man. Turnbull (34), in his provocative field work with the Ik,
described what may happen under adverse circumstances. Specifically, he noted that, under the threat of starvation (and we
would add, the inability to affect their own destiny), the Ik lost
their capacity for any except exploitative relationships. Caring,
goodness, loving, and hope disappeared as family ties ruptured
and each individual became, in truth, an island. This extreme
form of social and family disorganization may result when a culture loses control of its own destiny, loses viable strength-giving
myths, and becomes helpless to effect change. It is our view that
studies relating to optimal family functioning can provide significant information for a society concerning the business of
evolving a structure—specifically, family structure—that is most
adaptive to changing environmental demands.

At a time when authors such as Laing (14), Esterson (15), and
Cooper (5) speak of the "death" of the family, we are struck by
the absence of any other readily available way to achieve what
Parsons (24) defines as the primary family tasks: the socialization
of the children and the stabilization of adult personalities. We
believe that those clinicians and researchers who conclude that
the family is invariably stultifying and often lethal in its impact
on the individual have experienced few, if any, adequately or
optimally functioning families. It is quite possible that a prolonged
clinical or research exposure to severely pathological families containing psychotic individuals may contaminate one's view of all
families. It is our view that the attempt to depreciate the prevalent

family system, in an effort to achieve a radically different method of producing competent adults, is premature if we fail to explore the healthy end of the family spectrum to delineate clearly those factors that make many current families competent. This is not to oppose experimenting with new family forms, especially those variations in social structure that allow people bereft of families to find and give nourishment in an intimate, formalized, and ritualized structure (19). Indeed, the criticism that the nuclear family system prevalent in the Western world excludes many single individuals and places a great demand on individual autonomy is well taken. It is our hope, however, that information about successful family systems will enable us to achieve intelligent change rather than use the family as a convenient "whipping boy" for personal developmental failures.*

A third source of stimulation for our research was the need for interactional norms for family health. Because of this striking deficiency in our knowledge, there is no realistic perspective for understanding dysfunctional families. Do features of family interactions which appear to characterize dysfunctional families occur as often, to a lesser degree, or not at all in healthy families? If such features are noted, how do they differ (if at all) from those seen in dysfunctional families? Clinicians have not known, but only speculated, whether healthy families *invariably* demonstrate a single feature, a small group of features, or a wide variety of interactional features that distinguish them from dysfunctional families.

The historical preference for research in the pathological, as

---

* Cooper (5), for example, describes the family in this century as the ultimately perfected form of nonmeeting, specifying four ways in which the family has destructive impact upon its members. These are: 1) glueing people together based upon a sense of individual incompleteness; 2) predetermined roles rather than conditions which allow free formation of identity; 3) greater social controls than children need; and 4) the indoctrination of the children with an elaborate system of taboos.

Anthony Glyn (9) writes, "In the ideal British family, noncommunication among its various members should be as total as human ingenuity can make it." Certainly, such characteristics apply to a variety of dysfunctional families. We do not, however, find them descriptive of healthy families.

well as the relative ignorance of the functional, is, of course, common in research processes in all health fields. Because of the professional's humanistic interest in alleviating pain and suffering, his initial focus invariably is on the dysfunctional. As one example of this focus on the pathological, the mental health clinician has available to him much more data regarding families of schizophrenics than he does of healthy families. In addition, Burton et al. (4) and Henry et al. (13) have suggested that mental health clinicians as a group are very likely to come from somewhat dysfunctional families. If this is so, they may have an unusually difficult time in conceptualizing realistic family treatment goals, both from the impact of their training and their own personal experience. This adds weight to the need for data about healthy family processes, skills, and limits.

A fourth factor which influenced us to undertake this work is shared with other researchers in the field of family study. This is the belief that early ego development, however significant, does not completely determine adult behavior. The experiences of the early years of life (or their counterpart in experimental animals) are sometimes decisive, but more often must be considered within their interactional context. Subsequent events may range from repetitive reinforcement to extinction of early behavior patterns. Rigid adherence to an explanatory model which seals man's behavioral fate at age six or ten simply does not attend to the potency of social system determinants. Such a model seems as erroneous as it is excessively pessimistic. We view family systems research as providing a complementary focus to that provided by developmental studies. This commitment to multi-level explanatory systems has been a pervasive and continuing aspect of our study of healthy families.

Still another urgent need for healthy family studies involves the search for preventive methodologies in the mental health field. As data develop regarding the roles social structures play in individual emotional illness, the thrust of professional efforts can be directed toward ways to avert such dysfunction. The family, young families especially, is a logical focus. In a useful analogy, young families may be likened to an infant. The family as an organism undergoes a series of developmental sequences. Over time, a family's characteristic style of reacting may become increasingly "fixed." Young families, therefore, are reasonably unencumbered by family developmental events and may represent organisms unusually responsive to education. Some current educational efforts are sponsored by religious organizations under the rubric of "family life education." Concern about the effectiveness of such programs prompted one church to support this phase of our work. Their commitment, and ours, to the dream of prevention rests on a belief that, if we can identify the kinds of interactions which characterize healthy families, such interactional principles can be taught—that competence in the maintenance of sanity and the rearing of children can be learned.

In reviewing existing studies of families, we found they might be classified as traditional psychological studies, reports regarding the control families from interactional studies concerned with families of identified psychiatric patients, sociological studies, and theoretical writings about systems. These different sources of information and hypotheses cross many disciplinary boundaries. Aldous and Hill (1) in reviewing over 60 years of published family studies cite 12,850 publications and over 7,000 authors. Of the works written in English, focus has included primarily microscopic studies of marriage and divorce, transactions with groups, and the family as a small group; most investigators have taken an individual-psychological perspective. Despite the diversity of sources, there are parallels in data and constructs. For example, findings in regard to power distribution, flexibility, autonomy, expressiveness and openness to change are threads which can be seen in many different studies. To acquaint the reader with some of these studies, we will present an example for each of several sources which has been of particular value to us from the standpoint of theory, methods, findings and/or similar populations.

The traditional socio-psychological studies typically use interviews or tests of individuals in a family to construct a composite picture of the family. This approach relies on what individual family members are willing or able to share with the researcher. Although such individually based studies rely mostly upon content and do not measure interactional sequences, they frequently provide rich insights and hypotheses (22).

A representative of this type of study which has been particularly stimulating to our research group is *The Silent Majority* by Westley and Epstein (35). They investigated the relationship between college students' emotional health and the organization of their families. In their pilot study, ten first-year collegians who lived within ten miles of the university were selected from a sample of 170. Their selection was based on assessments by psychiatric interview and psychological tests. Two of the group were twins, so nine families were studied in depth. Each individual in each of the families was interviewed by a psychiatrist and a sociologist and given psychological tests. The parents were interviewed for a total of 20 to 30 hours and the children less intensively. The researchers became convinced that the way a family organized itself was both a consequence and a cause of the mental health or illness of family members.

To test this hypothesis they enlarged their study by investigating 96 of 100 freshmen who fulfilled the geographic criterion. Using an interview and testing approach to assess individual psychological health, the researchers selected the 20 most healthy and 20 least healthy, plus 56 in between. A higher proportion of the parents of the healthier students agreed to participate. The focus of their research was on the families of the ten at the top and the ten at the bottom of their ranking on health. These families were middle- and upper-middle class, described as "typical urbanites, lacking in friends, distant from neighbors . . ." All were functioning, successful, responsible members of the community. It is noteworthy that all the students were living at home, were "very inexperienced sexually," and demonstrated no significant rebellion. They were good students, and 70 percent were the first or only child.*

---

* This study highlights the difficulty in sampling procedures. It is not clear, for example, whether the geographic criterion skewed this population in the direction of a more conservative family structure.

Westley and Epstein defined family organization as the durable modes of relationships between the family members. They studied five dimensions: 1) power, 2) psychodynamics, 3) roles, 4) status, and 5) work. Other investigators had demonstrated considerable consistency in their findings that families vary in the way power is distributed and that such differences are influenced by social class, ethnicity, individual competence, achievement, motivation, and psychopathology. In their own study, Westley and Epstein derived their data regarding power on estimates from individual family members. They found five patterns: father-dominant, father-led, equalitarian, mother-led, and mother-dominant. Of particular interest to us was the finding that the children of the father-led families had a greater chance of being healthy while 64 percent of the children from equalitarian families were in the emotionally disturbed group. In fact, Westley and Epstein stated, ". . . democratic family council . . . is no more or less than the evasion of responsibility, and families who make this choice often pay in indecision and structural chaos." They do, however, caution that the superiority of father-led families cannot be generalized to other samples.

Regarding psychodynamic organization, the authors suggested that the form of organization that meets all the needs of the family varies and, for any given culture and time, there probably is a form of family organization which is optimal. Under "family functioning and relationships" they subsumed a host of factors varying from problem solving, communication, affective expression, autonomy, presence or absence of psychopathology, degree of warmth, balance of parental dominance, to role projection by the parents. These family variables clearly distinguished the healthy and sick students, but with such a high degree of interrelationship as to suggest two groups of similar variables: problem solving and communication variables and balance of autonomy and dependency. These data suggested that if both parents are disturbed, the children almost certainly will be; if both parents are healthy, so will the children be; if one parent is healthy and one disturbed, the children will be healthy if the parental relationship is warm and supportive; that is, the factor critical to the emotional health of the children was the nature of the relationship between the parents.

Three other dimensions of family organization—division of labor, social class and mobility, and family roles—suggested another cluster of variables which correlate with the health of the children. Included were partial sharing of household responsibilities, a high frequency and satisfaction of parental sexual intercourse, the presence of one strongly accepting parent, and the participation of the parent of the opposite sex in the care and rearing of the child.

This excellent, traditional, socio-psychological study with an overview of healthy families, presumably urban, upper-middle-class, and conservative, had a population in some respects similar to our own sample. Its major dependence upon the content of individual responses is typical for this kind of study. The possible contamination of results introduced by having the same judges rating both individual and family health is a fairly common fault.

There were a number of variables that correlated with high degrees of health of the children. The parental marriage was successful, with considerable shared responsibility in the home and a continuing high level of sexual interest and activity. Within the family, power was more apt to occur in a father-led pattern. Problems were approached early and effectively; communication was open and direct. A balance of dependency and autonomy was achieved. Throughout this study, the centrality of the relationship existing between the parents was stressed as a major determinant of the health of the children.

A second source of data and hypotheses regarding family health is the information regarding control families from interactional studies. These controls, although frequently matched as to demographic characteristics, are often chosen on the basis of a single criterion, i.e., no member of the family is receiving treatment for an emotional disturbance. Health, or normality, is defined as the absence of treated pathology at the level of the individual. The presumption that such families are normal, or healthy, and comprise a homogeneous group against which families containing identified psychiatric patients may be contrasted is open to question, but it is a logical technique for screening families in the initial stage of family systems research and provides valuable clues regarding family health.

Typically, a small group of patient families and the control group of families are asked to respond to identical stimuli, solve an identical problem or resolve intrafamily disagreement. Responses are recorded and transcripts analyzed from several points of view, mostly interactional. Provocative differences in a large number of variables, such as intrusions, silences, communication sequences, and interruptions are noted between the two groups of families. The interpretation of these differences is unsettled, however. The presumption that such differences are etiologic in regard to the identified patient's disturbance must be counterbalanced by the possibility that the differences either are responsive to the presence of the patient in the families of one group or reflect differences in "set" between the two groups.

In a study marked by unusually precise methodology, Mishler and Waxler (20) report a long-range interactional study comparing three groups of families: families with a schizophrenic child with a good premorbid social adjustment; families with a schizophrenic child with a poor premorbid social adjustment; and a control group with no child having a history of psychiatric hospitalization. These families were studied in a session involving the parents and the schizophrenic child and a session involving the parents and a well sibling. Strodbeck's (31) Revealed Differences Technique was used to generate discussion among the three family members. There were approximately 1800 communication acts per session; 20 different interaction codes were applied to each act. The interaction codes, designed to measure aspects of communication, were clinically relevant to a perspective regarding the family as related to the etiology of schizophrenia. They included measures of such variables as affective expressiveness, imperviousness, speech fragments, interruptions, and silences.

The five major areas of interactional differences among the groups were: 1) expressiveness, 2) power: the strategy of attention control, 3) power: the strategy of person control, 4) disruptions in communications, and 5) responsiveness. They found that the control families were more expressive and more positive in affect, unselective in the target toward whom feelings were expressed, and flexible in terms of roles. There were clear generational boundaries: father held the most power, mother somewhat less, and the child distinctly least. The parental coalition was strong with a clear hierarchy, but power was not exercised in an authoritarian or rigid manner. Communications were more disruptive than in families containing schizophrenics. At the same time, control families demonstrated greater responsiveness to each other's statements than families with patients.

This very meticulously conducted study of the verbal interactions of three-member family groups demonstrates both the extremely tedious nature of research in verbal communication and the nature of the variables which appear to distinguish functional and dysfunctional families.

Another source of hypotheses about healthy families lies in the theoretical writings regarding family systems. Subsequent to the development of General Systems Theory, Buckley (3) reviewed that literature and attempted to develop a parallel conceptual framework from which to view sociocultural phenomena. Speer (28), in a paper questioning the concept of homeostasis as an adequate construct for complex, adaptive systems, reviews Buckley's concepts and attempts to relate them to a view of the family.

In this system, "feedback" is categorized as either negative or deviation-counteracting, which leads to homeostasis, sameness, or change-resistant operations, or as positive, deviation-amplifying operations through which growth or creativity may occur within a system. In order to survive, complex, adaptive systems must be capable of positive feedback, or morphogenic operations which lead to change in structure, organization and values. Such systems are open internally as well as externally. They are capable of self-direction rather than a limited responsive adaptability to external events. In terms of Buckley's theoretical system, a maximally viable social system (such as a healthy family) would be characterized by: 1) complex structural relationships, i.e., in communication and interactions; 2) a highly flexible organization capable of change from within the system; 3) highly autonomous components with a minimum of constraint in intercomponent relationships; 4) considerable intrasystem determinism and causality of system and component behavior; 5) the ability to tolerate basic change in the system; and 6) the necessity of a constant flow of a wide range of information, experience, and input into the system.

In his challenge of the usefulness of the concept of homeostasis in the understanding of family systems, Speer reviews several interactional studies which support his postulated relationship between family system viability (health) and flexibility, autonomy, and absence of rigid constraint in system structure. He emphasizes that it may well be that disturbances of homeostasis within a family are positive, and that homeostasis itself may be one form of dysfunction. Important to our purposes is his observation, "We know almost nothing about the satisfaction, closeness, meaning-achieving, autonomy, problem-solving, communication, change, and basic relationship-organizing processes of exceptionally well-functioning, broadly and deeply satisfied families."

We attempted to search out, from whatever source, those findings which were interactional, quantifiable, and crucial to the optimal functioning of families. We found that little is known systematically about the processes of healthy family systems, and that there was a real and primary need for interactional studies that investigate the system operations of healthy families directly.

ISSUES

A research group interested in studying health at the level of family systems encounters many complicated questions ranging from the philosophical to the methodological. Some, particularly those philosophical issues involving value systems and judgments, are solvable only in arbitrary ways. In this section we hope to present such issues and indicate our stance as clearly and explicitly as possible.

In saying "this is healthy and this is not," we are mindful that descriptive labels in regard to human behavior have grave potential for misuse. Currently, for example, debate rages regarding psychiatric diagnosis (one descriptive system). Szasz (32) calls for the cessation of all psychiatric diagnostic labels, both on the basis of the lack of precision of the terms and on the ground that social stigma frequently results, and Ryder (26) expresses concern over the destructive political use of diagnostic labels.

Some (6,8) point to the dangers of researchers projecting their own value system, rediscovering them as "objective" criteria of health, and then using them "against" populations of differing value orientations. Others (5) expressed concern that the social mediating function of the family is used to reinforce the power of the ruling class in an exploitative society. This can be accomplished by the family providing a controllable paradigmatic form for every social institution—school, union, university, etc. Halleck (12), in a pungent comment, points out that one cannot define normalcy without making a statement of what ought to be. He is concerned, therefore, that the power to define normality or health can be used either to encourage or to resist changes in society. Though these dangers exist, we feel that the understanding of a great deal of human suffering can evolve from the use of descriptive systems. In this we are in substantial agreement with Lennard (16) in his discussion of the purposes and values of such systems. He notes that they: 1) enable one to summarize diverse observations and separate out common aspects; 2) enable comparisons which may point out similarities and differences; 3) enable the testing of hypotheses and development of new hypotheses; and 4) encourage one to face and solve conceptual problems.

What is meant by "health"? What is meant by "normal"? These questions of definition raise a complicated issue. Each has been defined in a number of ways and they are often used interchangeably. Offer and Sabshin (21,27) have brought together the literature related to definition of these terms in a way we found helpful. Although their focus was on the construct of "normality," their system illustrates various approaches to the definition of "health." With some paraphrasing, their four perspectives yield the following: 1) Health defined as the absence of overt pathology, including the traditional medical and psychiatric approaches. To view health as a reasonable, rather than optimal, level of function may be attacked as simplistic. However, it may have research and conceptual advantages if pathology is easier to measure than health. 2) Health defined as "optimal functioning" determined by a theoretical system. This approach is typified by psychoanalytic theory. This conceptualization springs from Freud's (7) description of normality or health as an ideal fiction. It is finding increasing use by theorists in preventive medicine. Offer and Sabshin suggest that this framework may become more prominent as medical advances eradicate grosser forms of disease. 3) Health defined as average functioning; this approach is characteristic of normative studies of behavior. It is a statistically oriented concept that views the midrange, majority of a population as healthy and either extreme as deviant. 4) Health defined as process, a perspective which takes into account the changes in systems over time. Offer and Sabshin emphasize the interdependence of these four perspectives within the total field of the study of normality. In actual practice, investigators may adopt one of the more limited definitions in the early stages of their work and then move toward adopting a less cross-sectional approach. Parsons' (24) social-psychological theory of socialization is clearly based in this approach.

At various stages of our study of healthy families we also have used different perspectives. In our initial sampling procedures we selected families on the basis of absence of individual psychopathology; that is, health was defined as absence of individual symptomatology. To this group of families, however, we have applied a series of discriminating judgments which arranged our sample along a continuum of health-pathology. This ranking allowed us to begin defining health as optimal functioning as determined by a theoretical system. Finally, in the theoretical system employed, the processes involved in growth-promoting changes are specifically attended. Thus, we have attempted to evolve a system of judgment that is both theoretically coherent and also related to empirical data. By optimal functioning we mean not just a passive adaptability to circumstances, but rather a set that reaches toward change, intrasystem determinism and innovation.

Another question of definition concerned the term "family." Our current research focuses upon the nuclear family. Despite some experimentation, this is the model currently most used in the Western world. Each nuclear family evolves systematic ways of being a family: communicating, problem solving, meeting the members' needs for affection and intimacy, resolving conflict, and dealing with loss and change. We are particularly interested in those systematic processes which may be seen as the structural components of the family's functioning.

We do not believe that health can be defined except in reference to context. In particular, we respect the impact of culture, history, and social class on the definition of family health. We believe that psychological health cannot have a value-free, universal applicability. Any system for distinguishing the functional from the dysfunctional must involve a consideration of culture-bound values, and that which is adaptive or creative in one era, culture, or socioeconomic class may well be maladaptive in another.

The work of Spiegel and Kluckhohn (29) has been significant in ordering our thinking. Their system suggests four basic value orientations which may differ from one culture to another. These orientations reflect problems crucial to all human groups: 1) What is the relation of man to nature? Cultures may be classified as seeing man subjugated by nature, harmonious with nature, or master over nature. 2) What is the temporal focus of human life? It may be the past, the present, or the future. 3) What is the modality of human activity? It may be being, being-in-becoming, or doing. 4) What is the modality of man's relationship to other men? It may be lineal, collateral, or individualistic.

In this organizational framework for values, it appears that Western man prizes mastery over nature, the future, doing, and individualism. It is impossible to define health without reference to such important contextual factors. Representing the majority, or modal values, these current, essentially "middle-class" values may reflect an evolved response particularly suited for the idio-syncratic complexities of a technological culture (23).

Complicating the difficulty of describing values is the issue of historical relevance. As cultures change, values change (25), re-quiring that assessment of the temporal context in which family health is investigated be altered. This process of cultural evolu-tion presents no particular problem for the investigator as long as the rate of change is gradual, as perhaps measured in centuries. However, if our culture is changing as rapidly as some observers suggest (33), the relevance of data gathered currently may very quickly be out of date. Researchers may be in the position of parents of today's children whom Margaret Mead (19) describes as being like immigrants to a new land who must learn from their children how to get along in the new environment.

Evolution of the Healthy Family Project

Research often begins as a result of clinical observations or needs. In the early stages the developmental course of research in the mental health fields is often a tortuous one and frequently unforeseen circumstances have decisive impact. Ours was no excep-tion; factors bound up with the lives of the researchers influenced the direction our project took.

In 1966 two of the authors (JML, JTG) were involved in a major reorganization of an inpatient adolescent service of a psy-chiatric hospital. An increasing number of the referred adolescents represented treatment failures of prior outpatient psychotherapy or brief, crisis-oriented hospitalization. These youngsters presented severe psychopathology and their inpatient treatment often lasted many months. As a consequence, the treatment team came to real-ize that, over time, they would have the opportunity to interact with only a relatively small number of patients. This observation, augmented by the clinical interest in understanding more about therapeutic success and failure, led to a clinical commitment to follow each patient for at least five years after discharge. The aim initially was to learn, with as much certainty as possible, with whom and to what degree the staff had succeeded. For several years, therefore, the entire adolescent treatment staff devoted the time necessary for such follow-up data collection.

During those years, three of the authors (JML, JTG, VAP) initiated a more formal project (9a, 10, 11, 16a) attempting to relate three general groups of variables to the patient's functioning five years after the hospital treatment. The first group concerned the patient's psychopathology. A number of instruments were designed in an effort to measure as much of the richness and depth of this area as possible. The second cluster of variables had to do with treatment. Here the interest was the staff's relationships to and attitudes toward individual patients, as well as the more formal characteristics of the treatment process. The third group of variables involved the attempt to measure critical aspects of the functioning of the adolescent patient's family.

The last area of the research came about because, while the psychopathology of some of the youngsters we observed seemed clearly related to early developmental difficulties, for other patients psychopathology appeared to be most significantly influenced by severe ongoing family disturbance. For a great many, of course, both factors were evident. However, those patients who seemed more clearly to reflect primarily either early developmental defects or ongoing family pathology were of particular interest, both clinically and for research purposes. If the observations were valid, the treatment of these two groups of patients might have quite different emphases, courses, and outcome.

In distinguishing these polar groups, intensive interviewing of the patient and his family was adequate for clinical purposes. For research purposes, however, the transcripts of these interviews, while rich with clinical meaning, did not lend themselves to adequate comparison of families; that is, they were not quantifiable.

Our search for a research instrument which would allow us to collect data about families that could be quantified led to the growing literature in family systems research. The literature search encouraged us to proceed toward a more structured analysis of patient-family functioning. Accordingly, we designed a format for a videotaped interview which included two tasks reported by other investigators and three devised to explore other areas of our interest. A small series of families of consecutively admitted adolescent inpatients and a comparable control group participated in these videotaped family interactional tasks. The control families were volunteers from a local Protestant Church and were demographically comparable to the patient families. The interviews for this pilot study were conducted in the summer and fall of 1968.

This small sample of 23 families (12 patient, 11 control), each with a child in mid-adolescence, provided us with our initial family interactional data. Each family came to the research setting to participate, as a family, in the five-part interactional procedure which was videotaped. Our objective was to find a technique with which to quantify interactional data in order to compare families. By this means we hoped to assess the role of family interaction in the long-term outcome of hospitalized adolescents.

The findings from the first stage of our work will be presented in Chapter II. For purposes of describing the evolution of the Healthy Family Project, involvement with this sample of 23 families was itself a crucial experience for the research team. It was from the opportunity to see the group of families judged by raters to be most healthy that the interest of the research staff in the interactional study of healthy family systems originated. Our excitement, pleasure, and interest in studying such families grew. This interest was enhanced by the possibility of expanding the application of systems-based interactional theory to healthy families. As noted earlier, there were several sources of information about healthy families, but we did not find direct studies of healthy families using systems concepts and interactional measurements in the psychiatric literature.

This pilot project also brought the fourth author (WRB) in as a key member of the research team. Initially, he was one of the 13 raters who evaluated the videotaped segments. His ratings of family health-pathology were determined by a rating system he evolved that measured a number of discrete variables which were interactional in nature. He brought to the research team prior experience in family systems research and an evolving theoretical orientation about systems, families, and their relationship to the metapsychology of the individual.

The videotapes of the structured Family Interactional Tasks became a significant source of data for the Adolescent Treatment Evaluation Project, and they continue to be used also as a resource for the clinical staff. This instrument provided the investigators with an abundant source of comparable data regarding both severely dysfunctional families and families whom we have come to term "midrange" (2). With our interest stimulated by the most healthy families from the control group, it became obvious that further investigation of a larger sample of families would be of value in providing basic information about families over a wide range of functioning (from most healthy to most disturbed).

The pastor and staff of the church which had provided us with the initial group of control families were again a source of crucial help. They assisted in finding another cohort of families and included three years' fiscal support of the project in their church budget. The belief of this pastor and his staff in the importance of investigating life in healthy families, and their ability to communicate their belief to the appropriate board and committees of the church, breathed life into this study.

Selection of our subsequent sample of presumably healthy families was a two-step process. The first group was chosen, in part, on the basis of absence of individual patienthood. After their participation in the videotaped Family Interaction Tasks, the group was ranked as to global health-pathology. This process enabled us to select two smaller groups to be explored more intensively. One group was made up of six families judged to be at the most functional end of the rank; another group of six, though capable and competent, was not seen as optimal. This focus on families at different levels of function without, however, the presence of an "identified patient," allowed us to search for differences unrelated to either the presence of a patient or different family expectations about the testing.

A list of all families on the church roll containing an adolescent was surveyed by the church staff in order to exclude those known to have significant problems. Each of the remaining 137 families received a letter from the pastor informing them of the project and inviting them to attend a meeting with the research team. This meeting served to explain to the families the nature of the project and something of the time and energy required of those who participated. The criteria for participation included: 1) biological intactness of the family; 2) oldest child in mid-adolescence; 3) no family member in psychological difficulty for the past year as manifested by a self-acknowledged psychiatric syndrome, having received any psychological treatment, or being in legal difficulty. Thirty-three families who fulfilled these criteria volunteered to participate.*

Each family came to the research facility for the initial data gathering; a family interview covering the current life situation of the family members, an extensive medical history, and a videotaping of their responses to the five Family Interactional Tasks were completed. Each of the 33 families also was asked to make a detailed daily record of the state of each family member's physical health, including physical symptoms, medication, professional medical care, hospital days, and any related concurrent events. These records were maintained for six months by 31 families.

A segment of each videotape was viewed by four psychiatrists who independently rated the family's health at a global level. On the basis of these ratings, 12 families were selected for more intensive investigation. Each of the 12 families was interviewed by two experienced family therapists. Each therapist saw each family for three hours, the interviews were videotaped, and the therapists dictated summaries of their observations of each family. In addition to these videotaped exploratory family interviews at the research facility, the families were seen in their homes

---

*Although something is known of the volunteering process at the level of the individual, we are unaware of comparable systematic studies at the level of the family. Westley and Epstein found that a higher proportion of healthy families agreed to participate than of disturbed families.

for exploratory psychiatric interviews with the individuals. Those members over 13 years old (N=43) completed Minnesota Multiphasic Personality Inventories and Shipley-Hartford Intelligence Tests.

We have approached analysis of these data at three levels which reflect different degrees of clinical depth and quantification: the level of clinical evaluation, the level of rating scales, and at a microanalytic level. We wish to stress our awareness of the small size and the narrowness of our sample. All of our 44 non-patient containing families (11 pilot, 33 replication) were white, Protestant, middle- or upper-middle-class, and they belonged to the same large, urban church. Each family volunteered to participate in a project studying family health. They did so at the urging of their pastor and with the knowledge that the project was supported by the church budget. These factors limit the generalizations which can be made to other families and other contexts. We have used this sample because these families were available to us and shared demographic and cultural characteristics, but the homogeneity was an advantage since it diminished the cultural variables that must be involved to explain family differences. Our hope is to learn enough about this sample that we will be able to extend our investigation of variables that influence family health to families of different socioeconomic and ethnic backgrounds.

A characteristic of this group of families that was of great importance to us was their degree of commitment to the research. They were active, "doing" families, all very much involved with community, church, and school. At times, their commitment to our interests must have been burdensome; despite this, they gave up evening and week-end time, and accommodated our complicated arrangements. They were open and candid in discussing intimate, painful, or conflictual material. For most, there was little in the way of defensiveness. The research staff frequently experienced a sense of pleasure and excitement in response to the families. We felt this opportunity enriched our lives, since we, like most mental health professionals, have limited sources of information regarding families, deriving data from our own families of origin, our current families, and uncertain extrapolations from clinical work with dysfunctional families. None of these sources represents reliable information about health. It may be that exposure to the pathological in training and practice would be balanced better by a broader view, that experience with "health" is valuable in the development of a perspective for those who are committed to the helping professions.

Our primary goal has been to measure interactional data and our framework has been a systems orientation. However, we have also collected traditional, individually based, content-oriented data with which to compare and contrast the interactional data. Our information is cross-sectional in nature: we studied families at one time in their lives. Because of this limitation we hope to follow this group of families through their next developmental stage— their separation from their oldest child. Our larger goal is to be able to demonstrate that those variables which are necessary and significant in the development of capable, adaptive human beings can be identified, measured, and, hopefully, taught to those who will raise the next generation.

REFERENCES

1. ALDOUS, J., and HILL, R., *International Bibliography of Research in Marriage and the Family*, 1900-1964. Minneapolis: U. of Minnesota Press, 1967.
2. BEAVERS, W. R., LEWIS, J. M., GOSSETT, J. T., and PHILLIPS, V. A., Family systems and individual functioning: Mid-range families. Presented at the American Psychiatric Association Annual Meeting, Anaheim, California, May, 1975.
3. BUCKLEY, W. (Ed.), *Modern Systems Research for the Behavioral Scientist*. Chicago: Aldine Publishing Co., 1968.
4. BURTON, ARTHUR, ET AL., *Twelve Therapists*. San Francisco: Jossey-Bass, Inc., 1972.
5. COOPER, DAVID, *The Death of the Family*, New York: Pantheon, 1971.
6. DAVIS, KINGSLEY, Mental hygiene and the class structure. *Psychiatry*, 1:55-65, 1938.
7. FREUD, S., Analysis terminable and interminable, In J. Strachey (Ed.), *Collected Papers of Sigmund Freud*. New York: Basic Books, 1959.
8. GANS, HERBERT J., Some notes on the definition of mental health: An attempt from the perspective of a community planner. Unpublished Seminar, Mass. Gen. Hosp., Feb. 27, 1957.
9. GLYN, ANTHONY, *The British*, Life, 1970.
9a. GOSSETT, J. T., BARNHARDT, F. D., LEWIS, J. M., and PHILLIPS, V. A., Follow-up of adolescents treated in a psychiatric hospital: Predictors of outcome. *Arch. Gen. Psychiatry*, in press, 1976.

10. GOSSETT, J. T., LEWIS, S. B., LEWIS, J. M. and PHILLIPS, V. A., Follow-up of adolescents treated in a psychiatric hospital: I. A review of studies, *Am. J. Orthopsychiatry*, 43 (4): 602-610, 1973.

11. GOSSETT, J. T., MEEKS, J. E., BARNHARDT, F. D., and PHILLIPS, V. A., Follow-up of adolescents treated in a psychiatric hospital: Onset of symptomatology scale, *Adolescence*, in press, 1976.

12. HALLECK, S., *Politics of Therapy*, New York: Aronson, 1974.

13. HENRY, W.E., SIMS, J. H., SARAY, S. L., *The Fifth Profession*, San Francisco: Jossey-Bass, 1971.

14. LAING, R. D., *Politics of Experience*, New York: Pantheon Books, 1967.

15. LAING, R. D., and ESTERSON, A., Sanity, madness, and the family, Vol. 1 in *Families of Schizophrenics*, London: Tavistock, New York: Basic Books, 1964.

16. LENNARD, N. L., and BERNSTEIN A., *Patterns in Human Interaction*, San Francisco: Jossey-Bass, Inc., 1969.

16a. LEWIS, S. B., BARNHARDT, F. D., GOSSETT, J. T., and PHILLIPS, V. A., Follow-up of adolescents treated in a psychiatric hospital: Operational solutions to some methodological problems of clinical research, Accepted for publication, *Am. J. Orthopsychiatry*, 45 (5):813-824, 1975.

17. LIDZ, T., FLECK, S., ALANEN, Y. O., and CORNELISON, A., Schizophrenic patients and their siblings, *Psychiatry*, 26:1-18, 1963.

18. LIDZ, T., FLECK, S., and CORNELISON, A. R., *Schizophrenia and the Family*, New York: International Univ. Press, 1965.

19. MEAD, M., The American family: Reality or myth, The Scott Hawkins Lecture, Southern Methodist University, Dallas, Texas, March 31, 1970.

20. MISHLER, E., and WAXLER, N., *Interaction in Families*, New York: John Wiley and Sons, 1968.

21. OFFER, D., and SABSHIN, M., *Normality*, New York: Basic Books, 1966.

22. OTTO, H. A., Criteria for assessing family strength, *Family Process*, Vol. 2 (2), 329-338, Sept., 1963.

23. PARSONS, T., *The System of Modern Societies*, Englewood Cliffs, N. J.: Prentice-Hall, 1971.

24. PARSONS, T., and BALES, R., *Family, Socialization and Interaction Process*, Glencoe, Ill., Free Press, 1955.

25. RINDER, E. D., New directions and an old problem: The definition of normality, *Psychiatry*, 27:107-115, 1964.

26. RYDER, R. G., Psychology of the scientist XVIII, the factualizing game: A sickness of psychological research, *Psychol. Rep.*, 19:563-570, 1966.

27. SABSHIN, M., Psychiatric Perspectives on Normality, *Arch. Gen. Psychiat.*, Vol. 17, 258-264, Sept., 1967.

28. SPEER, D. C., Family systems: Morphostasis and morphogenesis, or is homeostasis enough?, *Family Process*, 9:259-278, 1970.

29. SPIEGEL, J. P., *Transactions: The Interplay Between Individual, Family and Society*, New York: Science House, 1971.

30. STABENEAU, J. R., TUPIN, J., WERNER, M., and POLLIN, W. A., A comparative study of families of schizophrenics, delinquents, and normals, *Psychiat.*, 28: 45-59, 1965.

31. STRODBECK, F. L., Husband-wife interaction over revealed differences, *Am. Sociol. Rev.*, 16:468-473, 1951.

32. SZASZ, J. S., *The Myth of Mental Illness*, New York: Hoeber, Inc., 1961.

33. TOFFLER, A., *Future Shock*, New York: Random House, 1970.

34. TURNBULL, COLIN M., *The Mountain People,* New York: Simon and Schuster, 1972.
35. WESTLEY, W. A., and EPSTEIN, N. B., *The Silent Majority,* San Francisco: Jossey-Bass, Inc., 1969.
36. WYNNE, L. C., and SINGER, M. T., Thought disorder and family relations of schizophrenics, *Arch. Gen. Psychiat.,* 9:191-206, 1963.

Chapter II

THE PILOT STUDY

OUR INITIAL INTEREST in recording and quantifying family interactions developed from the attempt to evaluate, in a systematic fashion, the influence of current family psychopathology upon the course and outcome of adolescent inpatient psychiatric treatment. Pursuing this goal, the research team conducted a pilot study investigation of 23 families—12 containing a recently admitted adolescent inpatient, and 11 controls. In this pilot study a series of basic questions were explored.

First were a series of "can-it-be-done" questions:

1. Independently observing ten minutes of a videotaped family interaction, can raters agree on the degrees of health or psychopathology of a family?

2. Can raters distinguish between those families containing a patient and control families?

3. Will these global ratings of the degree of family psychopathology correlate with the severity of the adolescent patient's individual psychopathology in the 12 patient-containing families?

4. Will ratings based on marital interaction (without the children present) correlate with ratings based upon the entire family?

5. Will the rating of presumed experts correlate with family members' estimates of the family level of functioning?

A second set of research questions might be referred to as those that follow from a demonstration of acceptable levels of rater reliability and validity. Having demonstrated that raters can agree about the overall levels of health or psychopathology in our sample of families, and having demonstrated that the raters' estimates of health-pathology relate respectably to other independent measures of family function, we wished to dig more deeply into the potential sources of the raters' judgments.

6. Were the raters relying primarily on visual or verbal clues to the presence or absence of a psychiatric patient?

7. Will the ratings based upon ten-minute videotaped segments correlate with ratings made by an experienced family therapist observing the full 50 minutes of family interaction?

8. Will widely differing levels of training and experience in psychiatric family work influence the degree of rater perceptiveness?

9. Will the ratings of family psychopathology be quite content-bound, or relatively independent of the specific family interactional task?

10. Will raters report using any family system observations in their Global Health-Pathology ratings, or will they tend to base their family evaluations on cues from individual family members?

THE SAMPLE

The sample consisted of 23 families, 12 of which contained a member who was one of a series of consecutive admissions to an inpatient adolescent service. Eleven demographically comparable families were obtained from a large, local Protestant church. The "patient" families were told to come for the family testing as a routine part of the treatment team's evaluation of their recently admitted adolescent. The "nonpatient" families were volunteers who responded to the urging of the church staff and an informal talk by a member of the research team explaining the need for systematic data about healthy families. Their stated reasons for participation were diverse; the underlying reasons were not sought. The only stipulation was that no member of the family was currently receiving any form of psychiatric treatment nor in difficulty with legal authorities. In both groups of families, all members over six years old and still living within the family home were urged to participate. Two families (one nonpatient and one patient) were unable to bring all their children.

In many respects, the two groups were strikingly similar. With two exceptions, they were all middle- to upper-middle-class, white, Protestant families. Even the parental occupations were very similar, as indicated below:

Patient Families	Nonpatient Families
3 Engineers	2 Engineers
3 Salesmen	1 Salesman
2 Career Army Officers	4 Executives
1 Executive	2 School Administrators
1 School Administrator	1 Architect
1 Delivery Man	1 Attorney

One family from each group contained a stepparent, and one set of patient parents was adoptive. The ages of the parents were comparable, with the majority being in their forties. In both groups, each family contained at least one adolescent of high school age; the nonpatient families had an average of 3.5 children, the patient families had an average of 2.6 children. The families differed, of course, in their "set" or expectations about the nature and purpose of the testing procedures.

The family testing occurred at Timberlawn Foundation, which is contiguous to Timberlawn Psychiatric Hospital. Families met with one of the experimenters (JML) for a brief explanation of the project. Each patient family was told that although the project was for research purposes, the findings would be reported to the hospital staff who were working with their youngster, and that this information was considered by the staff to be an important part of the adolescent's evaluation.

Questions were answered and consent forms were signed by each member of the family. At this point, background information was obtained from the nonpatient families. Each member was questioned about role performance, the presence of symptoms of emotional origin, and whether the testing day was a typical day in the life of the family. This procedure required from 20 to 60 minutes, and was not requested from the patient families because the information was available to the research team from the hospital records or from other treatment staff.

From this point, the protocol was identical for all families. Each member of the family completed two paper-and-pencil tasks independently. The first was a response in writing to the question, "What are the main problems in your family?" The second was to make quantified ratings about the family in response to a list of family characteristics.* This list contained 20 statements about families—15 concerned psychological or emotional· aspects of family life (e.g., "In our family, there is an opportunity for each member to express himself in his own way."), and five described economic factors (e.g., "In our family, there is enough money for special things."). Each statement was followed by a scale with five points varying from "Not at all" characteristic of our family to "very well" fitting our family. The papers were collected without sharing their contents.

The family and the experimenter then went to the videotape studio, a room with a one-way mirror for one wall. An audiotape recorder was clearly visible and was pointed out. The family was reminded that behind the mirror one of the investigators was operating a television camera which was videotaping their interaction. At this point, the formal interactional testing commenced.

The Videotaped Interactional Tasks

Our interview was designed after reviewing similar evaluation interviews from other research groups and consulting with local family therapists. Two of the five tasks were borrowed from other settings, while three were designed here. The entire family en-

---

* See Appendix A, p. 231.

gaged in four of the tasks, and the parents only in one. The experimenter was present during half of the tasks.

Main Problems

This task followed the procedure of Strodbeck (6). It consisted of the experimenter's indicating that he had read the individual responses to the question, "What are the main problems in your family?" He then said, "While there are areas of agreement, there is considerable disagreement about what the main problems are." He told them that he would leave the room for ten minutes, and asked them to discuss the fact that they disagreed. They were not asked to resolve the disagreements.

Plan Something Together

This task follows the method of Riskin (4). It was included because replication of Riskin's impressive demonstration of the predictive capacity of his microanalytic technique had not been reported. The task itself consisted of asking the family to plan something together. They were told that whatever they planned should be something they might actually do, and that the doing of it should take at least one hour. Again, the experimenter left the room and returned in ten minutes. Findings from this portion of the family evaluation are examined in detail in Chapter VI.

Marital Testing

The design of this section was based on the clinical concept that the nature of the interaction of the parental pair is an important determinant of a total family's health. This part of the evaluation was divided into two phases. The children were excused, and the parents were asked to separate by one chair. The experimenter explained that the focus of this part of the evaluation was on their relationship with each other. They were asked to respond independently to a paper containing six blocks designated, "Stages of Marital Relationship": 1, "Courtship"; 2, "Honeymoon Phase"; 3, "Before Children"; 4, "Children Little"; 5,

"Children in Adolescence"; and 6, "Children Gone." The parents were asked first to put a checkmark in the block which was "happiest for self," and second to place an "X" in the block in which he or she felt the spouse had been happiest. The experimenter collected the papers and shared the results with the couple. He told them he would remain in the studio during the ensuing five minutes and wished them to discuss their agreements and/or disagreements about marital happiness.

After five minutes the experimenter interrupted the couple to announce that he would leave the room for five minutes and wished them to discuss whatever was the greatest source of pain in their relationship.

Family Closeness

While the parents were engaged in the Marital Testing, the children were individually responding to the Closeness Board.* The materials for closeness testing consisted of a large, flat board, with a number of holes in it and peg dolls—male and female— sized to represent the members of the family. The holes were arranged in a loose, spiral pattern in an effort to minimize an arrangement of equidistant pegs. The family members were asked independently to place the dolls on the board to represent how close they felt to other members of their family. Following the testing of the children, the parents also privately responded to the Closeness Board. The researcher explained to each family member that the information would not be shared with other family members by the researchers, but that family members might discuss their placement of the pegs with each other if they wished.

The family gathered again in the videotape studio with the experimenter, who was present during the remainder of the testing. He asked them to "discuss what closeness means in your family."

---

* See Appendix B, p. 232.

Family Strengths

This section was designed because we felt the testing experience would be stressful and we wanted to end the family evaluation with a fortifying task. The family was reminded of the Family Characteristics Inventory they had responded to in the preliminary conference and were told that "many people" considered "many of the items" to be family strengths. Then they were asked to discuss "what is strong about your family?"

DATA ANALYSIS

Raters

The services of a series of raters were obtained. None of the raters were involved in the research project nor in providing treatment to any of the patient-containing families.

A—An experienced psychiatrist actively involved in family therapy, with prior experience in family research.

B—An experienced psychiatric social worker actively involved in the private practice of family therapy.

C—An experienced clinical psychologist, with a primary interest in individual psychotherapy and some involvement in marital counseling.

D—A young psychiatric social worker actively involved in traditional case work, and with some experience in family therapy.

E—An experienced psychiatrist, with particular interest in group psychotherapy.

F—The 40-year-old wife of one of the investigators, the mother of four children—two of whom were adolescents. This rater had no training or experience in any form of psychological treatment.

G—The 29-year-old wife of one of the investigators, with two small children, and no training or experience in any form of psychological treatment.

H—A young psychiatrist, several years beyond his formal training, who had no particular interest in family therapy.

I—A recently-graduated psychiatric social worker, with an interest, but little experience, in family therapy.

J—An experienced psychiatric social worker, presently involved in the private practice of marital counseling and family therapy.

K & L—Both psychiatrists, with several years of nonpsychiatric medical practice prior to psychiatric residency. Both were one year beyond their psychiatric residency. Neither had any specific training or experience in family therapy.

The Rating Process

The raters met at different times with members of the research team. Each responded to a segment of the videotape of each of the 23 families. The first two raters responded independently to the ten-minute Family Strengths segment; the second two to the five-minute Marital Pain section; the third pair to the ten-minute Main Problems section; the fourth pair to Main Problems; and the fifth pair to five minutes of Family Closeness. The videotaped segments were in a different randomized order for each pair of raters. Each rater was seated in a room alone in front of a television monitor. He knew only that some of the families contained "an identified adolescent patient," and others did not.

A ten-point Family Health-Pathology Rating Scale was used (see Figure 1).

Each rater was instructed to circle the number which most closely reflected his judgment of the family's overall health. Also, each was asked to write down any observations he used in formulating his judgments. The raters did not communicate with each other during the evaluations.

The initial ratings (Raters A and B, Family Strengths) required more than eight hours (due to time spent winding and rewinding tapes), and produced an apparent fatigue effect on the raters. Thereafter, the family videotapes were edited electronically so that each section appeared consecutively in different randomized orders with a one-minute interval between families. This meant that subsequent ratings required about five hours for ten-minute

FIGURE 1

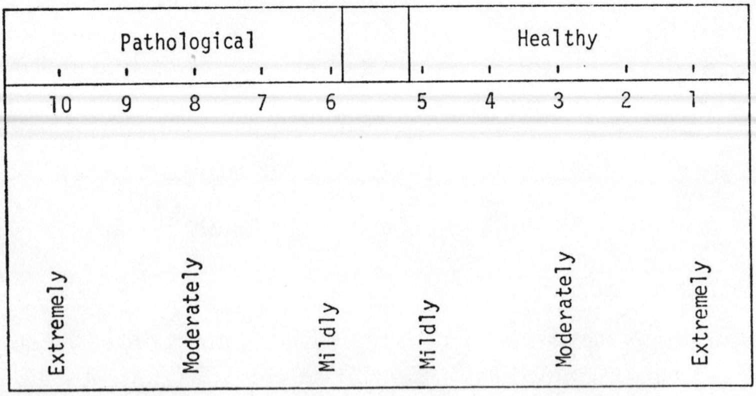

segments, and two-and-one-half hours for five-minute segments. Technical difficulties occurred during the testing of the initial family; for this reason, the N was 23 for all sections except Marital Pain, where the N was 22.

RESULTS AND DISCUSSION

1. *Independently observing ten minutes of a videotaped family interaction, can raters agree on the degrees of health or psychopathology present in a family?*

Correlations between judgments of various raters of whole family groups or marital pairs are based on independent evaluations of the family, or marital pair, on the ten-point Global Health-Pathology Scale (Figure 1). This scale was ordinal; therefore, the numerical ratings were converted to rank orders, and the Spearman Rank Order Correlation Coefficient (rho) was employed. The statistical significance of the obtained rho's was evaluated according to the table provided by Snedecor (5).

As can be seen by reference to Table 1, each pair of raters viewing the same segment of family videotapes independently agrees with high reliability as to the relative degree of health

TABLE 2-1

Interrater Reliability

Raters	Test Section(s)	r	p
A & B	Family Strengths	.75	<.001
E & B	Main Problems	.90	<.001
B & B	Strengths/Problems	.75	<.001
F & G	Main Problems	.65	<.001
H & I	Family Closeness	.78	<.001

reflected by the particular families. The fatigue effect, noted earlier, was apparent in raters A and B, and may have lowered the correlation coefficients for the A and B ratings, as well as the correlation of B viewing "Family Strengths" with his judgments three months later regarding "Main Problems." Checking more specifically for a fatigue effect, we divided A and B's evaluations of Family Strengths into those during the first four hours and the last four hours. A and B correlated .70 (p <.01) during the first four hours of rating, but only .26 (p <.05) during the last four hours.

2. Can raters distinguish between those families containing a patient and control families?

Seven sets of expert judgments were available for each family; that is, two raters' (A and B) judgments on the Family Strengths section of the interview, two raters' (E and B) judgments on the Main Problems section, two (H and I) on the Family Closeness section, and one (J) on the entire hour of videotape. These seven ratings were totalled, yielding an overall family score which could range from 7 to 70. Low scores would indicate psychological health in the family system, while higher scores would indicate more pathology in the family system.

It is striking that there was no overlap between the two groups.

TABLE 2-2

Rank Order of Families by Sum of Global Health-Pathology
Ratings of Seven Expert Judges

Nonpatient Families	Health-Pathology Scores	Patient Families
N1	16	
N2	17	
N3	21	
N4	26	
N5	26	
N6	29	
N7	30	
N8	32	
N9	35	
N10	36	
N11	42	
	45	P1
	49	P2
	50	P3
	52	P4
	55	P5
	55	P6
	56	P7
	56	P8
	57	P9
	58	P10
	60	P11
	62	P12

The nonpatient families ranged from 16 to 42, while the patient families scored from 45 to 62. A Mann-Whitney U Test for this difference between the patient and the nonpatient groups was significant at $p < .001$, with the nonpatient families being judged more healthy.

3. *Will these global ratings of the degree of family psychopathology correlate with the severity of the adolescent patient's individual psychopathology in the 12 patient-containing families?*

At the time of the completion of several weeks of extensive psychodiagnostic evaluation of the 12 adolescent patients, diagnoses were made. Eight of the 12 adolescents were given behavior disorder diagnoses, while four were considered to be psychotic. While there may be, and often is, a degree of overlap in the severity of psychopathology between these groups, it is a general finding that, on the average, psychotic patients are more severely disturbed than those with characterological diagnoses (1). Taking the average Health--Pathology scores from the seven expert judges, and dividing the patient group of 12 at the median, it is striking that all four of the psychotic adolescents are located in the six families judged to be most disturbed. A Fisher Exact Probability Test indicates that this location of the psychotic adolescents is statistically significant at $p < .05$.

4. Will ratings based on marital interaction (without the children present) correlate with ratings based upon the entire family?

Raters C and D independently viewed the five-minute Marital Pain section of the videotape. They used the same ten-point Global Health-Pathology scale to evaluate the marriage that other raters used to evaluate the family. The correlation between the ratings of C and D was .54 $(p < .01)$. Table 2—3 demonstrates the relationships between marital interaction ratings of C and D and the family's Global Health ratings from the other family raters.

It can be noted that both of the raters of Marital Pain (C and D) correlate significantly with each of the expert raters of the whole family. This finding is consistent with the clinical concept that the relative degree of psychological health in the parent's marital interaction is related positively to total family health.

5. Will the ratings of presumed experts correlate with family members' estimates of the family level of functioning?

As mentioned above, each member of the families completed a Family Characteristics Inventory. This list of 20 descriptive items, with a range of scores on each item of one to five, yields

TABLE 2-3

Correlations Between Marital Health Rating and
Global Health Rating of the Total Family

Marital Rater C	Family Raters	Marital Rater D
.55 p < .01	A Family Strengths	.48 p < .05
.55 p < .01	B Family Strengths	.47 p < .05
.62 p < .005	E Main Problems	.59 p < .005
.58 p < .005	B Main Problems	.56 p < .01
.59 p < .005	H Closeness	.50 p < .01
.58 p < .005	I Closeness	.44 p < .05

an overall score of 20 to 100 by each family member. The scores of all individuals in a family were averaged to give an overall "family score."

The nonpatient families' average scores ranged from 73 to 94 (higher scores represent greater health), with a mean of 84; whereas patient families were 63 to 89, with a mean of 73. The ten "highest" self-scoring families contained only one patient family, and the ten lowest self-scoring families contained only two non-patient families. The individual raters' evaluations correlated with family self-appraisals from .36 to .68 (p < .05 to .001), with a mean of .52 (p < .01). In every case, there was a significant, positive correlation between the clinicians' judgments of overall family health and the families' average response to the paper-and-pencil questionnaire. In addition, a Mann-Whitney U Test on the data in Table 2-4 indicates that the average self-ratings of the patient families were significantly lower (or more patholog-ical) than those of the nonpatient families (p < .001).

TABLE 2-4

Family Characteristics Inventory

Nonpatient Families	Mean Scores	Patient Families
N1	94	
N2	91	
N3	91	
	89	P1
N4	88	
N5	87	
N6	87	
N7	82	
N8	80	
N9	79	
	77	P2
	77	P3
	76	P4
	76	P5
N10	75	
N11	73	P6
	71	P7
	70	P8
	70	P9
	68	P10
	66	P11
	63	P12

6. *Were the raters relying primarily on visual or verbal clues to the presence or absence of a psychiatric patient?*

In 1968, when these families were videotaped, there were some apparent differences in adolescent boys' length of hair, adolescent girls' hemlines, and other grooming, clothing, and postural styles between the patient and control family members. The consistently high interrater reliability correlations obtained raised the question of whether visual or verbal clues to the patient's status in the families containing an adolescent patient had biased raters in observing those families; for example, judgments of family health or psychopathology might be affected by the length of an adolescent male patient's hair. Also, there were occasional verbalizations in the patients' families that clearly revealed patient status (e.g., "When do you think that Dr. X will let us visit with you?"). While these occasional clues to patient status did not appear to most raters to be particularly significant, we felt it necessary to obtain some ratings with all such clues removed. Accordingly, two raters (K and L) were asked to listen to five minutes of audio tape recordings of the Main Problems section of the interactional tasks. In the patient family tapes all verbal clues to patient status were erased—in addition, an equivalent number of verbalizations were erased in a random pattern from the nonpatient family tapes, so that the editing itself would not give clues as to patient status. Thus, psychiatrists K and L, with no visual input, listened to five minutes of edited audio tapes of the Main Problems section and made Health-Pathology ratings on each family using the ten-point scale. The interrater reliability between these two raters was $r = .39$ (p $< .05$). Rater K obtained correlations ranging from .23 to .67 with the previously mentioned seven expert raters. His median correlation with these seven other raters was .50 (p $< .05$), and six of his seven correlations were significant at less than the .05 level. Rater L obtained correlations ranging from .09 to .49 with the seven other raters. Four of his seven correlations were significant at less than the .05 level, and his median intercorrelation was .36, which was also significant at less than the .05 level. Rater K's judgments did not correlate significantly with family self-ratings ($r = .34$), but rater L's judgments did ($r = .36$, p $< .05$). Finally, adding rater K's and L's judgments for the patient group, the obtained median Health-Pathology score was 15.5, while the nonpatient group was given a median of 11. This difference was significant at p $< .01$ by the Mann-Whitney U Test, indicating that these raters also judged the nonpatient families to be more healthy.*

---

* These findings are in marked contrast to Haley's (2), and may reflect the use of longer tape segments (five minutes versus two minutes) or a less neutral task (Main Problems versus selecting the color of a new car).

TABLE 2-5

Interrater Reliability of Rater J and Judgments Based
on Various Segments

Rater	Section	Length	r	p
A	Strength	10 min.	.59	.005
B	Strength	10 min.	.60	.005
E	Problems	10 min.	.72	.001
B	Problems	10 min.	.68	.001
F	Problems	10 min.	.78	.001
G	Problems	10 min.	.54	.01
C	Marital Pain	5 min.	.60	.005
D	Marital Pain	5 min.	.64	.005
H	Closeness	5 min.	.72	.001
I	Closeness	5 min.	.62	.005
K	Problems (audio only)	5 min.	.41	.05
L	Problems (audio only)	5 min.	.49	.05

7. *Will ratings based upon ten-minute videotape
segments correlate with ratings made by an experienced
family therapist observing the full 50 minutes
of family interaction?*

Rater J, an experienced family therapist, was asked to observe
the 23 family videotapes in their entirety. He devoted 125 hours
to the examination of the tapes and provided ratings of psychological health, insights concerning family dynamics observed, and
suggestions about possible improvements in the interview structure and style. In addition, his observations and ratings provided
a check on the possibility that having all other raters observe only
five to ten minutes of family interactions might be introducing
some sort of systematic bias into their judgments (Table 2-5).

Rater J, observing the full 50 minutes tape on all 23 families
correlated with the other raters ranging from .41 on the 5 minutes
of edited audio tape of Main Problems to .78 on 10 minutes of
videotape of the same section. All correlations were positive and
significant.

8. *Will widely differing levels of training and
experience in psychiatric family work influence
the degree of rater perceptiveness?*

Degree of presumed expertness required to make reliable global appraisals of family health was the next problem explored. Expertness, in terms of the rating task, was conceptualized arbitrarily as being a reflection of the level of clinical training, years of general clinical experience, and specific experience in family therapy or research. On this basis, the three initial investigators (JML, JTG, and VAP) independently ranked the nine raters, whose services had been obtained at this point in the research process (raters A through I). The Kendall coefficient of concordance for the three rankings of expertness was .99 (p <.01). While raters presumed to have the most limited expertness (F and G) agreed at a significant level after viewing a ten-minute videotaped segment of family interaction, raters of greater presumed expertness (B and E), viewing the same videotaped section, have a higher reliability (.90 for B and E versus .65 for F and G). The difference between these two correlation coefficients was significant at the .05 level. In general, there does seem to be a positive relationship between the degree of expertness and the degree of inter-judge agreement, although all judges agreed at a significant level with each other.

9. *Will the ratings of family psychopathology be quite
content-bound, or relatively independent of the
specific family interactional task?*

The tasks given to each family were similar in that they involved verbal instructions to discuss a given content area, but the areas varied widely (Family Strengths, Main Problems, Family Closeness, and Plan Something Together). However, the intercorrelations between judges' ratings did not seem particularly influenced by the specific tasks given to the families in our study. Such a finding lends support to those family investigators who suggest that virtually any segment of family interaction will render more-or-less representative data, and that family assessments, therefore, are not heavily dependent upon the particular task with which the family is presented. Certainly there must be limits to this generalization, but within the context of our study, and at the level of global health-pathology ratings, it would appear to hold (3).

10. Will raters report using any systems observations in their Global Health-Pathology ratings, or will they tend to base their family evaluations on cues from individual family members?

It has been the opinion of this research team that a major part of our contribution to family research has been a consistent focus upon family system interactions, rather than upon individual members' characteristics (such as "Father is paranoid," or "Mother is compulsive."). However, this bias on the part of the research team could not be expected to extend to raters unfamiliar with our research goals. As a preliminary exploration into those cues consciously available to our raters, we asked each to write statements on the rating form, indicating their on-the-spot impressions of the characteristics that were influencing their judgments of family psychological health. Post hoc categorization of the 1,642 raters' statements obtained into large categories indicates that 36 percent of these statements relate primarily to individuals (e.g., "Father is very hostile."), while 64 percent seemed to relate more directly to family system-level analysis (e.g., "They are ignoring the middle boy."). This finding suggests that, at least at the level of raters' self-perceptions of the sources of their ratings, our testing procedure does elicit behaviors that will generate systems-level observations in expert raters.

SUMMARY

The results of the pilot study encouraged the research team to feel that we had developed a technique that would yield reliable and valid discriminations between patient-containing and control families, and that we had been able to elicit and observe family styles of interaction characteristic of varying levels of family health and pathology. In the patient-containing families, the global ratings of family psychopathology related meaningfully to independent evaluations of the adolescent patients' severity of disturbance; judgments of the quality of marital interaction compared closely with those of overall family functioning for the entire sample. Family members' judgments of the strengths and weaknesses in their own family were in reasonable agreement with the mental health professionals' ratings. The particular videotaped task observed seemed to have little impact on raters' judgments, and brief segments of videotape (or even of audiotape only) provided sufficient input for raters to make an evaluation. While relatively inexperienced raters could discriminate levels of family function, greater training and experience in family work was clearly an asset. The verbal interactional tasks seemed to provide raters with information of both an individual and a family process nature upon which to base judgments.

SUBSEQUENT FAMILY EVALUATIONS

During the months of analysis of data from the pilot study sample, research interest in understanding the impact of current family psychopathology upon the course and outcome of adolescent inpatient treatment was enriched by contact with the 11 "control" families. As we explored the styles and dynamics of healthy functioning in greater detail, two serious methodological problems in our data became clarified. First, although it appeared that judges could reliably and accurately distinguish between families containing an adolescent inpatient and those that did not, we did not know whether judges could differentiate between levels of functioning within the nonpatient, or presumably healthy, group. Second, differences in "set" between our patient and nonpatient groups made it very difficult to determine whether or not differences in family functioning might be due to difference in stress of the interview. Our control families were coming to help us, and they had the expectation that we were looking for signs of health.

Our patient families came within a few weeks after the placement of one of their children in a psychiatric hospital, and came expecting to be examined for information that would help the treatment team understand their youngster's psychopathology. The levels of stress between these two different sets of expectations are markedly different.

Accordingly, a second sample of 33 nonpatient families was obtained (see Chapter IV).

As a result of the experiences gained in the pilot study family testing, several changes were made in the family evaluation procedures. First, the instructions were tape recorded to eliminate the effect of an interviewer in the videotaped family evaluation. Second, the Main Problems task was dropped and a new task inserted. Finally, the Marital discussion and the order of tasks were changed. The resulting five-part format of the new family evaluation was conducted in the following order:

1. *Family Strengths*

This task was presented in essentially the same manner as in the pilot study.

2. *Threatened Loss*

A brief, audiotape-recorded vignette, portraying a hospital scene in which an unidentified male family member appears to be in imminent danger of dying, is presented to the family. The vignette stops on an ambiguous note, and the family members are asked to make up an ending to the story. A theoretical background for the inclusion of this section and data gathered relating to this section will be presented in Chapter VIII.

3. *Marital Testing*

With the children excused to complete the Closeness Board, the parents are asked in this ten-minute section to discuss what had been the best and worst in their marriage.

4. *Family Closeness*

This task is presented in essentially the same way as in the pilot study.

5. Plan Something Together

This task, a relatively emotionally uncharged one, was shifted to the last.

Initially, two raters were asked to observe the first five minutes of family interaction and to rate the family on the same ten-point Health-Pathology Scale used in the pilot study. The first two raters were E and I from the pilot study. Their numerical ratings were converted to rank orders. The two resulting rank orders correlated .54 (p <.005). At this point, the research plan called for the six highest and the six lowest ranking families to be selected from the larger sample of 33. Accordingly, the numerical ratings from the two judges were averaged, and the 33 families were then rank ordered, with the top and bottom six being selected for further detailed investigation. There was no overlap between the groups, as the top six families all received Health-Pathology ratings of one to four, while the bottom six families all received ratings of six or seven. In spite of this high degree of agreement and the clear separation between the two sets of six families, the research team experienced some anxiety over continuing a detailed investigation of these 12 families, having used only two judges. Two additional judges were then obtained (C and K from

TABLE 2-6

Correlations Between Rank Order of 33 Families'
Global Health/Pathology by Four Raters

Raters	r*	p
E : I	.54	.03
C : K	.38	.10
C : E	.28	.10
C : I	.45	.06
K : E	.47	.05
K : I	.39	.09

* Spearman Rank Order Coefficient

the pilot study) . These two judges observed the same five minutes of each family's interaction, and followed the identical rating and ranking procedures. Table 2-6 gives intercorrelations for the four judges.

These results provide answers to the research team's concerns. First, it was possible for raters to agree significantly on the level of health of a family system, even when the families came from a rather restricted range of adequate functioning and did not contain any possible cues to disturbance that might follow from containing an "identified" psychiatric patient. Second, the elimination of the "patient-evaluation" set for some families also did not prevent raters from agreeing on relative degrees of psychologically healthy family functioning.

These findings encouraged further detailed examination of the final group of 33 families reported in the following chapters.

REFERENCES

1. GOSSETT, J. T., LEWIS, S. B., LEWIS, J. M. and PHILLIPS, V. A., Follow-up of adolescents treated in a psychiatric hospital: I. A review of studies, *Am. J. Orthopsychiatry*, 43 (4) :602-610, 1973.
2. HALEY, J., Critical overview of present status of family interaction research,. In J. Framo (Ed.), *Family Interaction: A Dialogue Between Family Researchers and Family Therapists*. New York: Springer Publishing Co., 1972, p. 27.
3. JACOB, T., and DAVIS, J., Family interaction as a function of experimental task, *Family Process*, Vol. 12 (4), 415-428, Dec., 1973.
4. RISKIN, J., and FAUNCE, E. E., Family interaction scales, *Arch. Gen. Psychiat.*, Vol. 22 (6), 504-537, June, 1970.
5. SNEDECOR, G. W., *Everyday Statistics*, Dubuque, Iowa, Wm. C. Brown Co., 1950.
6. STRODBECK, F. L., Husband-wife interaction over revealed differences, *Am. Sociol. Rev.*, 16:468-473, 1951.

CHAPTER III

A THEORETICAL BASIS FOR FAMILY EVALUATION

W. Robert Beavers, M.D.

PSYCHIATRIC RESEARCH HAS MADE great advances toward embracing a systems view of emotional illness. In years past, focus was on the individual social deviant—classifying his characteristics, developing syndromes, and constructing a taxonomy of pathology, while paying little attention to the unique qualities of the individual's developmental environment. Later, focus moved from classification and description to individual psychodynamics—not just *what* was wrong, but *why* the person behaved differently. Psychiatric theory based on individual psychodynamics remains the cornerstone of treatment of emotional ills; and even empirical therapies, such as electroshock or psychoactive drugs, are often explained in a psychodynamic framework.

Over many years, the theoretical base has broadened further; first anecdotally, then systematically, families were noted to differ

At this point in the evolution of our research study, W. Robert Beavers, M.D. joined the research team. First a rater in the pilot study and then a central team member, he brought an evolving theoretical system about families. Over the course of the years of research, this original theoretical system has been tempered by team dialogue and the accumulating data. At its core, however, it is Beavers—and this is the only chapter which commands individual credit and responsibility. It is presented at this point in the book because it is the theoretical structure from which much of what follows evolved.

in style and functioning, and these differences were correlated with syndromes found in their offspring.

Though there are many factors contributing to this broader, systems-oriented approach, two seem especially important. The child guidance clinic movement centered attention on whole families, and the identified patient came to be seen as one symptom of a larger family problem. In addition, the psychiatric research units studying schizophrenia became interested in attitudes, patterns of communication, and behaviors found in the families from which schizophrenic patients emerged.

Quite recently a few studies have appeared describing the characteristics of healthy family systems, an area previously neglected by psychiatric theorists and practitioners.

A discussion of family systems may begin appropriately by a brief discussion of general systems theory (5,8) which is based on the concept of *entropy*, a complex term, referring to the state of organization and available energy present in a system. In a *closed* system, with no energy coming from outside, everything goes downhill, i.e., becomes more entropic. In a world without an external source of energy, the mountains would fall into the sea, structures disintegrate, and a steady state of total disorganization (maximum entropy) would result. Life is possible only in an *open* system. Even a one-celled organism is an open system, receiving energy from the less organized and less structured (more entropic) outside world, which it uses to develop and maintain its structure and flexibility. The miracle of life is possible because of negative entropy—"negentropy"—the utilization of energy to develop structure and fight the inexorable downhill pull found in any closed system.

Structure and flexibility are found in viable systems; the more an organism develops structure and flexibility, the more negentropy is demonstrated. Cells in an organism proliferate, specialize, integrate, and cooperate with greater power to interact with the environment. Kill a living organism, mount it on a slide, and observe its fabulous structure. It is still more complex than the material from which it developed, but it has lost its ability to change. Categorization of systems up the ladder of complexity (the degree of negentropy) can be conceptualized as moving on a continuum of organization from *chaos,* through *rigidity* with some differentiation of parts, toward greater *flexibility* with further evolution of coherent structure. This somewhat simplistic description of the characteristics of an open system as it increases in negentropy corresponds quite well with what is actually seen in family systems (from severely disturbed to healthy).

"Family homeostasis" is a term which has been used to describe the functioning of family systems, and once was thought to be descriptive of healthy families. Bateson (1) spoke of the family as a "biosocial feedback-governed, error-activated system"—suggesting the importance of keeping things as they are. But Speer (30) convincingly points out that this dreary, laborious attempt to maintain the status quo is characteristic of disturbance, and terms such as attempt *morphostasis*—the stagnation of structure. Stagnation, stillness, changelessness are not descriptive of all families, certainly not of healthy families, but rather of those disturbed units whose children often show that combination of regression, negativism and retreat to fantasy we usually call schizophrenia.

Speer rejects the concepts of homeostasis or morphostasis as a useful model for any but disturbed families and makes a plea for stability with built-in opportunities for change (positive feedback), as a more accurate systems model for healthy family functioning. His concept is termed "morphogenesis," and he cites studies showing that healthy families are more spontaneous than are disturbed ones. He describes a model with flexible structure, open to growth and change, and responsive to new stimulation.

It should be noted that the family qualities we will describe as related to the development of capable individuals do not make absolute distinctions between families that produce schizophrenic, non-psychotic but limited, or normal children. Rather, variables are described at three points on the continuum with low and high ends. If a family is low on several of these variables, it is generally least successful at child-raising, and the children are most vulnerable to social failure. The variables (which are not mutually exclusive) are described at three positions, arbitrarily labeled severely disturbed, midrange, and healthy.

The most *seriously disturbed* or chaotic families are quite entropic—timeless, repetitive in interaction, clinging in a sticky lump (the amorphous family ego mass), having little vital interaction with the outside world and little change in the family world. Dreams, fantasies, and a studied unawareness function in place of goal-directed, active negotiation among persons. Data for this low point on the continuum are taken from studies of interaction in families who have a process schizophrenic member, and from the author's clinical material. However, family characteristics are not seen as the sole source of an offspring's socially disturbed state, for several reasons. Foremost, it would be a negation of the overall position taken: a systems approach, open to as many variables as are determined to be important. Though the biochemical approach to schizophrenia has been disappointing to date, new developments may be more significant. Also, recent studies of Kety et al. (13) strongly support a genetic factor (general, not specific) in the production of process (but not reactive) schizophrenia.

Midway on the continuum of structure are those families in which the children are "sane" but limited (having greater negentropy than do severely disturbed ones). Their structure is relatively clear but *rigid,* and thus poorly adapted to change. Control is the watchword, and biological drives in parents and children are usually seen as threatening to the family structure and direction.

Successfully avoiding the timeless, murky swamp of meaninglessness, these families exhibit a degree of Speer's "morphogenesis." They do think of a future and want their children to behave well and perform well at some future time when they will be on their own. However, mistrusting feelings and drives, they find growth painful and continually inhibit or thwart it. Working with such *midrange families,* one can imagine some primitive sea animal with one large muscle attached to a jaw—successfully adapted so long as food floats by, but so limited as to be terribly vulnerable. Families in the middle range on the continuum include those who produce reactive psychotic, and non-psychotic psychiatrically ill children (neurotics and behavior disorders). As with the seriously disturbed family, the data are derived both from research studies on such family units and from clinical material.

Stierlin (31) introduced the concepts of centrifugal and centripetal vectors within the family as influencing adolescent separation. These styles are related to the degree that family members tend to leave the family (centrifugal) or cling together (centripetal). The concepts appear to have applicability and explanatory usefulness across the entire range of family competence, but may be of particular value in understanding the system variables of those families with heavy loading for either neurotic or behavior disorder children. The families in the midrange group with the centrifugal style will usually produce behavior disorders, and the centripetal families will usually produce offspring labeled neurotic.

Healthy families show the characteristics of a highly negentropic system. Structure is clear and flexible, but carried lightly. *Function* is the greater concern. Changes in direction are not threatening, and even the smallest children are considered capable of contributing. They enjoy negotiations and welcome new input into the system—examine, evaluate, but nevertheless welcome. Most significant is an open respect for biological drives. The need for intimacy is not seen as weakness. Anger is responded to as a sign that something needs to be changed or corrected. Sexual interest is considered a generally positive force. Westley and Epstein (32) noted that frequency of sexual intercourse between parents correlated positively with the emotional health of their children! When an organism is not at war with itself (whether that organism is a person or a family) and is able to accept and affirm its basic qualities, the most negentropic state is attained: structure with flexible, adaptive function. This group, at the high end of the continuum of functioning, includes families whose members have no evidence of psychiatric pathology. Data come from published studies, clinical observations by our research group members, and research at Timberlawn Foundation.

Technology and social structures are not only altering, but at a more rapid rate than any time in our history. Margaret Mead (20) dramatically describes today's parents as being like immigrants to a foreign land, forced to rely on their children for much of the new information necessary for successful acculturation. In this position, a rapidly adapting family system becomes more of a necessity than a luxury.

This chapter deals with five family qualities considered important in the development of capable, adaptive, healthy individuals: 1) power structure, 2) the degree of family individuation, 3) acceptance of separation and loss, 4) perception of reality, and 5) affect.

1. *Family Power Structure*

All social systems have structures which determine who wields power and what the hierarchy or "pecking order" is expected to be. Families vary greatly in their power structures, and the differences are closely related to family health. The continuum of family power moves from the low end of such poorly defined, delicately balanced interaction that little or nothing can change or develop, up the curve of organization to rigid, inflexible holding of power by one member who is recognized and accepted as dominant. In the most flexible family structures, power is shared and competence in relating develops from experiencing generous and benign leaders.

A strong determinant of family system capability is the assumption of members as to the probable nature of human encounter. Disturbed families behave as if encounters will be oppositional; competent families behave as if encounters will be affiliative. Indeed, it is the author's view that a clinical estimate of this underlying assumption will be of assistance in determining the degree of disturbance in family systems and individuals, without regard for diagnostic type or labels.

Assumptions about the nature of man underlie the methods and amount of control seen as necessary: if one sees himself and others as essentially evil or aggressive-destructive, he concludes that all people (including himself) must be viewed as threatening and intimidating; that husband-wife, parent-child, sibling-sibling, and in fact all relationships are likely to be oppositional.

There is, of course, no direct or objective way to determine these shared family assumptions; but the manner and style of family structure are observable phenomena and quite closely related to these assumptions. If encounters are seen as painful but necessary, a structure will be developed in which one must be either dominant or submissive (acting out the assumptions of opposition). If one has a more benign view of man, seeing his biological essence as unthreatening and accepted, children are guided and directed, and family rules are enforced without recourse to threat and intimidation. If encounters are seen as likely to be affiliative, then power may be shared and the structure will be more egalitarian.

Since deviation from a cultural norm is a powerful factor in determining whether an individual or a family is considered pathological, family structure and its relation to "normality" is extremely sensitive to cultural variations. Most of our research literature is based on North American, predominantly middle-class families, and we must be cautious in extrapolating these findings to other social classes and cultures. Sanua's (26) study of sociocultural factors in families of schizophrenics underscores this need for caution, stating that "While the findings in sociology and anthropology have, in the past few years, given impetus to the development of social psychiatry as a field of investigation, their effects are still minor, particularly in the purely psychiatric literature." Subsequently, family researchers have made efforts to overcome this narrow view, but our information and assumptions still tend to be confined to middle- and upper-middle-class caucasian Americans.

Another factor relating generally to family structure concerns completeness. In those families without one parent, or those who have had a child die, the incidence of child-rearing failure increases. Rosenzweig and Bray (25) found, in a study of schizophrenic males, that 39 percent had experienced the death of a sibling—twice the percentage found in controls. Lidz and Lidz (19a) studied 50 schizophrenic patients and found that 40 percent had lost one or both parents by the age of 19, a much higher incidence than in the general population. It is difficult to avoid the conclusion that a whole family generally is better than a part family. Identity formation seems more difficult without family role models and opportunities to observe adults of both sexes functioning intimately within a framework of mutual commitment.

A. *The Severely Disturbed Family*

In the most severely disturbed families, the father has little power (5). Garmezy and Rodnick (11) note that if the father in a schizophrenic's family is dominant, this correlates with better premorbid adjustment and prognosis. Mishler and Waxler (21) find that passivity and relative powerlessness of the father are frequently compounded by a coalition between mother and child, usually a male child, and usually the identified patient. When a child wields greater power than a parent, with the resultant breakdown of generation differences, the parent takes a sibling-like role described beautifully by Lidz and Fleck (19) as a "skewed" family. The skewed family breaks generation barriers with a powerful parent-child coalition. In "schismatic" families, parents war with each other, scrambling for interpersonal power, leaving their children fearful of tipping the precarious balance.

Lidz et al. (18), in a paper discussing schizophrenic patients and their siblings, comment: "When siblings were close in age—and even when they were identical twins—they were subjected to very different intrafamilial influences. The child who becomes schizophrenic may become a pawn or scapegoat in the parental conflict; he may be caught between the conflicting needs and wishes of the parents who become irreconcilable introjects; he may invest his energies in seeking to salvage the parents' marriage and to satisfy the needs of both; he may insert himself into the split between the parents and become a needed complement to one parent. The patients' energies during their developmental years were deflected from developing an integrated, independent ego, and failure of closure of their oedipal attachments left them prone to incestuous conflicts during adolescence. The influence of the siblings upon one another may create more or less precarious circumstances and greater or lesser vulnerability."

Day and Kwiatkowska (9a) found that the "well" sibling of a schizophrenic also showed severe psychological disturbance, though usually he functioned fairly well. They address themselves to this puzzling question of how he does as well as he does. "Possibly the very constriction which gave this offspring less of a subjective sense of conflict allowed him to move out of the family emotionally at an early age. Also, since he was not a participant in the family struggle in the same way as the rest of its members, he was able to make a fair number of childhood friends (unlike the patient). It is expected that these friendships would have the same shallowness which we have noted in our relationships with him. Yet through pseudo-identification with his peers and imitation of them, the sibling may find some support outside his family; when he marries, he does not have to rely on his parents."

It seems, then that the most inept families have a powerless father, with strong coalitions between mother and child, usually the one to become schizophrenic. Winning the oedipal battle is truly a Pyrrhic victory! This gives us some insight into the ways one or more siblings can escape the fate of the relatively self-less sibling, soon to be labeled schizophrenic. In a murky, confusing, and mystifying family communication system, the very structure that helps produce an identified patient—a parental coalition offering one child all the special attention, attachment, and significance in the family scheme—can serve as a modest protection for other children who are freer to reach out into the wider community to find meaning and identity.

B. *Midrange Families*

In less disturbed families, generation barriers are not broken overtly; when coalitions exist between parent and child, they are covert, usually illicit, and relatively impotent. Neither does a strong coalition exist between mother and father. Families obtain their characteristic rigid, authoritarian structure through dominance (32). Several lines of evidence (11,22) suggest that mother-dominated families are generally less capable of producing effective offspring than father-dominated ones (23). Authoritarian families (run by either parent), however, lessen the opportunities for development of autonomy; and severe conflict, overt or covert, is inevitable. Openly expressed, the product is unfriendly and competitive interaction and explosive behavior; hidden and constricted, it is a depressive, compulsive atmosphere emphasizing control of spontaneity (24).

Families of behavior disorders characteristically have a centrifugal style and a shifting pattern of dominance with neither parent able to wrest consistent control from the other. The parents typically invite transient coalitions with children, providing a context for everyone to learn manipulative and exploitative techniques.

This elusive, kaleidoscopic pattern of expressing power provides little hope of consistent control—either of one's self or others. It is ideal, however, for frustrated plans and failed hopes with blame and insult occurring frequently. Bursts of energy and efforts at control are usually unsuccessful.

In contrast, the families with a centripetal style do establish a stable hiearchy of power with one parent in charge. This allows for effective control and little opportunity for manipulative efforts to succeed. Technical proficiency is encouraged in such stability. Homes are kept neat, money is made, but feelings are threatening and therefore repressed. Spontaneity is rare. These families characteristically produce children given a neurotic diagnosis.

Neither the centrifugal nor the centripetal midrange family style offers a model for negotiation and compromise—extremely important skills in successful interpersonal relationships (4).

C. The Healthy Family

In our study of capable, middle-class families, those with a clear hierarchy of power, with leadership generally in the hands of the father, and a viable coalition with the mother as the next most powerful person, are most successful (32). The children are less powerful but their contributions are attended and usually influence family decisions. As a result, defensive power struggles are not necessary and family tasks are undertaken with cooperativeness, good humor, and effectiveness. This principle has been demonstrated in research settings by asking families to "plan something together" (24). Neither the child-centered home nor the father- (or mother) knows-best attitude emerges from studies of healthy families. With little fear of being run over, excluded, or stripped of dignity, the children can accept their lesser power with equanimity.

The empirical fact that the father-led pattern is described more frequently as most successful in family studies thus far does not mean that this is universal. The culture may influence successful family qualities; where the broader culture, or viable subcultures, have different definitions of a successful man or woman, the results may be different.

II. Degrees of Family Individuation

Family systems vary in the degree that individuation is tolerated and encouraged. This system tolerance for individuation is closely related to the autonomy of family members. In the western world, a great premium is placed on behavioral manifestations of a personal sense of autonomy. The autonomous person knows what he feels and thinks, and he takes responsibility for his personal activity. He interacts with others with a reasonably clear notion of where his skin ends and the other person's skin begins; that is, he has ego boundaries. He is able to think, most of the time, in terms of cause and effect. Only in unusual circumstances does he rely on magical explanations of interpersonal phenomena. In a study of the characteristics of healthy families, Westley and Epstein (32) state: "Autonomy seems to be essential to the development of a satisfactory ego identity, for one must be permitted to consider oneself a separate person, and to experience oneself as such, to find an identity. Without such autonomy, it seems likely that the child will be unable to solve the basic problems of separation from his family of orientation and will remain over-dependent."

Tolerance for individuation is reflected in several more discrete qualities of the family system. These more specific, observable, and researchable qualities include:

> 1. "I-ness": The ability of individual family members to express themselves clearly as feeling, thinking, acting, valuable and separate individuals and to take responsibility for thoughts, feelings, and actions.
>
> 2. Respect for the unique experience of another: The recognition and acceptance that others may perceive differently.
>
> 3. Permeability to others: The ability to hear and respond to others within the system.

A. *The Severely Disturbed Family*

In contrast to the family orientation which promotes autonomy in its members, severely disturbed families behave like mutually intimidating members of an illicit gang, checking each other out if a question is posed, and making quite sure that any response from one member is not "out of line" and does not involve one person's being obviously different from the others. With enough practice, this becomes automatic and family members are truly not aware of how much "group think" they do and how little respect is paid to individual perception and feeling. Bowen (7) termed such families as having an "undifferentiated family ego mass." He observed: "The ego fusion is most intense in the least mature families. In a family with a schizophrenic member, the fusion between father, mother, and child approaches maximum intensity. Theoretically, the fusion is present to some degree in all families except those in which family members have obtained emotional maturity."

Whether investigators of families with schizophrenic members use terms such as Bowen's "undifferentiated ego mass" or Wynne's "pseudomutuality" and "rubber fence" (33) or Laing's "mystification" (15), these labels refer to different aspects of the same phenomenon—the failure of a family to help its offspring develop autonomous action and boundaries of self which allow a relatively clear and coherent identity formation. This failure is not passive but active, a group "conspiracy" to avoid coherence and meaning. The process of mystification is found most pervasively, but not exclusively, in families which produce children later diagnosed process schizophrenic. It blurs boundaries among members and operates as a cognitive and emotional swamp from which extrication seems impossible. In fact, one reasonable and fruitful way of viewing schizophrenia in adolescence is as a desperate attempt to leave the family's murky, quicksand-filled communicational swamp.

In these poorly differentiated families, negotiation becomes a senseless concept. Relationships are maintained unclear and unchanging. The members of these disturbed families behave as if human closeness is found by thinking and feeling just like one another; therefore, individuation is tantamount to rejection and exclusion. Their children grow up haunted by the impossibility of obtaining two goals made incompatible in such a system—the goal of being an individual and the goal of acceptance and companionship. This unresolvable conflict is pathognomonic of process schizophrenia and severe borderline offspring.

All of us struggle for both of these satisfactions, and even if we have a fairly satisfactory early family experience, we often find larger social structures frustrating in this respect. Employees cannot be "themselves" around many bosses. Parents cannot express dissonant opinions in the PTA without risking social ostracism. Students who point out contradictions between democratic ideals and school policy risk expulsion. But such frustration is mild indeed compared to the powerful social pressures in families. If one cannot be "himself" in his own family, he may have no self at all.

In a study published some years ago, characteristic communication patterns of mothers of adolescent schizophrenics contrasted sharply with patterns in mothers with non-schizophrenic psychiatric patients (3). Asked a question about subjective feelings, these mothers of patients seemed unable to respond openly or clearly. A high percentage of their responses were evasive. For example:

Q. How did you feel about your son's continued thumbsucking?

R. Well, my husband was never happy about it.

Or, there were shifts, statements immediately disqualified by subsequent statements; for example:

Q. How did you feel about being pregnant for the first time?

R. Oh, I was happy all through my pregnancy. I had morning sickness continually and even had to go to the hospital. I was so sick.

Exasperating shifts negate any comprehension of previous statements and avoid shared meaning. This is part of the process of mystification: failure to recognize individuality, and continual undermining of possible autonomy by confusing, frustrating incomprehensibility. No family member is victim or villain: *all* are caught up in a nightmare without end.

An early conceptualization of these confusing patterns of relating was Bateson's concept of the double-bind (2). He suggested that a double-bind occurs when a child receives two related but contradictory messages, cannot comment on the contradiction, cannot leave the scene, and is punished whatever response he makes. Because of the child's need for the parent, the double-bind exerts a powerful malevolent effect. Only the presence of a rescuer, in the form of an effective, significant other person can mitigate the destructiveness. Bateson considers double-binds to be recurrent and reinforced by still other double-binds that necessarily become more comprehensive and inclusive.

In a broader framework, Heller's novel *Catch 22* (12) illustrates the frustrating "no-way-out" pattern seen in disturbed families. Yossarian is caught in a terrible double-bind in which he can stop flying only if he is crazy. If he wants to stop flying by saying he is crazy, he is obviously sane since no sane man would want to continue to fly and risk death. His only solution is to escape the system entirely; but if he cannot, he risks disintegration (becoming "crazy") which is taken as evidence of sanity by his superiors.

Let us examine the more specific manifestations of the general concept of tolerance for autonomy in the seriously disturbed family.

1) *"I-ness"*

In the most disturbed families there is a striking failure of members to take personal responsibility for their own feelings, for past actions or motivations, and for future goals. In addition, they are characteristically unclear, operating in a defensive and elusive fashion, using words much as a squid uses his inky fluid—to avoid possible harm.

The principal mechanisms in this indirect use of power (the control of interaction without declaration of personal feelings, thoughts, or responsibility for action) are:

a. Question-asking. Mishler and Waxler (21) found a much higher incidence of question-asking in the interaction of families containing a schizophrenic as compared with control families.

b. Evasions and shifts of meaning, as described in studies of communication patterns of mothers of schizophrenics (3).

c. Diffuse, unclear, but effective attacks on others' positions. Mishler and Waxler describe such subtle sanctions in family interaction as pauses: a person's value can be diminished successfully by having his words fall flat, with no response occurring for a period of time—an effective means of controlling without responsibility.

d. Sarcasm and ridicule are also powerful means of controlling without "tipping one's hand." Both Singer and Wynne (29) and Mishler and Waxler found hostility levels highest in the most disturbed families. This hostility usually serves double-duty: it is couched in slippery language designed to discourage counterattacks, and is a model for other family members to evade and obscure their own unique experiences.

2) *Respect for Other's Experience*

A second variable which is important to individuation is respect for the unique experience of another. At the lower end of such a continuum is found invasiveness. Just as the members of severely disturbed families treat their own unique thoughts and feelings shabbily, they show little or no respect for the worth of the other's experience. Such parents inform their children what to think or feel. Riskin and Faunce (24) term these invasive, rapacious statements "mind-reading" comments (for example, father says: "Mary, you're not hungry.") , and found them present almost exclusively in their multi-problem families. Lennard and Bernstein (16) found a similar clustering of this destruction of another's experience in their most disturbed families, with a high incidence of statements from one family member to another telling him what he feels or thinks.

Invasiveness is devastating to the development of personal identity. It is the most dramatic method of maintaining a group ego without individuation, making it impossible to be a separate individual and remain acceptable in the family group. Invasive communication can be physical, as in infancy when a mother feeds a child when she herself feels discomfort rather than responding to cues from the child. Continued later into symbolic interaction, such invasions destroy confidence in one's ability to know his own mind and body. "You don't really feel that way. You really love your sister; you don't hate her." "What do you mean, you feel lonely? You've got lots of friends. You are very popular." These invasions frequently contribute to double-binds. If one fights, he is considered ungrateful and uncooperative. If he accepts the invasions, his unique experience is mangled, and chronic, pervasive confusion results.

3) *Receptiveness*

This third family quality related to individuation is receptiveness or openness to others. At the lower end of this continuum is impermeability—the lack of acknowledgment of the other's perceptions. In seriously disturbed families, individual views are seldom shared. Parallel discussions produce ritualized encounters in which no negotiation occurs. Lennard and Bernstein noted, in families with a schizophrenic member, a pattern of interaction striking in its changeless repetitiveness. Studied at six-month intervals, families had a dreary sameness in sequences of interaction, length of speeches, and the pattern of who-speaks-to-whom. Mishler and Waxler found the disturbed systems scored lowest on complete acknowledgement of a previous speaker's remarks.

Studies by direct observation of family interaction (7) dovetail with the reconstructive approach of Bruch (9), who concluded that mothers of children later to become schizophrenic were remarkably insensitive to cues coming from their infants. A growing child cannot develop security concerning his inner world without awareness of his own unique perceptions and responses. Rather, he develops mistrust of self, diffusion of self, and a pervasive lack of clarity (6,27).

B. *The Midrange Family*

Family systems which are midway on a continuum of capability may be described as coherent with rigidity; they do allow the development of a coherent identity, but at the expense of much that is delightful in human behavior. They produce offspring with modest repertoires of interpersonal skills and constricted, generally guilt-laden self-images. Psychiatrists may label these products "neurotic" or "behavior disorder," attempting to describe the nature of the limited behavior patterns which result in emotional pain and/or social failure. Midrange families have more tolerance for individuation than the severely disturbed but much of their humanness is disavowed. Typically, they are clear and unambiguous in a given interaction at the expense of honesty about their own reality.

An illustrative midrange family was that of a young woman who presented herself to a psychiatrist manifesting marked hysterical features and overt depression. Her mother, having come from a lower social class and marrying into wealth, felt intimidated and eager to be "right." She was extremely harsh, prudish, and judgmental, pressing ever harder toward control. The father generally backed his wife in her efforts at limit-setting when she was present, but privately he tried to "make it up" to his daughter. Clear and direct within a given communication framework, he was a hypocrite, unable to give honest expression to his feelings.

Control is the watchword of the midrange families. Standards of behavior, thought, and feeling develop which are pathetically inadequate to express the full reality of children or parents.

Lying behind and intertwined with the constant efforts to control (oneself, one's spouse, one's children) seems to be an assumption that man is essentially evil. The view is elaborated differently in the two midrange styles of families. The families with a centripetal style behave as if one who controls himself, is "good," hides, denies, and represses his animal (evil) side, will have virtue and be powerful.

Midrange families with a centrifugal style behave as if they believe that since nobody in the family is virtuous, then any effort to be "good," noble, or even competent is fraudulent. Bickering and blaming one another are their mechanisms to avoid being attacked. This uses up much energy—which in the more rigidly structured neurotic family is often channelled into social accomplishment.

Both groups of midrange families handle ambivalence poorly. The world is usually seen as clear-cut, black or white, good or bad. With this either/or view of the world and the assumption of man as essentially evil, scapegoating is frequent in both groups but is handled somewhat differently.

Centrifugal families scapegoat incessantly and their style of blame and attack may shift focus from one to another family member. Anyone may find himself "it."

Not so with the centripetal group: the better functioning of these develop stable *external* scapegoats; that is, people outside the family who are scorned for expressing that which "good" families keep hidden. The more poorly functioning of these families may develop a stable internal scapegoat; that is, one person within the family who becomes "Peck's bad boy." He absorbs the family's rigid rule system, but turns it about and becomes a mirror image of the family's ideal. This way, other family members can remain consciously virtuous by projecting their faults and hidden wishes onto their family scapegoat and he, instead of having the usual family dynamics of a neurotic, will be a flamboyantly visible behavior disorder.

1) "I-ness"

In midrange families, an observer can detect individuation, but there is an eerie sensation of an invisible "referee." If the individual's wishes and behavior coincide with this referee's rules, he can declare himself with impunity, even smugness. Statements which relate to other's behavior are common and relatively risk-free. "You're wasting our time, John," and "You're always interrupting." Negative declarations such as "I don't feel angry toward you," "I'm not unhappy," "I'm not going to act up again," are much safer than positive declarations of being.

Centripetal family members avoid responsibility for their own thoughts, feelings, and actions by shrouding pronouncements under the cloak of the referee: "You shouldn't ever speak poorly of your teachers." "I'm only punishing you for your own good."

Centrifugal family members, usually more obviously defensive, use blame to avoid personal responsibility: "You got me so rattled I forgot." "Of course I drink, who wouldn't with such a crummy family?"

2) Respect for the Unique Experience of the Other Person

The midrange families recognize the reality of the experience of the different members, but make strong attempts to limit and to bring everyone's inner life and behavior into agreement with the referee. Criticism is frequent. Rarely does the rule system limit parental control to the *behavior* of the children: discipline extends to attempted control of their feelings and thoughts. "You shouldn't feel that way about your sister," "No decent person has thoughts like that," or even, "You must be crazy if you want to do that."

In the presence of an interviewer, speaking for others is frequent, but this does not have the destructive power of invasiveness which is minimal at this level of family functioning.

3) Receptiveness

In midrange family interaction impermeability is a significant feature, but it is less blatant, grotesque, and overwhelmingly destructive than in more disturbed families. In the restricted, centripetal family, communication usually occurs by taking turns speaking, with few successful interruptions (16,21). Since the rigid rules will not accommodate reality, a communicational sub-system often develops among the children which is ignored by the parents. Impermeability is most apparent when family members try to intrude with feelings or concerns that would not be acceptable to the invisible referee.

Example: a mother sits with a friend, chatting pleasantly. Her nine-year-old occupies himself doing multiplication tables. He runs into trouble and asks his mother: "How much is 7 x 7?" The mother, hungry for contact with a peer and feeling that the son's concerns are outside the rules ("Children should be seen, not heard."), totally ignores him. The child repeats his question to the point of near frenzy before subsiding into silence. Such events, when often repeated, leave the child feeling unimportant and somewhat dull. When report cards come, the same mother feels extremely frustrated and demands better performance from the child ("My child should make A's").

The centrifugal family is no more permeable, but their style is different. Several conversations may go on at once with no attention to individual members as parts of the whole group.

C. The Healthy Family

Knowledge of the factors which produce unusually capable adults is incomplete. Much of our information about normal or "healthy" families comes from studies which include as controls families presumed healthy by lack of overt pathology in their children. Other data are available from a few studies of well-functioning individuals and their family systems (17). In spite of this limited data from healthy families, it is evident that the process of individuation is most complete in this group.

Immediately apparent are: the presence of autonomous interaction that is relatively free of unresolved conflict; a clear, yet flexible family rule system; relative freedom in communicating; skill in negotiation in which ambivalence is acceptable and agreement results from inventive compromise.

In an atmosphere free of intimidation, defenses such as projection, denial, blaming and scapegoating are infrequent and unnecessary since no individual needs to avoid taking responsibility for himself.

In family groups with a high degree of individuation, a coherent rule system coincides with tolerance of uniqueness. An unspoken but strongly held view that people, while responsible for acceptable behavior, can think and feel just about everything, removes the burden of control. As a result, the interaction seems almost effortless and is characterized by frequent interruptions and remarks incoherent to outsiders, but easily comprehended by family participants (21).

1) "I-ness"

Since healthy families are reasonably comfortable with uncertainty, ambivalence, and disagreement, members have the luxury of being visible and known. The system recognizes people as mistake-makers, and even parents can issue pronouncements that later prove to be in error without much loss of face, and children can fail without a negative self image. In such a system one can be candid, open, and vulnerable. Comprehensive expression of views and feelings is much more frequent in healthy families than in any pathological group (24).

2) Respect for the Unique Experience of the Other

In these fortunate families, there is a sensitivity to the subjective world view of the other. Individual family members experience respect for their own feeling and thought, and hence are likely to give others the same respect. Therefore, invasions rarely occur. When they do, they are quickly resisted, and even the smallest children are accorded respect for their subjective reality.

3) Receptiveness

Mishler and Waxler (21) found in the interaction of their normal controls the highest incidence of complete acknowledgement of family members' communications, even though they also had the highest incidence of fragmented sentences and unscoreable remarks. Indeed, even these fragments were a part of the communication pattern which had maximum receptiveness, openness, and acknowledgment of the other.

Such flexibility allows members of a healthy family to be aware of the experience of fellow family members. Mutual respect encourages openness and increases the possibility of new and useful input into family negotiations.

The beneficent features of successful individuation, 1) "I-ness" (the ability to state unequivocally one's feelings and thoughts and to take responsibility for action), 2) respect for the uniqueness of another's experience, and 3) receptiveness or permeability (openness to another's communicative efforts), combine to provide a powerful base from which to solve problems and learn from others. These qualities maximize the opportunity for developing a separate, unique identity without the threat of becoming a pariah.

III. Acceptance of Separation and Loss

A competent family self-destructs: children grow up, leave the nest; parents grow old, and having failing functions, die. Adaptation to these stark realities is successful only to the degree that individuation is complete. In such evolved people, a sense of capability does not depend on unchanging relationships. There is an ability to accept the future, to acknowledge and adapt to the great changes brought about by growth and development, aging and death. A family member can then operate with respect for his own dignity and that of others. He can have joy in encountering a loved one, even though that very encounter brings awareness of the implications of loss in passage of time. When individuation is incomplete, separation is resisted and family pain and functional difficulty increase.

A. Severely Disturbed Families

Searles has written movingly (28) of the relationship between madness and the fear of death:

> The ostensibly prosaic fact of the inevitability of death is, in actuality, one of the supremely potent sources of man's anxiety, and the feeling responses to this aspect of reality are among the most intense and complex which it is possible for us to experience. The defense mechanisms of psychiatric illness, including the oftentimes exotic-appearing defenses found in schizophrenia, are designed to keep out of the individual's awareness—among other anxiety-provoking aspects of inner and outer reality—this simple fact of life's finitude. Various characteristics of our culture serve to maintain our obliviousness to this fact of inevitable death and the psychodynamics of schizophrenic illness in particular serve as strong defenses against the recognition of it. Although the earliest roots of schizophrenia may antedate the time in the individual's life when death's inevitability tends to confront him, it is the author's impression that this particular deeply anxiety-provoking aspect of reality is one of the major threats which the schizophrenic process is serving to deny.

Searles was speaking of the individual schizophrenic patient, and not the family system from whence he came. Paul and Grosser (22), however, have similar views from experience with family systems with a severely disturbed (usually schizophrenic) member. They see the bizarre communication and disturbances of reality as resulting from a poorly handled loss of a loved one. They center treatment efforts around an attempt to help family members to grieve and to accept the previously unacceptable.

These severely disturbed families are the least individuated and family members have the least confidence in their ability to survive change. They will show the most maladaptive defenses in dealing with inevitable losses. The family clings together in its amorphousness, using fantasy and denial as bulwark against loss. These are essentially dishonest, illusory techniques for handling such powerful and inexorable forces as growth and development, aging and death.

B. *Midrange Families*

Neither can midrange family members abide separation of parent from child, child from parent. Usually the therapist of a neurotic or behavior disorder finds the patient's parents still caught up in a frustrating, conflict-ridden relationship with their parents, or still ineffectually grieving for an idealized parent, long dead. The midrange family product usually has the ability to find new relationships which are closely related in style to those he knew in the past. Rather than mourning his losses resulting from growth or death, and looking for new relationships, the midrange offspring keeps the memory of mother and/or father burning bright. He recreates them with considerable ingenuity and skill, utilizing susceptible people outside his primary family.

C. *Healthy Families*

The ability to accept separation and loss of loved ones is at the heart of all the skills of healthy family systems. If parents feel competent as humans, able to live without clutching a particular relationship (either of parent, spouse, or child), then it is unnecessary for them to blur reality, to live out fantasies, to insist desperately on timelessness and the perpetuation of never-broken bonds between generations. A strong parental coalition, always seen in healthy, intact families, allows the parents to break excessive bonds with their own parents and sets up the opportunity to have good generational separation in their own developing family.

However, the demands of living are only partially met by a gratifying husband-wife relationship. The ability to have meaningful encounters and relationships in the broader environment must be emphasized as a part of healthy family systems. These relationships, reaching into the wider community, are sources of stimulation to the family structure, putting "life" into the system. They strengthen the ability of parents to accept their own aging and the developing autonomy of their children with equanimity.

After observing many family systems along the continuum from most disturbed to healthy, it is considered important to comment on the significance of a transcendent value system in effective adaptation to separation and loss. This is a difficult variable to research and is usually approached from an a priori position. It is also a territory that produces anxiety in most honorable researchers, since "objectivity" is a transcendent value for this group, and value systems are stubbornly subjective. Another serious problem in obtaining meaningful data in this area is the fact that verbally stated values may have little to do with the internalized values that dictate behavior. People kill in the name of love, cower and tremble while adhering to a philosophy of the unimportance of earthy existence, and clutch children or parents with verbal statements of a belief in a separate individual relation to a deity ("The Lord is my shepherd. I shall not want.").

Nevertheless, clinical work suggests that, in addition to a good marital coalition and meaningful contacts outside the family system, a functional transcendent value system is necessary to handle object loss capably. If family members have an extended identity that reaches beyond their own bodies and those of loved ones, they are not so dependent on meaning derived from a particular person who is irreplaceable.

IV. *Perception of Reality*

Just as individuals vary greatly in their ability to operate within a shared context and framework with their fellow man, so do families vary in this extremely significant skill. It is important to emphasize that any conception of an absolute reality is rejected since the very nature of human interaction causes this concept to be *interpersonal* and, therefore, any effort to determine the degree of reality testing of an individual or a family is a social process. Indeed, a common expression of poor reality testing is the attempt to foist unique and different perceptions of the world onto resisting others, with little appreciation for the large amount of negotiation or naked power necessary to accomplish this feat. Families, because of their continual close relationship to one another, develop a shared world view which can be evaluated by an observer as being more or less like his own. Inevitably, this is an arbitrary effort fraught with the possibility that incongruity is due to the *observer's* failure rather than the family's; but with this caveat the attempt may still be made (just as individual interviewers in mental health professions perform a similar task with individual patients). Among the many aspects of a family's shared perception of reality, two stand out as especially significant in comparing and contrasting family systems: 1) the degree of congruence between the family mythology and the observed "reality" and 2) the degree to which a family "timebinds."

A. *Family Mythology*

Ferreira (10) defined family myths as "a series of fairly well integrated beliefs shared by all family members, concerning each other and their mutual position in the family life, beliefs that go unchallenged by everyone involved in spite of the reality distortions which they may conspicuously imply."

All families develop these ongoing and enduring myths about themselves. The nature and quality of the mythic aspects of family systems are very much related to the level of family functioning.

1) *Severely Disturbed Families*

Here we find the greatest disparity between family myth and "reality," often necessitating blindness to such obvious phenomena as having a family member who is overtly psychotic. Therapists who have treated families with a schizophrenic member are familiar with a pattern in which the member who is showing marked emotional pain and bizarre behavior is either ignored or treated as merely "obstinate."

The stubborn, unchanging quality to the myths defies the introduction of possibilities for change; e.g., "Father is inadequate," even though he has functioned well in the outside world for years, and/or "Mother is always capable," although she has just disintegrated after attempting to obtain release for her hospitalized psychotic offspring. The identified patient is "sensitive, capable, misunderstood," even though he has failed consistently in interpersonal relationships outside the family.

Incongruous myths in disturbed families are maintained by denial, obliviousness, and careful family teaching, with no corrective mechanism to adjust to broader social "reality." This incongruence is a potent source of mixed messages and confusion to a developing child. Individuals in all family groups live in two realities—the *mythical* and the *real* behavior of their members. When these are markedly different, it may be necessary to blot out the reality of one's own perceptions and develop a capacity to operate in the shared fantasy. Otherwise, one runs the risk of being unacceptable within the family system.

2) Midrange Families

The myths of these families, whether centrifugal or centripetal in style, are also at odds with reality, but the distortion is less severe. The incongruence is most evident in the area of feelings.

Families with a centripetal style are quite concerned with social power and being "appropriate," and, therefore, behavior is closely watched and controlled. This results in a mythology reasonably congruent in the area of performance. They are, however, most obtuse in recognizing and dealing with emotional pain in members.

Centrifugal midrange families define themselves as second-class and unworthy of much respect and social power, so they, too, have mythologies that are fairly congruent with behavior. The marked difference is, of course, that the behavior is often not "appropriate" —Daddy drinks and is unreliable, Mother is slovenly, shouts at the kids and tells them to get lost, children misbehave and are rude and unmanageable. In a manner similar to centripetal families, the incongruent mythology is most obvious in the lack of concern for or awareness of emotional pain. For example, a man showing his wife a group of houses which were $20,000 greater in value than their own, proudly compared their house as equal. The daughter indignantly insisted that her father must be crazy— anyone could see that the houses they were admiring were much more expensive. He gave her a crooked grin and said: "Well, honey, it's an art you have to develop." He had married a wealthy woman and had failed twice in business. The mother alternately supported and attacked the myth that her husband was a success- ful provider.

3) *Healthy Families*

The myths of healthy families are reassuringly similar to ob- servers' views of the family members' character structure and the quality of their interaction. In contrast to less functional family systems, they are quick to pick up emotional pain or unusual be- havior in each other, and approach problems with directness and an expectation that something can be done. In other words, myth is not used to cloud and distort reality perceptions. Instead, it performs a different function, that of filling in the gaps of observa- tion and providing a matrix of shared meaning. These myths, though helpful and reassuring, are not rigid and can be altered relatively easily; for example, that mother is incompetent in mathe- matics or that father is all thumbs in the kitchen. This corresponds with family behavior and yet when circumstances demand that an individual step out of his role, he is flexible and potentially skillful enough to do so. If mother becomes widowed, she is able to develop skills and manage the family finances. Congruence between myth and observed reality is relatively close and does not preclude change with new demands.

These myths about the family and family members are gentle and humorous. Generally man is accepted as a "mistake-making animal," which softens or obliterates the black or white quality of expecting people always to live up to their image (or live down to it). There is room for surprise and change in these myths.

B. *Timebinding and Timelessness*

Many years ago, Korzybski (14) defined man functionally as a "timebinder," noting this unique ability of man. Indeed, it separates man from other animals in the fact that, in the rough, each generation of humans, at least potentially, can start where the former generation left off. This capability is not, however, equal in all men or in all family systems' functioning, because there are compelling reasons why one might wish to deny the passage of time. Such denial, while perhaps alleviating pain, can lead only to greater dysfunction and denials of other realities.

The ability of a family system to tolerate the pain of loss due to growth and development, aging and death, opens up a panorama of possibilities for human encounter with awareness, acknowledgement and acceptance. Change is inevitable with the passage of time, and a true human encounter produces change in all the participants. Browning's question: "Can we love but on the condition that the thing we love must die?" suggests this intimate and poignant relationship between closeness and the awareness of finiteness and death. Family systems vary greatly in their ability to deal with these realities.

While there is considerable overlap between the function of timebinding in a family's perception of reality, and acceptance of the loss of loved ones (discussed in the previous section), it may be helpful to present them separately— with the recognition that such intellectual categorizations of complex, interrelated phenomena are arbitrary.

1) *Severely Disturbed Families*

Severely disturbed families are extremely reluctant to acknowledge the passage of time. These family members are most fearful of separation and loss, and use a variety of unrealistic (hence pathological) methods to obscure the evidences of change. The family atempts to "hold back the dawn" and, hence, the interaction is stereotyped, repetitive, and devoid of real encounter. Incongruent family myths are used in this effort. A boy of 15 may be seen as already grown with wisdom exceeding his father's at one moment, only to be seen as helpless and infantile the next. The face of the biological clock is obscured, and fantasy replaces reality in family consciousness.

Here is a description written by a severely isolated and lonely young woman, a product of such a family:

> I lived in absoluteness. My world moved in the slow, unchanging and unquestioned rhythm of a dream. It *was* a dream. Nothing moved in the basic outlines of our existence. Life was as absolute and predictable as the path we had beaten between our house and our grandparents. Relationships were secure. They were the same when I woke in the morning as they had been when I went to bed the night before. Life was slow then. We moved in a circle. Time belonged to the world, but we belonged to ourselves. We were frozen. I wore that rhythm like a ring around the faithful finger of my life.

With markedly unrealistic family myths and an enduring sense of timelessness, it is no wonder that severely disturbed families communicate oddly and function inefficiently, both short-term and and long-term in the larger world.

2) *Midrange Families*

In these families, the reality of the passage of time is distorted but not obliterated. There is difficulty in accepting growth and development, aging and death, but the reality is painfully and gracelessly accepted. Mothers in this group often compete with their adolescent daughters in sexual attractiveness ("Mirror, mirror on the wall, who is the fairest of them all?') or conversely, they submerge themselves in middle age, asexuality, and dowdiness. Similarly, fathers may compete zealously with sons, with varying degrees of success; or depressed, they may passively withdraw from the field.

An old psychiatric joke defines the psychotic as one who thinks $2 + 2 = 5$; the neurotic as one who knows $2 + 2 = 4$, but *can't stand it!* This parallels timebinding in the severely disturbed and midrange families. The midrange family recognizes time's inexorable passage, but such awareness provokes considerable pain.

3) Healthy Families

The members of these fortunate family systems have been able to develop a reasonable degree of self-confidence and autonomy, and, therefore, the pain of separation and loss is markedly lessened. One result of this is the family's grace in accepting and acknowledging the realities of time's passage—children growing up and becoming more powerful than parents, the parents' waning abilities, the inevitability of death.

The favorable consequence of this realistic orientation is an opportunity for closeness and a communicational openness unmatched by any system that depends on a shared myth of timelessness for equilibrium. Children not seen as competitors or crutches may be viewed with pride. Without the need to deny or grudgingly admit the powerful force of the biological clock, the growth and development of children is celebrated.

Because healthy families approach possibilities with curiosity, interest, and hope, they find out more and their myths are more congruent with reality. In these families, with a recognition and acceptance of the passage of time and the reality of change, both physical and emotional, in their members, true encounters can occur. The meaning of present transactions is acknowledged, always with a direction toward the future. Children are encouraged and expected to become more capable, more skillful, and more aware of possibilities in the future.

V. *Affect*

This variable encompasses the various aspects of feeling, both short and long term, expressed in families. This is most significant in itself as part of diagnosis in individuals or family groups, and has long been a focus of clinicians. Reducing pain is an honorable activity of therapists, traditionally as important as increasing functioning ability.

Feelings expressed in a family, however, are intimately related to system structure. Rigid and inflexible structure, unclear boundaries between family members, and resistance to acknowledgment of loss produce painful interactions and induce despair.

Just as an experienced automobile mechanic makes accurate predictions of engine structure and function by listening to the motor sounds, so does a clinician detect structural and functional problems by empathically perceiving feelings of the family.

There are several measurable aspects of affect in families. These include the prevailing mood or feeling tone, the degree of expressiveness of feeling, and the quality of empathy—the degree of sensitivity and responsiveness to others' feelings. Further, there are conflicts in all family systems. There may be, in addition, unresolved and apparently unresolvable conflict which is reflected in distortions of feeling tone.

The prevailing mood may vary from one of warmth and affection, usually with shared humor and an overall attitude of optimism, to various shades of negative feelings, such as stiff politeness, bursts of overt hostility, frequent anxiety or depressive affect, numb apathy, on down to the soul-searing and destructive expressions of cynicism and bitterness.

When discussing mood and feeling tone, perhaps an operational definition of warmth would be useful. This word, like many used in describing human interaction, is often left undefined, as if everyone shared the same view of its meaning. Unfortunately, such is not the case. Very few people, even mental health professionals, define it the same way.

A useful definition which includes the necessary elements is:

"human warmth is human need, honestly expressed, with a recognition of the limits of the other person." It is a *reaching out* and, therefore, is related to *need*. Many people confuse warmth with "giving"—which often leads to a virtuous sterility and emotional starvation. Needs consciously acknowledged, however, may go awry if they are not clearly expressed—if too opaque or expressed obliquely, disappointment rather than warmth results. Finally, if one's needs are expressed clearly but are unrelated to the other person's capacity for meeting those needs, frustration, anger, and guilt result rather than the possible warm interaction. To apply this definition to family interaction, one may say that a family whose interactions are characterized by warmth is one in which members are able to express their individual needs clearly, with an accurate recognition of the limitations of the others' abilities to meet those needs.

Mood, or feeling tone, may be separated and distinguished from the degree of expressiveness of feeling to a large degree. Some families with obvious cheerfulness and warmth have members who do not verbalize their feelings easily, or one may see families in which negative feelings pervading the family system are expressed with painful directness.

Finally, the ability of a family system to be empathic ranges from consistent empathic responsiveness through degrees of attempted empathic understanding, to a seeming absence of such shared feelings, to grossly inappropriate responses to feelings. The ability of a family to be empathic is usually closely correlated with the overall mood or feeling tone since warmth, or the absence of it, is so directly related to the degree of emotional sensitivity.

A. *Severely Disturbed Families*

Many researchers describe the negative affective climate that permeates severely disturbed families. When telling stories from a TAT card stimulus (29), families of autistic children demonstrated pervasive cynicism, open hostility, and sneering, deprecating attitudes. Parents of young adult schizophrenics had a mood of depression, hopelessness and despair, but without the bitter hostility seen in the families of autistic children. Lennard and Bernstein (16) were impressed by the disparaging and sarcastic comments and absence of affirmation in the interchange of families with a schizophrenic member. Riskin and Faunce (24) found their most disturbed families to have the most unfriendly and contentious atmosphere. Mishler and Waxler (21) noted this same discord in families with schizophrenic members.

This negative atmosphere seems inevitable in any group of people who have minimal individuation and much maladaptive interpersonal behavior.

B. *Midrange Families*

Midrange families show a variety of negative moods—sadness, depression, criticism, or low-keyed bickering with occasional explosiveness and argumentativeness (24). Singer and Wynne (29), in TAT stories given by parents of acting-out children, found many hostile tales, but they lacked the sadism found in the stories of parents of childhood schizophrenics. The stories of parents of withdrawn, neurotic children had a subdued mood without open hostility or warmth or joy. These groups of parents seem to be midrange in affect as well as in effectiveness in childrearing—able to get by but showing constant evidence of ineptness and constriction in emotional exchanges. Since unpleasant feelings frequently appear, family members are vulnerable to psychiatric disorders relating to feelings—depressive and anxiety states.

C. *Healthy Families*

The most capable families demonstrate open, direct expression of humor, tenderness, warmth and hopefulness to a striking degree. Expressions of negative feelings are made in the context of awareness of the other person and with a balancing supportiveness. This group of families are skillful interpersonally: the members work together reasonably well and their interaction appears to elicit pleasure with a resulting positive emotional tone. When conflicts arise they are recognized quickly and resolved effectively.

It is always more pleasurable to be involved in group activity where accomplishment rather than failure and frustration results. When an optimal family, with its individuated, clear, and flexible structure approaches a problem or a possibility, the concomitant sounds of positive feelings are easily seen to be a byproduct of effectiveness.

SUMMARY

This chapter presents a theoretical approach to family competence based primarily on structural variables seen from a systems framework. Family systems are related to one another in five different areas: power structure, degree of individuation, acceptance of separation and loss, perception of reality, and affect. Families are viewed as being on a continuum of functioning with three major levels distinguished—severely disturbed, midrange (with two very different styles, neurotic and behavior disorder), and health. Characteristic expressions of the five variables are described for these family types. This orientation encourages synthesis of data from various disturbed families and from healthy family systems with the goals of therapeutic intervention suggested by the approach. Based primarily on studies of middle-class white families (and limited in scope by this fact) the data suggest that families that produce adaptive, well functioning offspring have a structure of shared power, a great appreciation and encouragement of individuation, and an ability to accept separation and loss realistically. In addition, they have a family mythology consistent with the reality as seen by outside observers, a strong sense of the passage of time and the inevitability of change, and a warm and expressive feeling tone.

REFERENCES

1. BATESON, G., "The biosocial integration of behavior in the schizophrenic family." In N. W. Ackerman, F. L. Beatman and S. N. Sherman (Eds.), *Exploring the Base for Family Therapy*, New York: Family Service Assn. of America, 1961.

2. BATESON, G., JACKSON, D. D., HALEY, J., and WEAKLAND, J., "Toward a theory of schizophrenia," *Behav. Science,* 1:251-264, 1958.
3. BEAVERS, W. R., BLUMBERG, S., TIMKIN, K. R., and WEINER, M. D., "Communication patterns of mothers of schizophrenics," *Family Process,* 4:95-104, 1965.
4. BEAVERS, W. R., "The application of family systems theory to crisis intervention." In D. K. Switzer, *The Minister as Crisis Counselor,* Nashville: Abdington Press, 1974.
5. BECKETT, J. A., "General systems theory, psychiatry and psychotherapy," *International J. of Group Psychotherapy,* Vol. XXIII, No. 3, 292-305, July, 1973.
6. BIRDWHISTLE, R. L., "The age of a baby." In *Kinesics and Context,* Philadelphia: U. of Pennsylvania Press, 1970.
7. BOWEN, M. A., "Family concept of schizophrenia." In D. D. Jackson (Ed.), *The Etiology of Schizophrenia,* New York: Basic Books, 1960.
8. BRILLOUIN, S., "Life, thermodynamics and cybernetics." In W. Buckley (Ed.), *Modern Systems Research for the Behavioral Scientist,* Chicago: Aldine Publishing Co., 1968, 147-159.
9. BRUCH, H., "Falsification of bodily needs and body concept in schizophrenia," *Arch. Gen. Psychiatry.,* 6:18-24, Jan., 1962.
9a. DAY, J., and KWIATKOWSKA, H. Y., "The psychiatric patient and his 'well' sibling," *Bull. of Art Therapy,* Winter 1962.
10. FERREIRA, A. J., "Family myth and homeostasis," *Arch. Gen. Psychiat.,* 9:457-463, 1963.
11. GARMEZY, N., and RODNICK, E. H., "Premorbid adjustment and performance in schizophrenia," *J. Nerv. and Ment. Dis.,* 129:450-466, 1959.
12. HELLER, J., *Catch 22,* New York: Simon and Schuster, 1955.
13. KETY, S. S., ROSENTHAL, D., WENDER, P. H., and SCHULSINGER, F., "Mental illness in the biological and adoptive families of adopted schizophrenics," *Am. J. Psychiat.,* 128:302-306, 1971.
14. KORZYBSKI, A., *Science and Sanity,* Lancaster, Pa., The International Non-Aristotlian Library, 1933.
15. LAING, R. D., "Mystification, confusion, and conflict." In Nagy and Framo (Eds.), *Intensive Family Therapy,* New York: Hoeber, 1965.
16. LENNARD, N. L., and BERNSTEIN, A., *Patterns in Human Interaction,* San Francisco: Jossey-Bass, Inc., 1969.
17. LEWIS, J. M., GOSSETT, J. T., and PHILLIPS, V. A., "Studies of healthy family systems," *Timberlawn Foundation Reports,* Dallas, Texas, 1969.
18. LIDZ, T., FLECK, S., ALANEN, Y. O., and CORNELISON, A., "Schizophrenic patients and their siblings," *Psychiatry,* 26:1-18, 1963.
19. LIDZ, T., FLECK, S., and CORNELISON, A. R., *Schizophrenia and the Family.* New York: International Univ. Press, 1965.
19a. LIDZ, R. W., and LIDZ, T., "The family environment of schizophrenic patients," *Am. J. Psychiat.,* 106:332-345, 1949.
20. MEAD, M., "The American family: Reality or myth," The Scott Hawkins Lecture, Southern Methodist University, Dallas, Texas, March 31, 1970.
21. MISHLER, E., and WAXLER, N., *Interaction in Families.* New York: John Wiley and Sons, 1968.
22. PAUL, N., and GROSSER, G. H., "Operational mourning and its role in conjoint family therapy, *Community Mental Health Journal,* 1:339-345, 1965.
23. RICHARDSON, H. B., *Patients Have Families,* New York, Commonwealth Fund, 1945.

24. RISKIN, J., and FAUNCE, E. F., "Family interaction scales," *Arch. Gen. Psychiat.*, Vol. 22 (6), 504-537, June, 1970.
25. ROSENZWEIG, S., and BRAY, D., "Sibling deaths in the anamneses of schizophrenic patients," *Arch. Neurol. and Psychiat.*, 49:71-92, 1943.
26. SANUA, V. D., "Sociocultural factors in families of schizophrenics," *Psychiat.*, 24:246-265, 1961.
27. SCHAFFER, L., WYNNE, L. D., DAY, J., RYCKOFF, I. M., and HALPERIN, A., "On the nature and sources of the psychiatrist's experience with the family of the schizophrenic," *Psychiat.*, 25:32-45, 1962.
28. SEARLES, H. F., "Schizophrenia and the inevitability of death," *Psychiat. Quart.*, 35:631-664, 1961.
29. SINGER, M. T., and WYNNE, L. D., "Differentiating characteristics of parents of childhood schizophrenics, childhood neurotics, and young adult schizophrenics," *Am. J. Psychiat.*, 120:234-243, 1963.
30. SPEER, D. C., Family systems: Morphostasis and morphogenesis, or is homeostasis enough?" *Family Process*, 9:259-278, 1970.
31. STIERLIN, H., *Separating Parents and Adolescents*, New York, Quadrangle, 1974.
32. WESTLEY, W. A., and EPSTEIN, N. B., *The Silent Majority*. San Francisco: Jossey-Bass, Inc., 1969.
33. WYNNE, L. C., RYCKOFF, I. M., DAY, J., and HIRSCH, S. L., "Pseudo-mutuality in the family relations of schiophrenics," *Psychiat.*, 21:205-220, 1958.

CHAPTER IV

FAMILY SYSTEM RATING
SCALES

The research group spent many hours translating the theoretical family systems framework to a series of rating scales. After much preliminary scale design, the group used each evolving scale to rate segments of the videotaped interactional testing of the 23 families who participated in the pilot study. This led to a repetitive cycle of discussion, revision of each scale, and further testing of the scales. When the group's reliability in the use of the scales reached acceptable levels, other raters were introduced to the scales and asked to rate family interactions. Each of the 13 scales, along with the Global Health-Pathology Scale,* is presented individually along with a description of its relationship to the theoretical family systems framework.**

After observing from 10 to 50 minutes of videotaped interactional testing, the rater was asked to score the family regarding the basic power structure of the total family system. The manner in which the family dealt with the issue of power or influence was the organizing principle in the formulation. In keeping with the entropy model, the Structure Scale moves from chaos to rigidity

---

* See Appendix E, p. 235.

** Several scales (structure, parental coalition, closeness, invasiveness and conflict) are set up in reverse; that is, with the smallest numbers representing the most pathological end of the continuum. This was done to discourage the halo effect of raters' using the same rating on all the scales. These scale ratings were converted in order to arrive at a sum of scales.

I. Structure of the Family

A. Overt Power. Based on the entire tape, check the term that best describes your general impression of the power structure of this family.

1	1.5	2	2.5	3	3.5	4	4.5	5
Chaos		Marked Dominance		Moderate Dominance		Led		Egalitarian

If 2 to 4, indicate:
Who is #1 in power: Father........ Mother........ Child (specify)........
Who is #2 in power: Father........ Mother........ Child (specify)........

1 = Chaos: Leaderless; no one has enough power to structure the interaction.
2 = Marked Dominance: Control is close to absolute. No negotiation; dominance and submission are the rule.
3 = Moderate Dominance: Control is close to absolute. Some negotiation, but dominance and submission are the rule.
4 = Led: Tendency toward dominance and submission, but most of the interaction is through respectful negotiation.
5 = Egalitarian: Leadership is shared between parents, changing with the nature of the interaction.

to flexibility. A critical element in determining the rating was the concept of respectful negotiation.

B. Parental Coalitions
Check the terms that best describe the relationship structure in this family.

1	1.5	2	2.5	3	3.5	4	4.5	5
Parent-Child Coalition				Weak Parental Coalition				Strong Parental Coalition

This second of the scales measuring family structure asked the rater to make a judgment regarding the strongest power coalition observed in the videotaped family interaction. It was included because of the clinical and research data which suggest that the nature of the parental coalition is an important factor in the overall health of the family.

C. Closeness

1	1.5	2	2.5	3	3.5	4	4.5	5

Amorphous, vague and indistinct boundaries among members	Isolation, distancing	Closeness with distinct boundaries among members

The closeness rating scale proved to be one of the more difficult scales for raters to master, but also one of the most discriminating. The rater difficulty may be due to the fact that it involved two variables—the presence or absence of distinct boundaries between individuals in a family and the degree of closeness. Those family systems which, in their communication, reflected vague, amorphous boundaries or fusion were at one extreme of the scale; in the middle portion were those families in which the separateness of the individuals was clear, but associated with considerable interpersonal distance. Families which demonstrated closeness with distinct boundaries were rated at the other end of the scale.

The inclusion of two variables in this scale was based on a concept of ego boundaries: One must be separate in order to be close. The effectiveness with which the Closeness Scale discriminated between groups of families supported this view.

D. The power structure, or "pecking order" in this family is:

1	1.5	2	2.5	3	3.5	4	4.5	5

Hard to determine	Relatively hard to determine	Relatively easy to determine	Quite easy to determine

This scale differed from the others in that it told us about the rater rather than about the family, and it was therefore not included in a family's Sum of Scales. It was not predictive of any grouping of families.

II. Mythology

Every family has a mythology; that is, a concept of how it functions as a group.
Rate the degree to which this family's mythology seems congruent with reality.

1	1.5	2	2.5	3	3.5	4	4.5	5
Very congruent		Mostly congruent				Somewhat incongruent		Very in-congruent

---

The Mythology Scale rated a family on the degree to which
the family's concept of itself was congruent with the rater's appraisal of family behavior. Families which acted and talked as if
the family was "normal" despite the all-too-obvious presence of
severe conflict, pain, and despair were rated at one extreme. At
the other end were families who, independent of the level of family
functioning, saw themselves essentially as they were seen by the
raters.

III. Goal Directed Negotiation

Rate this family's overall efficiency in negotiation and problem solving.

1	1.5	2	2.5	3	3.5	4	4.5	5
Extremely efficient		Good				Poor		Extremely inefficient

This scale rated the effectiveness of the family's negotiations. As
such, it is dependent upon the presence of negotiation and effectiveness. We saw many dysfunctional families—usually with a
strong pattern of dominance-submission in which no negotiations
occurred and, therefore, in terms of this scale, such families,
though they could arrive at a solution to a task, were extremely
inefficient negotiators. Other inefficient families talked with each
other throughout the available time period, but came to no
shared solution.

IV. Autonomy

A. Communication of Self-Concept: Rate this family as to the clarity of disclosure of feelings and thoughts. This is not a rating of the intensity of feelings, but rather of clarity of expression of individual thoughts and feelings.

1	1.5	2	2.5	3	3.5	4	4.5	5
Very clear				Somewhat vague and hidden				Hardly anyone is ever clear

---

The Communication of Self-Concept Scale is the first of four attempting to evaluate family system characteristics involved in the production of autonomous individuals. It was based on the premise that one aspect of autonomy is the degree to which the family nourishes or discourages the clear communication of feelings and thoughts. It was the quality of clarity of disclosure which was important in this scale.

B. Responsibility: Rate the degree to which the family members take responsibility for their own past, present, and future actions.

1	1.5	2	2.5	3	3.5	4	4.5	5
Members regularly are able to voice responsibility for individual actions				Members sometimes voice responsibility for individual actions but tactics also include sometimes blaming others, speaking in 3rd person or plural				Members rarely, if ever, voice responsibility for individual actions

---

This scale, the second of four evaluating autonomy-encouraging family characteristics, measured the degree to which the family system reflected family members' acceptance of responsibility for their own feelings, thoughts, and actions. At one end we found families in which members avoided any communicated responsibility, whereas at the opposite end we found families in which "I did," "I will," "I feel" statements were frequent and characterized the functioning of the total family system.

C. Invasiveness: Rate the degree to which the members speak for one another, or make "mind reading" statements.

1	1.5	2	2.5	3	3.5	4	4.5	5
Many invasions				Occasional invasions				No evidence of invasions

This scale rated the extent to which a family system tolerated or encouraged family members to speak for one another. Its inclusion was based upon the concept that speaking for another ("What you really feel is . . .," "John, you are not hungry") impedes the development of autonomy in the other.

D. Permeability: Rate the degree to which members are open, receptive, and permeable to the statements of other family members.

1	1.5	2	2.5	3	3.5	4	4.5	5
Very open		Moderately open				Members frequently unreceptive		Members unreceptive

The fourth scale relating directly to the construct of autonomy was the Permeability Scale. This scale measured the degree to which a family system encouraged the acknowledgement of the stated feelings, thoughts, and behavior of its members. Impermeable families often failed to respond to members who repeatedly tried to be heard. Such obliviousness obliterated a sense of adequacy or autonomy.

V. FAMILY AFFECT

A. Expressiveness: Rate the degree to which this family system is characterized by open expression of feelings.

1	1.5	2	2.5	3	3.5	4	4.5	5

Open, direct expression of feelings	Direct expression of feelings despite some discomfort	Obvious restriction in the expression of some feelings	Although some feelings are expressed, there is masking of most feelings	No expression of feelings

---

The Expressiveness Scale was the first of four which measured various aspects of family affect. This scale measured the degree to which the family system encouraged the open communication of affect. It did not measure the quality of affect, only the openness of expression.

B. Mood and Tone: Rate the feeling tone of this family's interaction.

1	1.5	2	2.5	3	3.5	4	4.5	5

Unusually warm, affectionate, humorous and optimistic	Polite, without impressive warmth or affection; or frequently hostile with times of pleasure	Overtly hostile	Depressed	Cynical, hopeless and pessimistic

---

This scale asked the rater to make a judgment regarding the mood or feeling tone of the family interaction: From one end, at which family systems were characterized by a warm, optimistic feeling tone, moving toward hostile, depressed and hopeless moods. The scale refers to overall family system mood.

C. Conflict: Rate the degree of seemingly unresolvable conflict.

1	1.5	2	2.5	3	3.5	4	4.5	5
Severe conflict with severe impairment of group functioning		Definite conflict with moderate impairment of group functioning		Definite conflict with slight impairment of group functioning		Some evidence of conflict without impairment of group functioning		Little, or no conflict

In the Conflict Scale two factors were to be evaluated by the rater. The first was whether conflict, if present, was "seemingly unresolvable," i.e., during the videotaped family interaction there was either no attempt at resolution or, if present, the attempts were sparse and unproductive. The second factor estimated the effect of the conflict upon the functioning of the group; the problem was whether or not there was evidence of impairment in accomplishing the task at hand.

D. Empathy: Rate the degree of sensitivity to, and understanding of, each other's feelings within this family.

1	1.5	2	2.5	3	3.5	4	4.5	5
Consistent empathic responsiveness		For the most part, an empathic responsiveness with one another despite obvious resistance		Attempted empathic involvement, but failed to maintain it		Absence of any empathic responsiveness		Grossly inappropriate responses to feelings

This scale was used to measure the degree to which the family system encouraged its members to be aware of each other's feelings and to communicate this awareness. The scale moved from consistent awareness and responsiveness to occasional, absent and, at the extreme, grossly inappropriate responses to affect.

TABLE 4-1

Interrater Reliability Using Beavers-Timberlawn
Evaluation Scales *

	Raters A & B N = 36 **		Raters C & D N = 12 ***	
	r	p<	r	p<
Structure	.45	.01	.66	.01
Coalition	.20	NS	.67	.01
Closeness	.41	.01	.60	.05
Mythology	.31	.05	.60	.05
Negotiation	.69	.01	.65	.01
Clarity	.41	.01	.17	NS
Responsibility	.30	.05	.26	NS
Invasiveness	.21	NS	.73	.01
Permeability	—.17	NS	.71	.01
Expressiveness	.25	.05	.29	NS
Mood	.31	.05	.82	.01
Conflict	.36	.05	.65	.01
Empathy	.34	.05	.57	.05
Sum of Scales	.45	.01	.82	.01

* Pearson Product Moment Correlation Coefficient
** Randomly ordered population of 12 healthy families, 12 families with a child with a learning disability, and 12 families with an adolescent child who was in a psychiatric hospital.
*** Healthy families.

As can be noted, there was overlap between some of the scales; for example, a relationship between the Empathy Scale and the Conflict Scale. Despite these numerous areas of scale overlap, we felt that each scale contained a central construct useful in the assessment of family system functioning.

After demonstrating satisfactory interrater reliability within the research group, the scales were used by "outside" raters. We underestimated both the amount of training necessary for the use of the scales, and the influence of clinical or research experience with families upon the reliable use of the scale. These influences can be noted in the considerable difference in interrater reliability in Table 4-1. This table demonstrates reliability studies using two different pairs of raters and two different samples of families.

Rater A was a Registered Nurse in a graduate academic program; Rater B was a physician in his third year of psychiatric residency. Neither were experienced family clinicians or investigators and they achieved modest, but significant, reliability levels on 10 of the 13 scales. Rater C was an experienced psychiatric social worker. Rater D was an experienced psychiatrist with broad research experience. Both C and D received more training in the use of the scales. They achieved greater reliability and impressive correlations for 10 of the 13 scales.

In reviewing additional reliability data from other raters, we were impressed that four of the scales most frequently present difficulty for raters. These are: clarity of self disclosure, responsibility, invasiveness, and expressiveness.

Three of the four most difficult scales rated the autonomy-producing characteristics of the family system. Their difficulty may reflect the fact that mental health professionals are more experienced in dealing with power, coalitions, mythology, and expressions of affection than they are with the construct of autonomy, which is at another level of inference.

The use of the Global Health-Pathology Scale and data regarding its interrater reliability and validity was presented in Chapter II. The relationship between independent measures of global family health-pathology and the Family System Rating Scales is presented in Table 4-2.

The 33 healthy families were rated by an experienced psychiatric social worker, and the 70 families of hospitalized adolescents were rated by an experienced clinical psychologist. Each of these raters had demonstrated significant interrater reliability with a third rater, a Registered Nurse graduate student, who had scored subsamples of those two populations.

As can be noted, there was significant correlation for each of the Beavers-Timberlawn Family Evaluation Scales and the Global Family Health-Pathology Scale. The high correlation of the sum of the 13 scales with a measure of global family health-pathology supported the hypothesis that most of the relevant dimensions implicitly used by clinical raters were included in the 13 scales.

Table 4-3 demonstrates the relationship between individual

TABLE 4-2

Relationship Between Beavers-Timberlawn Evaluation Scales
and Global Family Health-Pathology Scales *

(N = 103: 70 Patient Families, 33 "Healthy" Families)

I.	Structure	
	Style of Leadership	.77
	Coalition	.70
	Closeness	.60
II.	Autonomy	
	Self-Disclosure	.52
	Responsibility	.74
	Invasiveness	.30
	Permeability	.68
III.	Affect	
	Expressiveness	.63
	Feeling Tone	.69
	Conflict	.78
	Empathy	.75
IV.	Perception of Reality	
	Mythology	.79
V.	Task Efficiency	
	Negotiation	.67
	SUM OF SUB-SCALES	.90

* Pearson Product Moment Correlation Coefficient, level of significance on each scale was $p < .005$.

psychopathology scores in hospitalized adolescent patients and the Global Health-Pathology Scale scores for the families of those patients. The adolescent patients' individual psychopathology scores were obtained independently by members of the hospital treatment team. They used a derivation of the Luborsky Scale (2) expanded and altered for applicability to adolescents (1). This scale yields an overall evaluation of the severity of psychopathology for adolescent patients (Appendix F). In Table 4-3, the hospital treatment team median scores, representing pooled staff judgments, are used.

This table demonstrates a significant relationship between the severity of adolescent patient psychopathology and a global meas-

TABLE 4-3

Relationship Between Individual Psychopathology Scores and Global Health-Pathology of Family *

	Global Family Health-Pathology Scale	Adolescent Psychopathology Scale 1
Scale Range	1-10	10-190
Sample Range	6-10	71-175
Sample Mean	8.1	134.9
Sample Standard Dev.	1.05	17.0

Pearson Product Moment Correlation Coefficient = .52, p <.005

1 Score is the Median Score assigned by members of the Adolescent Treatment Staff, Gossett-Timberlawn Adolescent Psychopathology Scale (1).

ure of family competence for a series of 70 adolescent admissions to a psychiatric inpatient facility. The magnitude of the correlation (r =.52) is surprisingly high in that constitutional, temperamental and developmental factors are not directly involved in the measure of family competence; i.e., it is a here-and-now measure.

Table 4-4 demonstrates the relationship between the Beavers-Timberlawn Family Evaluation Scales and the Gossett-Timberlawn Adolescent Psychopathology Scales* when applied to the same 70 patient families described in Table 4-3.

As anticipated, all of the correlations were positive and 8 of the 13 correlations were statisticaly significant. The correlations were modest: to find greater correlations between single family variables and an overall measure of adolescent patient psychopathology would be unanticipated. The individual scales with the greatest correlations were: the family style of leadership; the degree of closeness; the capacity of the family system to encourage its members to assume responsibility for their thoughts, feelings, and actions; and the family capacity for empathy. The sum of the 13 scales correlated slightly better than the four most highly correlated individual scales. Indeed, the scale measuring closeness within

* See Appendix F, p. 242.

TABLE 4-4

Relationship Between Beavers-Timberlawn Family
Evaluation Scales and Gossett-Timberlawn
Adolescent Psychopathology Scale*

I. Structure		
Structure	.31	<.005
Coalitions	.11	NS
Closeness	.41	<.005
II. Autonomy		
Self-Disclosure	.15	NS
Responsibility	.35	<.005
Invasiveness	.11	NS
Permeability	.25	<.025
III. Affect		
Expressiveness	.14	NS
Feeling Tone	.28	<.01
Conflict	.22	<.05
Empathy	.33	<.005
IV. Perception of Reality		
Mythology	.19	NS
V. Task Efficiency		
Negotiation	.24	<.025
SUM OF SUB-SCALES	.42	<.005

* N = 70

the family correlated at essentially the same level as the sum of
scales.

Table 4-5 compares mean values for each of the Beavers-Timberlawn Family Evaluation Scales in four groups of families (healthy,
and families containing a neurotic, behavior disorder, or psychotic
adolescent).

Although the numbers of "neurotic" and "psychotic" families
were not large, the findings were impressive. The Global Health-
Pathology Scale scores were in the anticipated direction and the
differences were statistically significant. The Gossett-Timberlawn

TABLE 4-5

Mean Values of Beavers-Timberlawn Evaluation Scales in Diagnostic Categories

Scale	Healthy N = 33	Neurotic N = 7	Behavior Disorder N = 45	Psychotic N = 18	Significant Levels T-Test +					
					H-N	H-B	H-P	N-B	N-P	B-P
Global										
Health Pathology	4.0	7.3	7.9	8.9	.01	.01	.01	.01	.01	.01
Adolescent[1]										
Psychopathology	n.a.	117	133	147	—	—	—	.01	.01	.01
Family System Rating Scales										
Sum of Scales	31.0	44.5	46.9	50.4	.01	.01	.01	.60	.20	.20
*Structure	2.1	3.3	3.4	3.7	.05	.01	.01	—	.60	.40
*Coalition	2.0	3.3	3.4	3.8	.02	.01	.01	—	.40	.20
*Closeness	2.5	2.9	3.0	3.6	.20	.01	.01	.80	.05	.01
Mythology	2.0	3.8	4.1	4.6	.01	.01	.01	.60	.10	.10
Negotiation	2.7	3.2	3.8	4.0	.20	.01	.01	.20	.20	.60
Clarity	2.7	4.0	3.5	3.9	.01	.01	.01	.40	—	.20
Responsibility	2.3	3.4	3.8	4.3	.01	.01	.01	.40	.05	.10
*Invasiveness	2.0	2.0	2.3	2.7	—	.20	.01	.60	.01	.20
Permeability	3.0	4.1	4.1	4.4	.01	.01	.01	—	.60	.40
Expressiveness	2.9	4.2	3.7	4.0	.01	.01	.01	.05	.60	.10
Feeling Tone	1.9	2.4	3.0	3.6	.20	.01	.01	.20	.02	.05
*Conflict	2.1	3.2	4.4	4.4	.01	.01	.01	.05	.05	—
Empathy	2.9	3.6	3.8	4.3	.01	.01	.01	.60	.10	.05

[1] Scores are medians of the Gossett-Timberlawn Adolescent Psychopathology Scale rated by adolescent staff members.
* Set up in the inverse direction on the scale, these scores are adjusted here to parallel the other scales: higher scores indicate greater pathology.
+ Student's t: one tailed test

Adolescent Psychopathology Scale scores revealed similar findings.

Each of the Beavers-Timberlawn Family Evaluation Scales mean scores was in the anticipated direction except that the seven families containing neurotic patients obtained higher (more pathological) mean scores on clarity of self-disclosure and on expressiveness of affect than did the behavior disorder and psychotic patient-containing families. With few exceptions, the differences in the means between the healthy families and the patient-containing families were statistically significant. The small number of exceptions to this finding is particularly impressive considering the variation among the healthy families (Chapter V).

A small number of the differences between the means were significant within the three groups of patient-containing families. Scales measuring family closeness, feeling tone, and conflict were most apt to demonstrate significant differences.

The Invasiveness Scale was most useful for scoring families containing a psychotic member. There was little difference in mean values between "neurotic" and "behavior disorder" families. While very destructive when it did occur, invasiveness was infrequent outside the most disturbed group.

The data reported in these five tables provided evidence for the construct validity of the family system theoretical framework described in Chapter III. The Beavers-Timberlawn Family Evaluation Scales had, with few exceptions, a reasonable degree of interrater reliability. The correlations between these scales and measures of global family health-pathology and individual adolescent patient psychopathology added weight to the usefulness in both research and clinical practice. The differences between the mean values across a continuum of family competence were impressive.

In discussing the Beavers-Timberlawn Family Evaluation Scales in relation to healthy families, we wish to emphasize that the 33 families were not a homogeneous group and the use of mean scale scores from the entire group of 33 families tended to minimize the differences between the healthy families and the patient-containing families. Despite this, the data supported the view that families judged to be healthy in their functioning did differ from patient-containing families across a wide variety of family variables. It was this very clear difference that we interpret to be the most striking finding. Healthy families were more likely to demonstrate a structure of shared leadership—tending toward (but not achieving) egalitarianism. The parental coalition was clear. Closeness was obvious. In their self appraisal, such families were decidedly more congruent with an outside judgment. They demonstrated skill in effective negotiation; were clear in their expressions of feelings and thoughts; accepted responsibility for their actions; demonstrated little in the way of invasiveness; were openly expressive, and reasonably permeable to each other. Healthy families tended to be warmer, more optimistic, and reasonably empathic with each other. There were low levels of conflict in such families.

It appeared from rating scale data that health or competence in family systems was the outcome of many variables. Despite obvious overlap among the variables, the data presented in this chapter suggest that we have identified a usefully discriminating number of those crucial variables.

REFERENCES

1. GOSSETT, J. T., and BARNHART, F. D., "Preliminary analysis of adolescent psychopathology scale data," *Timberlawn Foundation Reports*, No. 73, Dallas, Texas, 1974.
2. LUBORSKY, L., "Clinicians' judgments of mental health: A proposed scale," *Arch. Gen. Psychiat.*, 7 (6), 407-417, 1962.

CHAPTER V

CLINICAL OBSERVATIONS

THIS CHAPTER PRESENTS observations of 12 families derived from viewing six hours of family interaction on videotape. Each of these 12 families was seen separately by two experienced family therapists on two occasions each for 90-minute interviews. The family therapists were instructed merely to "learn as much as you can about each family in two 90-minute interviews, using any approach you wish to take." They both chose to rely upon fairly standard, verbal, exploratory interviewing techniques.

The investigator (WRB) who responded to the resulting 72 hours of videotaped interviews approached the task with a strong investment in the theoretical framework of family systems described in Chapter III, but with a deliberate effort to set the theory aside as much as possible, and respond to the family interviews at the lowest level of abstraction. In effect, he wished to keep in mind as many different "sets" and hypotheses as possible. This deliberate effort was made in agreement with Popper (2) that it is impossible not to have a hypothesis, and that unacknowledged hypotheses are the most mischievous.

The investigator dictated ongoing commentary while observing the videotapes, which, when transcribed, produced a 254-page document. In addition, a summary statement was made regarding each of the 12 families. Finally, these summaries were scored in a manner allowing numerical comparisons. Each of the investigator's comments was initially categorized as one of three types: comments regarding individual family members, comments regarding two-

99

person interactions (parent-to-parent, child-to-child, child-to-parent), and comments about the family system as a whole. Each of these types of statements was then assigned a positive, negative, or neutral valance. The valances represented a judgment regarding the power of the observed behavior either to further or to detract from human capabilities.

When the data analysis at this clinical level was reviewed, eight variables useful in evaluating competent families evolved. These eight variables, considered as continua and listed in what is considered descending order of importance are: 1) affiliative versus oppositional attitudes in the family system; 2) respect for one's own subjective world view and that of the other person versus disregard for the unique in one's self and others; 3) openness and directness versus distancing, obscuring, or confusing mechanisms; 4) a firm parental coalition with no evident competing parent-child coalition and a tattered parental coalition; 5) an understanding of varied human motivations and needs versus a rigid, control orientation; 6) spontaneity of interaction versus the repetitive and stereotyped; 7) initiative versus passivity; and 8) unique, impressive individual characteristics versus bland, "plain vanilla" qualities.

The first variable, the affiliative versus oppositional attitudes, refers to what family members seem to expect of human encounter and is a striking, emotion-laden variable. When these expectations are affiliative, they propel people into engagement and increased interest; when oppositional, distance is maintained and anger and fear are sensed. Measurement of this variable reflects a complex synthesis of behavior pattern, voice tone, and context. Indeed, a simple way to describe either group or individual pathology might be the degree to which the group or an individual acts as if the next human interaction will be oppositional, because this can be a very powerful, self-fulfilling prophecy. Since we live in the world ambivalently and no one experiences exactly the same feelings or perceptions about the outside "reality," the nature of such predictions is powerful in creating either productive, cooperative interaction, or painful, destructive, inefficient human transactions.

The second variable is respect for one's own and others' subjective world views versus oblivious, insensitive lack of appreciation for the uniqueness of individual perceptions. This variable also is complex and has many manifestations. Respect for one's own views is illustrated by comfort in expressing feelings and even disagreement; respect for the other shows up in such ways as really listening and supporting others even in disagreement, and never speaking for others or attacking their inner selves. Such respect may be destroyed if a family relies on rigid family "referees" extensively (referred to in Chapter III). With the spurious assumption that there is a "right" way to feel or think, one or more family members become the spokesman for the inhuman referee. For example, if parents tell a child that they do not punish him because his behavior offends them, but because his behavior is "just not right," they effectively annihilate their own unique view and also that of the child. He perceives a real human being objecting to his behavior, but is told that it is response to an external standard. This acts as a foreign body, a thing apart, and dehumanizes interaction. With the referee orientation, guilt in the parent is common and usual. He often lashes out, "You didn't follow the rules," and then reverses himself as guilt becomes conscious, "I'm sorry" (thinking, "He is no worse than I").

It should be noted that in families with only a modest investment in a referee as inhuman rule setter, power is usually expressed as part of the person rather than as isolated and separate from the person. Decisions, judgments, and enforcement of rules become increasingly effective as they reflect the humanness of the acting person.

Thirdly, verbal openness and directness versus obscuring, distancing, and confusing interaction: this communication variable is seen as an important aspect of a family's ability to negotiate. Part of the sensation of joy the observer feels in observing the interaction of healthy families is the obvious lack of calculation, the openness of honest feeling and thought on the part of different family members—especially the children. There is freedom without chaos—a feeling of a three-ring circus, yet with everything under control.

Number four, a firm coalition between parents without competing parent-child coalitions versus shaky parental coalition and obvious competing parent-child coalitions. This variable reflects the quality of the parents' relationship. Does it provide teamwork in matters of discipline and setting family rules? Does it include mutual gratification? Does it have areas of strength and areas where the coalition breaks down? Related directly to the strength of the parental coalition, and inseparable from it, is the degree that a child persists in attempts to vanquish the same-sex parent as a rival for the affections of the opposite-sex parent. This group of healthy families shows much less unresolved oedipal conflict than any group of pathological families, but this is not to say that oedipal problems are resolved completely in all these families. In fact, they were present frequently enough to encourage the view that rigid, stereotyped behavior patterns and marked conventionality of sex roles are related to the absence of oedipal resolution. That is, the more seriously these families took a narrow and stereotyped view of maleness and femaleness, the more apt we were to see unresolved oedipal difficulties. Consistently there was a close correlation between the estimated quality of the parental relationship and the estimated competence of the family systems.

Fifth, understanding varied human motivations and needs versus a rigid, control orientation. Does the family system operate with many possibilities and several strategies, or rely on a single one—direct control? Most disturbed families have a linear view of cause and effect and how one should approach problems in relating to others. A simple example: A child bites his nails and the parent says "Stop." The child continues to bite and the parent moves from the less severe punishment to beating. Such linear response to a family problem is common in incompetent family systems. In more effective families one sees the use of varying approaches. If force does not work it is considered that perhaps the approach is wrong, or perhaps the behavior can be ignored (as nail biting, stuttering, etc.) . These assumptions about multi-factoral human interaction are always found in optimally functioning families. Rarely in these most effective family systems does one see a parent attempting to use raw power alone to pursue his goals. If there is a marked difficulty in seeing eye to eye, the family members try to back up, reevaluate, and redefine the problem. However, in every healthy family there was a "core" of superego beliefs that were unquestioned and unchallenged. It would have been aesthetically and theoretically pleasing to find that the optimally functioning families did not have this core of superego, this bit of the referee system—but such was not the case. Although it was clear that such a fixed and linear core is smaller as family systems improve in effectiveness, a remnant seemed either necessary or inevitable.

Sixth, spontaneity versus repetitive and stereotyped interaction: People are much more fun when their responses to each other are fresh and ingenious, not drearily predictable. In disturbed families, this predictability is especially frustrating since it is associated with negative feelings and inept operation. The stereotyped, conventional and the obviously neurotic are a part of the same phenomenon, the difference being in terms of ability of the system to function. Whether a family system has a pattern that is stereotyped, repetitive, rigid, yet effective, or whether this rigid pattern of the interaction among family members is dysfunctional, the rigidity still inhibits the joyful, the spontaneous and the free. A major concern about the famly that is quite predictable and rigidly structured is whether the system will be able to adapt as needs and demands change.

Seventh, the active-constructive versus the passive: This variable refers to the family's orientation toward the outside world. Is the outside world seen as threatening or is it a "smorgasbord" to be enjoyed selectively and brought into the family? Though varying in their interests, optimally functioning families reach out to the larger community, and this is important in evaluating effectiveness. Whether the contrasting passivity of the less well functioning families is biological or an inhibition of functioning developed by past threats is not easy to say, but our impression is that most disturbed families are not biologically stunted, but system stunted.

Eighth, unique, impressive individual characteristics versus the bland and mediocre. It is hard to be unimpressed with a family that produces a particularly responsive, creative, and active-constructive human being; and even a modestly effective family has a bit of luster if it has one or more outstanding members.

These variables, as well as those discussed in Chapter IV, are not mutually exclusive. For example, the ability of a family to allow or encourage spontaneity is obviously related to each member's respecting the subjective worlds of other individuals. Expectations of positive encounters are related to the experience of being dealt with openly, of being able to trust that the apparent is indeed real. Although the variables interact, they are sufficiently different to allow separation, estimation, and evaluation. Descriptions of the 12 families are presented as two groups of six—the "optimal" families followed by the moderately effective, "adequate" families. This separation is made to facilitate presentation and should not be misconstrued to represent a sharp dichotomy. Rather, these families are seen as representing a continuum of competence.

The Optimally Functioning Families *

1. The *Comfort* family consisted of a relatively young set of parents in their mid-thirties and children aged 14, 13, and 11. Overall, this family's interaction seemed capable, easy, understated, and somewhat bland. Though the family was clearly quite happy and effective, and they did command the observer's attention, their style was rather like that of a Cadillac idling: the strength and power were there, but variation was modest. The family did not make difficult challenges for itself. Hence, it had potential power with all the members content to enjoy their ease and not extend

---

* Names, number and sex of children, and other identifying characteristics of each family have been changed in this Chapter to protect confidentiality.

themselves. Anxiety is painful, and they had great skills to avoid such pain.

There was a striking sense of "we-ness," an expectation of affiliative encounter. Evidence abounded that they supported and affirmed one another, responded favorably, and frequently reached out to each other. Oppositional exchanges were nearly nonexistent.

They had a clear and obvious deference to outside authority. They had the ability to get their needs met within what they considered a proper and benign social order, and viewed people who deviated from that structure as being either foolish or threats to the community. This may explain their small concern about changing or affecting the larger world. They saw themselves as important and they took care of themselves and each other, but they didn't consider themselves as potentially powerful as *"real"* authorities (who are other people who decide the rules, wisely and benignly, and that's perfectly all right). The Comforts were reminiscent of the Betas in Huxley's *Brave New World* (1)—they defined themselves as better than most, but not at the top. Their family system incorporated a very strong sense of right and wrong in a most humane way.

This family had the most continually overall positive mood of any family studied.

In interacting with each other, these family members illustrated a belief in human dignity. They respected each others' world views though that world was small. They did not have a great deal of interest in disparate views outside the family; since they related only to those they consider similar, they remained affiliative in almost all of their activities. There was a strikingly warm and caring mood with an optimistic and cheerful tone. There was little evidence of unresolved conflict, and no evidence of any continued anger or underlying depression.

Verbal openness was evident. The children were direct about their feelings, and expression of anger was acceptable in the system. The superego structure was not foreign and isolated, but skillfully integrated in their everyday functioning. Rather than inhibiting their ability to be themselves, it seemed to be a framework around which they distributed their self-definition. This allowed leeway in expressing feelings, but this system does not reward individual thinking. However, since it was otherwise so rewarding, no one needed to be deviant.

There was a very capable coalition between the parents with no evidence of any favoritism for one or another child. The family was father-led, but father's attitude towards his wife was one of interest, concern, and respect, with no attempt to subjugate or to parade a more powerful position. Mother was modest in her efforts to be autonomous or to lead, at times, but not to the point of inefficiency.

The family did not talk about abstract concepts and displayed little interest in intellectual approaches to the world. Because of this, one might overlook their understanding of human motivations and needs, but it was clearly revealed in their behavior.

This family handled some functions less well. Because of the powerful, though integrated, superego structure in the family system, there was a conventional tone to the family that diminished spontaneity. Very little surfaced in the way of unique views of the world. This was not due to modest intellect; both parents were college graduates and the father had built a business with a good income. Their intellect had been used to make their life comfortable. This conventionality did, however, reduce the observer's admiration for their general interpersonal skills.

The family was socially active and especially involved in organized sports. Though showing no interest in activities having to do with ideas or concepts, they had a great deal of ability and shared their enjoyment of the world with others who were similar.

Mr. Comfort was a sensitive, sturdy, and flexible man. He expressed feelings easily, was physically relaxed, and quite responsive to others. The other family members had similar evidence of personal capabilities. It was clear that the parents saw being adult as a pleasant and gratifying state and rewarded their children by allowing them to do more grown-up activities. This was most significant in the growing family. The parents enjoyed their life and saw the adult stage as one of contentment, ease, and happiness and did not find their responsibilities painful. Father stated that the main thing he wanted to impart to his children was respect and consideration for others. He saw the reason for problems in the world as personal immorality. This orientation may produce adaptive human beings, but not great achievers.

Table 5-1 lists the ratio of positive and negative comments made during observation of the videotapes in the summary which parallels this description. The small number of negative and positive statements reflects the vanilla-like conventionality yet interpersonal effectiveness of the Comforts.

2. The *Powers* were a young family; mother and father are in their early thirties with three children, 14, 13, and 9. The father, an aggressive, successful businessman, set the tone of the family interaction. Though he often tried to dominate, Mrs. Powers presented herself as competent and usually held her own with him. The oldest child was quiet; the middle and youngest children were active and aggressive much like their father. The family members had a warm responsiveness to one another, and a truly affiliative orientation, interspersed with some chafing at father's great power and occasional outright dominance. Though pleasant and positive overall, the family had a high level of anxiety. They operated well with this anxiety level, and it seemed to be a spur for all except, perhaps, the oldest child, who had a different style and tended to respond to anxiety by moderate withdrawal. He was quiet and somewhat unaggressive. The family accepted this difference, and he was not scapegoated. They showed reasonable empathy, but also some concern over this child's difficulty in making friends.

There was a definite respect for different viewpoints in the family. This tolerance and respect encouraged a vigorous marketplace of ideas. Father set the tone of aggressive, direct expressions of positions, but he really attended to other family members and responded to their communications, both verbal and behavioral. Mother and children were heard, and attention was paid to them, but they must scramble for the floor. Mrs. Powers was an energetic person who, encouraged by her husband, was furthering her education. Mr. Powers had a family tradition of active women, so

his wife's activity outside the home was quite consistent with his
view of the world. Overall, there was a high degree of respect for
each others' perceptions and feelings.

Communication in this family was open and direct with little
confusion or obscuring. The one apparent exception to this was the
oldest child who was a "marginal commentator." For example,
when one of the interviewers asked him if he ever got angry with
his father he responded, "well no, not really." Then he went on
and in a pseudodutiful fashion remarked, "they get angry with
me for good and just cause," and then also commented, "yes, only
for just cause," with an ironic inflection that was not lost on the
rest of the family—and was accepted. There was a game-like quality
in the way the oldest child presented himself as one-down to his
siblings and the world in general, but it was a pleasant game; he
was able to enjoy himself and seemed to have adequate self-esteem.
There were no sarcastic, cutting messages.

There was a firm parental coalition in this most physical couple
of all of the families seen. When together they moved toward one
another and touched in a warm way; no evidence existed of favoritism of one child over another, or unresolved oedipal feelings.
Generation barriers were clear. Mother, though involved outside
the family circle, was most invested in the family. She often seemed
to be the family cheerleader.

The family was insightful and verbal with great appreciation
of human complexity and an excellent capacity to express this
understanding both in behavior and words.

There was an unusual degree of spontaneity and the unexpected
was almost anticipated. Each person was a well differentiated individual, and there was a prevailing presumption of autonomy.
Two areas of repetitive, stereotyped interaction centered around
father's power and the oldest child's withdrawal. Mother seemed
a bit hard-put to keep up with the aggressiveness of her husband,
and the oldest child tended to fringe family interaction as he
apparently fringed outside groups. He was, however, quite witty
and a major contributor of the unexpected.

This family was the most constructively aggressive of any family in this group. Contrasting with the Comforts, a family equally high in competence, their capabilities were due not to skillful avoidance of intrafamily friction, but rather, to keeping friction moderate while reaching out into the world. They were movers, doers, and changers.

Both parents had impressive individual characteristics. The father was driving, aggressive, creative, and never really content. Mother also showed this pushing quality in her considerable outside activities. The two younger children were also active and aggressive; but the oldest marched to a different drummer and came across as different rather than inferior. This was a kinetic, striving group, offering each other enough mutual support for the struggle to be rewarding.

On Table 5-1 the positive observations far outweigh the negative, reflecting a family that had both skills and tensions.

3. The *Kings* were a family with parents in their early forties, with girls 14 and 13 years old, and a 7-year-old son. Initially, the system was puzzling because of a large amount of ambiguous language. It was well understood by the family, but required some familiarity before being fathomed by an observer.

Mother viewed herself, her husband, and the family as having evolved and grown over the years. This was a family of integrated contradictions. Father presented as a very rigid and authoritarian person in his speech, but his behavior was quite flexible. They defined him as "Archie Bunker," but with comfortable laughter that belied the statement. They described themselves as "conservative," but appeared rather liberal in many respects, and father enthusiasticaly supported minibikes and motorcycles for his children. It was a family where father, a great bear who growled a lot, said the only reason that his children behaved when most children were going to hell was because they feared him. Yet, the children (with the exception of the youngest) spoke up, laughed at him, and he received this in good humor. Father was a college graduate, yet everyone had a low evaluation of books and the intellect. In another reverse twist, the parents were concerned about the poor grades of two of their children. Their stated belief was that a family succeeds through structural rigidity and hardnosed threats, but actually theirs was run with caring and guidance with tolerance for individual feelings and differences.

The overall impression was one of an affiliative family system and a positive emotional climate—with the exception of occasional evidence of a conflictual relationship between father and son. However, the overall impact was of a group that had pleasure in one another's company.

The family members paid high respect to one another's subjective views (again, with the limitations seen in terms of father's deprecation of his son). However, this tolerance was not immediately apparent to an observer. The father made a pretense of being dominant, harsh, and insensitively dictatorial—known to be false by everyone in the family. He made sweeping statements about the terrible state of the world and the necessity to rule with fear. Behaviorally he negated this by showing clear respect for his wife's and his children's viewpoints. He was sensitive to his wife's feelings, and she was affirming of his own competence and capabilities. She seemed to be aware of his early emotional deprivation and provided a good deal of mothering for her husband as well as for her children. He basked in this warmth.

The older daughter, an outspoken girl, was not punished in any way for the expression of her own views, though they did not appear to fit the family expectations. For example, she was quite lucid in her description of discomfort with her grandmother's touch and withdrawing from it. As she described her responses, she was supported by the rest of the family. The family was unusual in the dimension of verbal openness that they frequently communicated; although the style was ambiguous, the messages were decoded with skill.

The parental coalition in the King family was solid. The father had difficulty in acknowledging his own needs, but over a period of years he had learned to receive much from his wife, who was content to be nonintellectual, emotional, and affectionate. Mother was reasonably warm with her son and somewhat more accepting of his human imperfections than was father, without this seeming to have a preferential favor.

The family did not rate high in their ability to acknowledge verbally complex human motivations or needs. They were limited in describing human interactions, with the exception of the oldest daughter, who stood out as having learned to express subtle feelings in words. This family's functioning ability was admirable, even with this tendency toward simplistic and surface explanations of human behavior.

The people in this family were interesting to talk with and had a good deal of spontaneity. Their high activity level was an important strength. This was an optimistic, energetic group reaching out to the world by activities, with a resulting enrichment of family interaction. The family did not appear to have unusual or outstanding individual personalities, though the parents were impressive as having grown from modest beginnings.

To summarize, the Kings were an interesting, active family with spontaneity and autonomy. They were verbally more simplistic than their behavior indicated, and they had a peculiarly complex communicational system that was difficult for an outsider to decode. The parents encouraged one another to grow and increase their abilities, and were proud of this fact. The ratio of positive and negative observations (Table 5-1) reflects this summary with a large number of both positive and negative statements.

4. The *Ponder* family. This family had the oldest parents and children in our series; the parents were in their early fifties with two children 17 and 13. This family was intellectual, verbal, and interested in the larger world, with lively and energetic discussions of human problems, social structure, and their own values. It was the most egalitarian family observed, and it was quickly evident that every member of the family considered his own feelings and judgments important, expected to be heard, and was not to be pushed around. The mother was quite independent and autonomous. She had interests different from the average housewife, which made for a more complex interaction between the parents. The father had two relationship patterns, one quite controlling,

the other warm and affable. He sometimes attempted to control others' behavior, but more often he presented a perceptive, egalitarian orientation. The children, each in his own way, were successful human beings. The older was talented in music and had many interests that were pursued with ability (although not as well as the family thought possible). The younger child was more physically aggressive and socially outgoing; the parents respected the children's differences and did not attempt to force them into a mold.

There was an impressive respect for each other's subjective view of the world. Conversation was spontaneous and deep, with a high degree of affiliative expectation. There was good humor and an overall positive mood in the family. There were, however, bursts of irritation—especially toward the research team—and they were able to be open about their annoyance. Some of this anger, however, was mildly disturbing when, in a gamelike fashion, it was directed toward family members. For example, the children's characteristic way of relating to mother was with a mildly hostile, somewhat deprecating manner. Basically, they seemed to respect her, but their banter generally left her to fight from a one-down position. Mother accepted this beleaguered position and related this same way to one of the interviewers. There was a modest depressive mood at times, apparently related to this family's having aspirations higher than their abilities (large as they are) allowed them to reach. They were a marked contrast to the Comfort family which gave the impression of having many more skills than aspirations. Negative feelings were handled well by this family, however, and the impact was one of caring and respect. On balance, expectations were positive except in the area of household responsibilities. Here, a referee orientation was apparent, clearly a blind spot that produced continued, intermittent friction. Father abandoned his egalitarian style and flipped into an ineffective authoritarian mode, resisted by the children in a passive and negativistic fashion. This family had some fights when their usual reasonable, respectful orientation was abandoned; and the father, not conscious of his changing styles, was continually puzzled about his ineffectiveness in this area. Otherwise, the family was quite high in respecting individuals' own subjective views.

There was a fairly high degree of verbal openness. However, mother did have a much more complex way of communicating than the others. She frequently played the game of being beleaguered and criticized, and then showed her stronger qualities by aggressively fighting out of a hole. Father supported her efforts to express herself as a competent human. The family members commented on this pattern, and Mother spoke of frequently feeling "odd-man-out," perhaps because as the only female there may have been somewhat more pressure on her than on other members of the family.

Obviously this couple respected and cared for one another, and had a sound parental coalition. Each had been independent and autonomous for several years before marriage, and they came together with a mutual respect for each other's intellect and capabilities. She saw herself as having a career and as much "professionalism" as her husband.

Though not destructive, Mother and the older child had a special quality to their relationship. Mother saw herself as artistic, and she saw this child's artistic interest related in a particular way to her, and accordingly was somewhat protective of this child's "differentness." Mother was not a plain-vanilla female; nor was the child. This lingering specialness that she had for the child seemed not to interfere significantly with her relationship to her husband.

More than any other family, the Ponders verbally expressed understanding of human motivation and needs, often talking of the "whys" of human behavior. They consciously perceived their own ambivalence and complexity, though their behavioral responses to each other were not equally outstanding. If this family had difficulties, it would be relatively easy for a therapist to add to their skills.

The family was spontaneous and interesting; they were discussers and arguers. Each of them had active interests in the outside world and both parents tried to make significant contributions.

The children were aggressive in different ways, the younger was active in the conventional fashion, being interested in sports and social activities. The older marched to a different drummer and was more the dreamer. This was not passivity, however, since the dreaming was related to actual artistic activities.

As a result of this active orientation and the tremendous expectations that family members had for themselves, each contributed individually toward a respect for the quality of the family as a unit. Each was a unique individual with unusual abilities. Implicitly, the family motto seemed to be "Man's reach should exceed his grasp, or what's a heaven for?" There was more adventure, and more productiveness—and more pain in the system than if they had had modest aspirations.

The number of both negative and positive observations (Table 5-1) are high, consistent with a complex system with problems and many strengths.

5. The *Reasoner* parents were in their early forties with four children—18, 17, 16, and 12. This family was an unusual combination of different systems involving the two oldest children and the two youngest children. The father and mother came from rather authoritarian families, and in their early years of marriage were severe disciplinarians, an approach that developed two well-behaved and respectful older children who were somewhat intimidated and had less spontaneity and freedom. The parents saw themselves as having evolved over the years, maturing and becoming more flexible. By the time the two youngest children were born they were able to be less rigid and less demanding. This view fit well with the greater spontaneity and openness, directness, and general affection exhibited by the younger children. In the earlier period of tight control, the two older children developed resentment that had not been completely resolved. The second child particularly was frequently sullen and hostile. Mother was unable to let him withdraw, but continued to pick at him in order to try to get him to behave "pleasantly." The oldest child, although less hostile, seemed inhibited and lacking in confidence.

The capability of the family system as a whole was somewhat hampered by the "chickens coming home to roost."

Consistent with the sensation of "two families" (which was recognized and described in detail by the family) the parents related in a different fashion to the older and younger children. They seemed to expect (and get) opposition from the older pair and, in turn, responded to the sullenness and withdrawal with irritability and nagging. There was a more positive expectation of the younger siblings.

The family was reasonably direct with feelings and thoughts, except for the expressions of anger. Mother came from a quarreling family and she did not want any of that in her family. She married a quiet, self-effacing man, and she acted as a damper on direct angry feelings. Mother and Father were somewhat wordy people who were apt to intellectualize feelings, but this ability had also assisted in their growth. For example, Mother spoke of her professional work and described in some detail her failures and her efforts to improve. Father described his considerable interest in leadership and many years of effort to be more sensitive to feelings and more capable as a leader. The two older children reflected one aspect of their parents with their stiffness and overcontrol; the younger children expressed another side with their relative ease of expression.

Confusing communication was minimal. The father had a habit of being a marginal commentator, making asides almost to himself about his own feelings or what he saw going on in the family. This did not seem to be confusing to anybody, but was generally unattended.

There was a strong coalition between the parents, who had a nearly equal amount of power. Mother was verbally active and reported participating outside the family as an autonomous, competent person, a role that pleased her husband. There was no evidence of any lingering oedipal ties in any of the children. Indeed, the children were notably autonomous. Perhaps because of the previous authoritarianism in the family, the two older children seemed to be speeded in their separation, almost acting as guests in the family group—accepted guests, but ones who were reluctant to remain. The parents had struggled hard to add to their understanding of human needs and were torn between their old style of authoritarianism and what they had tried to develop: an open communicative system that also attended feelings. Mother was more apt to rely on direct, intimidating efforts to control; Father expressed remorse for his past heavy-handedness.

The family members varied in spontaneity. Father was intellectually spontaneous and often quite clever with his irreverent, marginal commentary. The two younger children seemed to have reaped benefits as the family loosened up and they showed a good deal of freedom of expression.

This was an active-constructive group. All the members were energetic and filled with projects as they interacted with verve and ability in outside projects. The two older children, while inhibited within the family, were quite capable in performing outside. However, it was partly this very capability that produced mild resentment at having their Sundays interrupted by being involved in the family research. Both parents were committed to contributing outside the family and did so with superior ability. Father was quite involved in his career, and yet did not see this as diminishing his efforts to be a good father. Mother invested herself in raising the children, yet found energy to pursue a part-time career outside. They placed a high premium on individual and autonomous action.

The favorable impression of the overall functioning ability is indicated in Table 5-1, with 62% positive observations and only 30% negative ones.

6. The *Adams* parents were near forty, with three children, 16, 12, and 10. The most striking thing about this family was the verbally active mother, a vivacious woman with a strong sense of family history. She was powerful, especially in conversation. Her husband, no patsy, expressed power by silence and they almost caricatured a complementary pattern. The oldest boy, a handsome young man, seemed to have a mind of his own and was not afraid to express himself. The oldest girl was poised and able to battle

effectively to be heard. Indeed, she poked fun at her mother's ways without sounding impertinent. The youngest child spoke softly and had difficulty in expression. One could be autonomous in this family, but it took effort.

The emotional tone of the family generally was positive. There was genuine warmth frequently expressed between family members and disagreements were modest in intensity. Most of the time they expected good things from each other, partly due to the rather precise and definite control that was a part of the family system, engineered primarily by Mother. There was some fear of people's inner impulses and, therefore, an effort to preach and shape proper behavior.

As one result, this family was not high on the variable of respect for the subjective world view of one's self and others. Within this family with a strong control system, children were heard and attention was paid, yet every family member vacillated between attentiveness to others and a good deal of obliviousness. Part of this resulted from mother's verbosity. The children listened respectfully, but obviously paid diminishing attention after the first few paragraphs. Mother had high expectations for people; she, herself, did not measure up to these standards, and the children were bold enough to point out her failings. She accepted their words, but did not let these comments penetrate effectively into comprehension. The father was, at times, sensitive to other family members and at other times withdrew into his own reverie or plowed ahead without attention to others. He was comfortable with a professed lack of understanding of people and used this alleged blind spot as a shield.

Communication was clear—excepting, however, some degree of denial on Mother's part. All family members described her as hiding her true feelings, but in such a way that they really understood what she felt. There was much joking about her tendency to be sweet when she was angry. She was intellectual in her understanding of people, but this cognitive understanding was not quite matched by behavior. If she had really set the family style of communicating, it would have been a very confusing group indeed, but she did not. The father spoke less often, but spoke directly, and when the children made fun of their mother's obliqueness, this was not punished, but rather was comfortably accepted. The parents, when with the children, had a capable coalition. Although Mother seemed to have more social power than Father, the sensation persisted that whatever power she had was given to her by this generally silent father who showed no hesitation in intervening occasionally. When they were alone together, the coalition seemed less capable. The father behaved as if he were slightly afraid of his wife, and they communicated intellectually with a small amount of warmth. Father reported being attracted to his wife because of her physical beauty and seemed to relate to her as a beautiful, but remote, mountain that could be approached and even climbed, but with difficulty. There was no evidence of unresolved oedipal ties with the children. The two oldest children were evolving sexual identities and separating reasonably well.

A considerable degree of understanding of human motivations and needs was expressed in the family members' behavior toward one another. Although the father professed ignorance of such "deep subjects," he had confidence in his family's ability to grow and develop without his maintaining a rigid, controlling posture. Mother talked of understanding, but never ceased to try to control her children's behavior. This was effectively resisted by the children.

The parents had a restricted view of what people *should* be like, but were able to present this to their children in an acceptable way. They were content to follow patterns laid down from previous generations. There was no evidence in either parent of past rebellion or questioning their own families' values. Because of their high personal self-esteem, the parents viewed their children as capable and had a high expectation that they would do well. This was a powerful factor in the family's effectiveness. It was clear that the family had a referee and was wary of people who were individualistic or rebellious, but the referee had served both parents well, and the children felt similarly. The older daughter spoke disparagingly of girls her own age who were "wild," and did not obey their parents and got into trouble. This family illustrated well what was seen in all the healthy families—some scapegoating turned toward the outside world.

The family did not exhibit a great spontaneity or expression of unique feelings and perceptions. Mother and Father had a conventional, stereotyped view of what man and woman should be. As a result, while family members seemed healthy, sturdy, and capable, they generally repressed any feelings or thoughts that did not fit into their constricted model. The family was restricted in receptivity to the outside world and they had successfully trained the children to ignore ideas not stamped "approved."

This was not a passive family group, and yet the activity was spent primarily in maintaining the status quo. An anecdote may illustrate an overall impression about the family: A cellist practiced for hours daily, weekly, playing the same note again and again. His wife, unable to stand it longer, suggests to him that she has observed other cellists who placed five fingers on the string and ran the bow over all the strings. Her husband responds, "Aha, but they are *looking* for the note. I have *found* it!" Just so, this family communicated that they have found the *proper* way to behave and their energies were spent in maintaining that way. However, the parents were competent and one expects the children to follow in that pattern.

The score on Table 5-1 of 40% positive observations and 55% negative ones reflects a lower assessment than the overall clinical impression. Most of the negative comments related to the excessive control Mother attempted to maintain and to the resulting obliviousness in the system.

SUMMARY OBSERVATIONS ABOUT THE OPTIMAL FAMILIES

These optimal families scored well in most of the eight categories chosen for evaluation. Although the Reasoners showed some stubbornly oppositional quality in interaction involving the two older children, and the Adams parents displayed a less intense affectional bond, all six families were impressive in their affiliative orientation. The Ponders, the Powers, and the Reasoners seemed to include more of the outside world in this orientation, while the Comforts, the Kings, and the Adams were insulated, by choice, from encountering dissident views and people.

Consistently there was a high degree of respect for the uniqueness and specialness of one another, but with the exception of the Ponders and Reasoners, there were obvious restrictions to being open to novel thoughts from the outside world being brought into the family for discussion.

Each couple had a firm parental coalition, with no evidence of unresolved family romances between any parents and opposite-sex-children—a striking group of successes in helping children through the oedipal developmental period.

The people in this group showed high levels of individual initiative, but it was expressed in very different ways. The individuals in these families varied a great deal not only in comparison to each other, but also in comparison to other families. The Comforts had a paramount concern with satisfaction in closeness and did not seek encounters in the outside world. The Ponders valued satisfaction in intellectual activities and in risk, and accepted a good deal of friction and frustration along the way. The Kings valued the satisfaction found in performance and were almost contemptuous of ne'er-do-wells. The Powers had needs for achievement, social power, and recognition. They, like the Ponders, accepted a good deal of discomfort and anxiety in obtaining these satisfactions. The Reasoners were socially conscious and were concerned with being effective in the larger community. The Adams were traditional, conservative, and effectively maintained tried-and-true values.

The variable of openness was not so consistent. The Comforts' and the Powers' communications were quite easy to follow and decode; the Ponders had some repetitive games that obscured feelings, particularly in mother-son interactions, and the Kings' communicative style was even more complex. The styles varied and the effort to understand needed to be greater with the Ponders and the Kings, but the results seemed clear—these people understood each other well. The Comforts and the Kings stood out as being a bit less aware of human complexity and tried, generally successfully, to simplify their perceptions of each other and the outside world. The Reasoners showed a transitional quality in reference to openness—they had made great strides in developing a closer, clearer, and more flexible family system, but spoke of earlier rigidity that seemed concretized in interaction with their two older children.

The Adams family had openness and communicational clarity with definite limits built into the family rules as to what was possible for "good people" to feel or think.   •

These families were impressive in their operational understanding of human complexity and varied motivations, but differed in their ability to verbalize such knowledge. The Powers, Ponders, Reasoners, and Adams were adept at speaking of such matters and, indeed, the Reasoners' and Adams' verbal competence seemed to exceed their functional ability.

The Comforts related gently and skillfully, but with a maximum of objectified verbal discussion of their interaction. The Kings also had difficulty in verbalizing a sophisticated awareness of the complexity of human needs and responses, relying rather on simplistic authoritarian statements. Their behavior, however, belied these verbalized shortcomings and the interaction was respectful and subtle. It was apparent that while the verbal facility relating to the complexities of human interaction is useful, it was not necessary for highly effective family functioning.

These six families contained a number of individuals with what appeared to be special characteristics—creativity, broad interests, and much curiosity about the world.

THE ADEQUATELY FUNCTIONING FAMILIES

The second group of healthy families is described as "adequately functioning" families; that is, not pathological but having considerable pain and more modest interactional skills.

7. The *Cooper* parents were in their mid-forties with a girl 15

and a boy 13. The most striking quality of this family was the mother's persistent, anxious, and rather unhappy conversation, characterized by a defensive, mistrustful quality with self-denigration. Her husband was quiet and let her talk without being either challenging or supportive. The son was modestly depressed in appearance and was unusually sensitive. Perhaps this was necessary in order to live with such a mother, for she was frequently unhappy with great defensiveness, and it took a reasonably sensitive person not to cause her to feel poorly treated. The daughter varied in her appearance; for long periods she was quiet and seemingly immature for her age, but at other times, there was a shyly seductive quality in her interaction with Father. When she did speak up, she seemed to have more self-confidence than her mother. This was not a happy family, but they maintained reasonable satisfaction by a marked degree of external scapegoating. Mother and Father continually talked about other kids who "run wild and use dope," and they were proud that their family did not do such things.

The emotional tone in the family was not pleasant. There were times of general anxiety, especially when Mother had the floor and rattled on in her fashion. Frequently, there was a depressive tone to the interaction and yet, for some stretches of time, they appeared warm and caring with each other and with some very positive interchanges. An especially tender interchange occurred as the sister spoke genuinely and proudly of her brother's abilities. The family assumed that there would be opposition in encounters with the outside world and with each other. Mother constantly assumed that Father was depriving her by working long hours. She seemed to expect more positive responses from her children than from her husband.

The family was somewhat peculiar in its evidence of respect for each person's subjective world view and that of others. Since Mother was hypersensitive to criticism, it had produced children who were sensitive to her moods, but unfortunately this often led them to be unaware of their own feelings. Mother complained frequently and Father tuned her out, showing long periods of inattention to her. He also appeared to be unaware of his own feelings.

There was not a great deal of verbal openness in this family. Mother especially contributed to an overall impression of distancing and confusing verbal interaction. Although she spoke clearly enough at times that both family members and observers could understand her, she frequently shifted, switched, backtracked, disqualified, and generally made her verbal output confusing and impotent. The two children had found roles as diplomats and their own verbal output was cautious. Father spoke infrequently, hiding a lot of his feelings, but when he did speak, he was clear.

There was difficulty in the parental coalition; they did not look well together, either with or without the children. Mother's theme was that she was ignored and her feelings unattended. Father responded by tuning her out, neither reaching for her nor being angry. Mother expressed ambivalence about whether they should have gotten married. Though they worked together as parents with shared concern for the children, their coalition was poor in meeting each other's needs. As a result, there were unresolved ties between mother and son and father and daughter. More genuine warmth appeared in the interaction between father and daughter than between father and mother. Further, the son had accepted his role of being the supportive male figure for his mother. These coalitions were less sticky than they might have been, however, because the parents encouraged autonomy on the part of the children.

There was little understanding of the complexity of human needs and motivations and the family members assumed relatively stereotyped roles. Father felt that a man should be energetic, capable, striving, and hard working, and should not dally with fantasies, dreams, or feelings. It was remarkable that this was not accepted by Mother. She saw a woman's role as limited to the home and dependent upon her husband for gratification, but was unhappy with this and believed her lack of pleasure was due to her husband. As a result of these rigid concepts of adult roles, the family interaction had a minimum of spontaneity. This family seemed able to be fairly content with this paucity of interactional richness because they used external scapegoating. Their unspoken theme seemed to be: "We have troubles and we don't have much fun, but we sure are better than most other people who run around and use drugs and get into trouble."

This family was modestly active-constructive, with the family members stoically maintaining the status quo in the presence of chronic emotional pain. Mother was concerned about doing a good job in the home, but presented herself as a relative failure and seemed to be propped up by other family members. The work ethic brought into the family by Father allowed him to be unusually capable in his career. This encouraged the same values for the children, and the son also appeared unusually competent, interested, and active in the outside world.

This family was seen more positively than would be suggested by the number of positive and negative statements (Table 5-1). Most of the positive features expressed absence of negative elements: they did not get into quarrels, but instead they tended to withdraw. They did not rebel, but instead conformed. They did not challenge each other's adequacy, but instead scapegoated the outside world. These negative virtues functioned as strengths for the Coopers.

8. The *Prosper* parents, in their mid-thirties, had two children, 15 and 11. The most prominent feature of this family was its dedication to control. Father was a tense, self-controlled person; Mother and the children frequently cast anxious, furtive glances at Father for clues as to how to react. The family did reasonably well in spite of a rigid father-dominated control, and Mother and the children did not appear browbeaten.

The family was not a happy one; but episodes of warmth were interspersed with the depression, tension, and controlled anxiety. Their laughter was rarely shared in a joyful fashion, but used to lighten negative statements. Recounted stories of past frustrating interaction highlighted the subdued anger. The stories always ended with Father's being tyrannical, insensitive, and taking over. Father expected opposition as he encountered family members and frequently used force and threats. Mother also expected opposition from her husband, but had developed successful ways of coping with it. The children had learned Mother's style and seemed reasonably content in this structure.

This family was low in respect for each individual's own subjective world views. The father embodied the family referee whose rigid rule system made it impossible to have a great deal of sensitivity for individuals. However, within this system, they did show interest in and concern for each other. For example, Mother and Father participated with the children in varied recreational activities, not only because they enjoyed these activities. but also because they cared deeply about the children.

The family communicational process was direct, with no confusing sequences, and the ever-present control was expressed in precise language. Their iron-bound rule system, administered primarily by Father, created considerable distancing and resulted in fear of Father. Though communications were clear and direct, it was obvious that much of what was felt was not said.

There was a stable, functional parental coalition. They agreed on the rules and rarely argued as to what "should" be done. The mother's submissiveness appeared to be acceptable to her, though it did not encourage closeness. Father remained tied to his own mother. He was poor at acknowledging his own feelings and, therefore, expected little warmth or tenderness from others. Mother expressed more warmth toward the children than toward her husband. The parental coalition seemed technically effective, but with little expression of feelings, and this encouraged a high emotional intensity in the relations between mother and son. In keeping with this mother-son coalition, Father expressed much more harshness toward his son than he did toward wife or daughter. There was no evidence, however, of an intense father-daughter relationship.

The family was relatively low in understanding the complexity of human motivations and needs. This system relied heavily on a linear aproach to human problems: the rules were clear, deviations met with physical punishment or withdrawal of privileges. However, there was no rebellion in the ranks, apparently because of the parents' behavioral evidence of care and concern.

There was a high active-constructive orientation. The father was an admirable person in many ways: hard-driving, creative, and successful. He reached into the outside world with considerable impact. Mother also was active—in the family, in business, in socializing, and sports. She had, in these pursuits, that peculiar combination of submissiveness and autonomy that all good master sergeants possess. The children emulated their parents, socializing and engaging in sports with skill and enthusiasm. They were productive and capable, but had a poignant lack of awareness of their feelings and fantasies.

On Table 5-1, there are 39% positive and 57% negative observations compatible with an effective family that had friction, unresolved conflict, and anger. The strengths related to their pervasive belief that this was an unusually capable group, superior in intellect and physical abilities, who would be winners. The soft, the gentle, the dreamy—those things that cannot be disciplined—were left out, except where it was presumably "appropriate" (as in Mother's role with the children).

9. The *Medders*. Father and Mother were in their mid-thirties with two children, 16 and 11. Both parents came from quite authoritarian families. Each had rebelled by marrying the other and had attempted to develop a less rigid family. However, with little experience in any other family style, they tended to slip into authoritarian patterns, did not like it, and frequently were uncomfortable. Mother expressed her discomfort in what she termed "chronic nervousness," and Father felt guilty over his angry outbursts. He feared he might hurt family members if he did not control himself. The power was in the hands of the parents, especially Mother—due in part to the parents' shared view of her social superiority. She was better educated and more skillful verbally than her husband. Although he had done well in business, he often had a hangdog appearance in relating to his wife. The family functioned with some continued pain, but the parents had worked

hard to develop a family structure that seemed significantly better than what each knew as children. The observer felt great empathy with their struggle. A contributing factor to their modest success was that each married against early patterning; Father had married a woman from a mother-dominated family, and he had experienced a father-dominated family. In their struggle with each other to evolve a workable relationship, there was the tension that exists in developing new skills.

The family was action-oriented, talked about *things*, avoiding discussion of feelings and relationships. They had a strong referee orientation and had difficulty filling in the gaps of such a rigid structure with needed skills.

The mood in the family fluctuated from depression to open anger to real warmth with humor. Frequently there was evidence of an attitude of opposition toward each other. Father saw his function as controlling himself and controlling his children, but seemed wary that his wife might control him. This assumption of opposition was softened by the marked unresolved ambivalence of all the family members, and often there was evidence of tenderness and warmth with positive expectations. Though shuttling between these two orientations made for pain, there was a strong undergirding of caring. The Medders family had a conscious awareness of the need to respect each others' views, but under stress this awareness was replaced by obliviousness and insensitivity. The parents frequently talked *at* the children with little concern about a response. This was more obvious with the father, while the mother more often tended to act as a mediator between Father and children. "Oughts" and "shoulds" abounded in the family dialogue with attendant anxiety and resentment.

This family had a peculiar communicative style because of the unintegrated ambivalence. From moment to moment they were very clear in expression of feelings and viewpoints, but confusion and obscuring resulted from contradictions negating the speaker's own position. No one in the family acted as an interpreter to get things clear. For example: Father insisted that he wanted to avoid the terrible authoritarianism that he had experienced, and then later talked earnestly of the necessity of taking belts to children to punish them.

The parental coalition was rather shaky, with continual efforts to control one another, many differences of opinion, and a moderate amount of unresolved conflict. For example, in the marital section Father stated that the children were the best part of their marriage, and that they were what kept them going, because otherwise, with his temper, he might impulsively divorce. He perceived that his wife's response was angry, and modified his position by saying that he was much more hot-headed and impulsive early in their marriage. Each played parent to the other, using the pointing finger, and neither was able to listen well. Obviously, however, they had affection for each other, and the generation barriers between them and their children were well maintained. There was no special relationship between either parent and a child.

The family members were only modestly aware of the complexity of human motivations and needs. They relied heavily on "shoulds" and "oughts," and depended on linear methods to solve family problems, quite often using threats or force. Both parents talked about "spoiling the children rotten," with the marked implication that to love "too much" was to be destructive. This family seemed to operate on the assumption that man is essentially evil and must constantly be threatened in order to become civilized.

There was little spontaneity in the interactions. The children were inhibited and imitative, laughing when the parents laughed, remaining quiet most of the time, and speaking only when spoken to. Occasionally, the rigid control orientation thawed and bits of humor and individuality were visible.

Strengths of this couple were their energy and continued efforts to be constructive. (Both parents have initiative; the father striving hard for material success, and the mother trying hard to be effective as a homemaker.) These efforts and hopes were handicapped by lack of skill. Though the level of the family interaction was far from optimal, it was a tremendous accomplishment for two such emotionally deprived people.

In summary, this was a family started by two very needy people with few interactional skills who, by tremendous efforts and drive, had increased their own self-esteem and had raised children to adolescence who knew that they are cared for—but who were fearful. A reflection of this tenuous family system is seen in the summary on Table 5-1 (28% positive statements and 69% negative ones).

10. The *Baker* parents were in their early forties with sons 14 and 13, and a daughter 10. Mother was a talkative woman who had a style of attempting to control others, and then putting herself down to a laughable absurdity. The father was quiet and controlled and left little doubt that it was he who had the power. The oldest son was a chip off the old block who also tended to isolate himself.

The parents illustrated what, in a symptomatic family, would be termed a "hysteric-compulsive" match; that is, Father was a caricature of maleness, strong and silent; Mother caricatured a female by being quite emotional, but seeming relatively powerless. There was an unresolved family romance, more obvious between Father and Daughter than with Mother and Son. The specialness of the daughter to the father was openly acknowledged, and the daughter smugly stated that the father never got angry with her. The style of interaction was continually mild, irritable, and complaining, only rarely interspersed with genuinely warm feelings. There was warmth, but usually it was soured a bit with sarcasm or mild put-down. The family was relatively close because they were even more contemptuous of the outside world than of each other. The general attitude of the children seemed to be that "this isn't too good, but it is a lot better than being out on the street."

An expectation of opposition was a permanent feature in the family interaction. When the interviewer focused the discussion on theoretical matters such as what was important in family life or in values, they agreed, either actively or passively, and it was during these periods that they looked best. Otherwise, they bickered, and Mother sought continually and ineffectively to control the feelings and thoughts of her children. In turn, the children

complained of Mother nagging. This open bickering did illustrate
a certain respect for each other's point of view, however, since it
implied that feelings were important and not controllable. Except
for their constant resistance, the children behaved well in the
interview and appeared to accept the basic family rules which were
clear and enforced.

The family was midway on a continuum of verbal openness.
There was a gamelike quality to their communications: they gave
lip service to a rigid system, yet Mother and children openly described going around the system and joked about the necessary
deceptions. Father was accepted as the embodiment of the family
referee. When he complained that secrets in the family were being
kept from him, everyone insisted that nothing was kept from him.
This was both true and false since they openly discussed times in
the past when important facts had been hidden from the father.
As Mother was coaching her younger son in answering an interviewer's question, she added: "Don't you think that honesty is
important?" He responded quietly and undefensively, "Well, you
know I'm honest." It was believable and reassuring. In spite of the
bickering, the degree of trust was high, these people trusted and
understood one another at bedrock, but in everyday interactions
a contradictory, gamelike quality intruded. Significant parts of
each of the individuals were hidden as they played out restricted
roles. This, of course, indicated a reduction of respect for each
other's subjective view of the world.

Father was remote from Mother, and this encouraged emotional
distancing in all the family. Father's idea of real enjoyment was
solitary activity. Mother constantly reached for her husband, was
rebuffed, and blamed herself. They gave each other enough to
survive, but there were unresolved coalitions with Father and
Daughter, and Mother and the older son. These parent-child ties
did not operate powerfully enough to threaten realistic generation
barriers. Mother and Father cooperated well enough to maintain
family rules, but Daughter expressed smug joy over her ability to
handle her father, and mother demonstrated preferential treatment

of her older son. Both of these parents had hungers not met in the parental relationship that were fed by the children.

The Bakers had moderate ability to understand human motivations and needs. A marked rigidity of roles reflected a cognitive approach to family problems that was linear. There was, however, behavioral evidence of an awareness that people in the family needed love and caring, and that kept frustration under control. Mother was aware of this need and, though she hungered for more herself, she continually tried to provide it for others. Father was aware of the need for order and predictability, and tried to provide that. Like Jack Spratt and his wife, between the two they provided both structure and some warmth.

This was a relatively unspontaneous family; as the interaction unfolded it became predictable. Few degrees of freedom were allowed—the watchword was not growth, but stability, and heightened anxiety attended any family member's getting out of line.

Though the family members were active and involved in the larger world, none of the individual personalities stood out as unusually skillful. They were adequate and they survived with modest pleasure and some frustration. Their goals and rewards were modest and they were reasonably content. The many negative statements on Table 5-1 along with many counterbalancing positive comments, reflect painful stereotyped patterns coupled with underlying caring.

11. The *Day* parents were in their mid-forties with three children, 15, 9, and 8. The striking overall impression was of another family with a classical "hysteric-compulsive" parental relationship: Father being both husband and parent to the wife, and the wife consistently seeming helpless and, at times, even more powerless than her daughter. There was evidence of an unresolved triangle as Mother and Daughter battled for Father's preference; the daughter fluctuated between winning and losing. When she was the winner she was coy, provocative, and appeared older than her real age, with many flirtatious mannerisms directed at Father. When she was loser, Mother and Father got along better and Daughter was somewhat withdrawn and depressed. The daughter

responded to this difficult and somewhat tenuous relationship between Father and Mother at every point, and when she was most successful she was anxious to glue her parents together, even physically holding each of their hands at the same time. The sons were less involved in this intense family interaction and seemed to be somewhat isolated emotionally. They did not appear to be damaged by this and perhaps were better off since they were allowed to go their own ways. Father did not offer them much support and frequently was competitive. However, though the personal pain of all the family members was obvious, this family drama never got out of hand—it had limits to its oscillation—and this was a strength.

The mood during the interviews varied, sometimes a somewhat depressed feeling, occasionally controlled anger, and at times a good deal of anxiety. Rarely was there strong evidence of tenderness or warmth, and spontaneous, joyful laughter was almost completely absent. Since control and stereotyped role playing were the rule, family members expected opposition. Both Mother and Daughter had some confidence in their ability to obtain Father's favor if they were seductive and unchallenging, the sons had confidence in their ability to stay out of the way.

This family group showed little respect for individual viewpoints or feelings. Their concern was with form: proper words were considered important and the reality behind those words was not given much consideration. This family was very superego-oriented, with the father being the referee, which made little allowance for expression of subjective world views.

The communication system was largely closed to expression of honest feelings. Father rarely expressed any feelings, but instead laid down the law. Both Mother and Daughter frequently disguised their true feelings and placated and played up to Father; the sons were rather isolated and did not express feelings.

The parental coalition was rather tenuous. The constant anger was managed rather poorly, usually by withdrawal and silence. Father was extremely limited in his emotional repertoire and was proud of his intimidating use of silence. His wife, on the other hand, was emotive in a little-girl manner, always attempting to diminish the distance from her husband. Father appeared not to see his wife as being successful or as powerful as he. The mother agreed with this and described herself as being terribly helpless when they first met, giving her husband credit for helping her to grow up. Because of the emotional distancing of the parents, resolution of oedipal ties had not occurred and the daughter, particularly, was caught up in the family drama and had a somewhat tenuous self-definition outside its boundaries. Mother, however, did not relate seductively to her sons, though she was a buffer between Father's frequently caustic and hostile feelings toward the younger boy and the boy's need to feel significant.

With relatively little insight and understanding of human motivations and needs, the family was concerned with form and structure. They did not disintegrate, but the pain was evident. For example, a striking interaction occurred when the younger son was reduced to tears as the father angrily criticized him. This son was somewhat scapegoated by all other family members. However, the family had some ability to deal behaviorally with human needs and Father frequently rebuffed the daughter's blandishments and supported his wife. On balance, however, there was much narrowness and obliviousness.

There was relatively little spontaneity in the interaction. Father was consistently distant, powerful, remote. Mother was consistently ingratiating and child-like. The daughter was either depressed or actively and successfully competing with Mother for Father's favor, and at the same time being the peacemaker who was obviously anxious about any marked distance between Mother and Father. The older son had a few more degrees of freedom in his behavior since he was less tightly enmeshed in the family drama. He had a very active sports life outside the family, and frequently interjected comments that were unexpected and refreshing. The younger boy appeared to be even less caught up in the family struggle.

A family strength was their activity and energy. Father, though unemotional and inexpressive, was active and successful in his work, and wielded the power in the family. The mother was not beaten down by her child-like role and continued to reach out energetically to her husband and to her sons. She had a respectful-competitive but not very effective relationship with her daughter.

These individuals were capable but not outstanding. They functioned in spite of a good deal of interpersonal pain within their family, but with structure and predictability that prevented them from being symptomatic. A great deal of expressed emotional hunger went unmet, but there was no clinically significant depression.

To summarize, the family showed many of the characteristics that are found in obviously neurotic families, but their energy, effort and tenacity in maintaining the family and continuing to be concerned about its welfare prevented them from being overtly pathological. The summary of positive and negative statements parallels these impressions (Table 5-1).

12. The *Abbott* parents were in their late forties with daughters ages 15 and 11, and a son age 12. The overall impact of the family was of anxiety, with parental inactivity and passivity and nervous movement in the children. The youngest child was somewhat regressive in his behavior. The older daughter was more energetic and frequently dominated and controlled the interaction in the family. The younger children were physically calm but engaged in anxious monologues in an earnest, but failing, attempt to control the interaction.

There were few sequences in the interaction when there was a sense of ease and warmth. The mood of anxiety was varied occasionally by open anger, some depression, and bursts of relatively joyless laughter. Instead of being reassuring and infectious, the laughter had a hostile, cutting edge. The family system responded to strong expectations of oppositional interaction by isolation and imperviousness.

The family members were not skilled in respecting their own or others' inner life. Each was cut off from satisfying contact with others. The younger daughter indicated this by childlike clutching; the older girl by her intrusive showmanship and center-stage activity; the son by his tense, stiff posture and high-pitched monologues; the mother by her powerful, but passive, stolidity; and the father by a fixed smile with which he expressed a whole gamut of emotions from hostility to tenderness.

This system showed the largest amount of confusing and incomprehensible dialogue. There were disqualifications, imperviousness, and a zaniness of language style. For example, the son was told that his sister might pull his leg, and he moved from abstract to concrete: "If she pulls my leg, I'll pull hers." This zaniness might have been humorous, but no one responded. All of the family members made tangential references to subjects unintelligible to the clinician and not responded to by other family members. The only family member who had "rational" discourses was the son, but since they were ignored this only added to the observer's vertigo.

The parental coalition was complex and puzzling. Both married in their thirties. Mother had been a very energetic worker, Father a loner who was reasonably successful in his work, and they came together with modest expectations of intimacy. There was minimal emotional sharing; distance was the cornerstone of their relationship. Mother was powerful and treated her husband alternately as an honored guest or as an inadequate handyman. The parents' isolation from one another was clear, but not disruptive. Mother did not put her husband down overtly, and he seemed reasonably content with this relationship. The son apparently was not involved with any oedipal tie with Mother, rather he seemed related to the family system as a visitor—almost a boarder, but less welcome than Father and without his esteem or usefulness. The hostile rivalry between Father and Son was expressed in cutting humor. When the parents interacted without the children, the distance was dramatically expressed by the two empty chairs between them. Father's most positive remark about their relationship was, "If I thought it was bad, I would leave. Maybe that is why we get along." His oedipal tie to the older daughter was a bit more sticky. She was a showoff and her father liked her liveliness and ignored her destructiveness.

The lack of awareness of human needs and the strong degree of obliviousness resulted (in contrast to other families) in a high toleration for the "inappropriate" behavior of the two girls. The son ineffectually attempted some "parental" control, but was not supported by his parents. His verbal efforts at control were ineffective, and at one point, rather deviously, he twisted the younger girl's arm. The parents saw him as having been quite willful when younger, but he appeared to have changed into a more compulsive style. Perhaps he had obtained so little gratification from his previous aggressivity that he was attempting (with little success) to gain approval by pseudo-maturity.

It was difficult to place this family on the continuum of spontaneity. Mother and Father behaved in a very predictable fashion; that is, distant with little discussion of feelings. The son, treated a bit like a live-in maid, was stereotyped in manner. The two girls seemed to do whatever they pleased and, therefore, might be termed spontaneous. But this seemed to have a tinge of chaos, with little of an interactional quality and it, too, became predictable.

This family was moderate in productive activity. Father was passive in the family, yet was capable in his career; Mother was efficient in meeting the physical needs of her group, but apparently was unaware of their other human needs. There was a sad quality to the family interaction due to this pervasive distancing and in the continual complaints of the children that they never did anything that was fun. The parents defined themselves as "breadwinner" and "child caretaker" and no spark of uniqueness or creativity emerged. The son was severely inhibited in peer relationships though the two girls reported having friends.

Review of the overall impact of this family system showed a high degree of distancing and communicational confusion. The strengths of the family that allowed for modest success lay in the very obliviousness that might, in other families, be seen as a liability. With a studied unawareness of the pain and isolation present, the family persevered and functioned. The observation scores on Table 5-1 reflect the overall impression of large areas of difficulty coupled with modest strengths.

SUMMARY OBSERVATIONS ABOUT THE ADEQUATE FAMILIES

These adequate families scored rather low on seven of the eight categories of evaluation. All were quite deficient in spontaneity, with rigid and stereotyped patterning usually replacing the unplanned and joyful. Generally, there was an oppositional orientation with only modest respect for the subjective realities of individuals. The families possessed few individual members who stood out as creative or as contributors to the larger society. The fathers of the Cooper and Prosper families were exceptions to this "plain-vanilla" impression, both being diligent, productive, and outstanding in their careers.

One family of this group was intermediate on the scales of openness, parental coalition and an understanding of varied human motivations, while the other families were low in these categories. The one category that these adequate families scored well on was initiative. They were generally energetic and purposeful.

It became apparent that families can function with the presence of a good deal of stereotyped behavior, limited skills, and obliviousness. Even painful, predictable, gamelike interaction may be present; indeed, these families designated "adequate" showed characteristic patterns found in acknowledged dysfunctional families. The Prospers, the Coopers, the Bakers, and the Days exhibited a strained parental coalition with definite evidence of unresolved parent-child coalitions. The Prospers' parental coalition works reasonably well because of the submissiveness of the wife. The Medders evidenced extreme efforts to control feared destructive impulses; and the Abbots exhibited confusing communicational sequences. These maladaptive patterns existed, yet they were handled by the family systems and function was maintained. What contributed to this toughness, this tenacity in survival and functioning? Predictability of structure, perhaps. There was a greater trust of the known difficulties in the family than the unknown dangers of the outside world. This seemed to be especially evident with five of these families. The parents of the sixth seemed to compare themselves less to a dangerous outside world than to their

TABLE 5-1
Observations Made During Six Hours of Family Interviews

Family	Total No.	% Positive	% Negative	% Neutral
OPTIMAL				
Comfort	31	74%	16%	10%
Powers	74	54	30	16
King	65	55	35	10
Ponder	85	57	26	17
Reasoner	71	62	30	8
Adams	65	40	55	5
ADEQUATE				
Cooper	55	29	56	15
Prosper	74	39	57	4
Medders	54	28	69	3
Baker	82	39	56	5
Day	82	39	56	5
Abbott	73	12	84	4

own painful and frustrating families of origin, and found pride and comfort in such comparisons. In addition, some real self-esteem was apparent in all of these family members. The parents valued their parenting role; and, though their skills were modest, they persevered. Further, each family was headed by a father with skills in which he took pride and which provided economic structure for creature needs to be met and freed his wife to meet, in some fashion, the children's needs for human warmth. Consistent presence and a view that the job of parenting was important were able to compensate for the lack of interpersonal skills. *Trying is important if that trying is continual and predictable.*

REFERENCES

1. HUXLEY, A., *Brave New World*, New York: Harper & Row, 1932.
2. POPPER, K., "Science: Problems, aims, responsibilities," presented at the 47th Annual Meeting of the Federation of American Societies for Experimental Biology, Atlantic City, New Jersey, April 17, 1963.

CHAPTER VI

MICROANALYSIS

OUR RESEARCH PLAN INCLUDED three levels of data: the clinical level, the level of rating scales, and the microanalytic level. Approaching the data in this manner afforded us the opportunity for comprehensive analyses and comparison across levels. The levels themselves were seen as reflecting continua of richness and quantification. The clinical level (Chapter V) represented observations and impressions of an experienced family therapist and researcher upon viewing six hours of videotaped, exploratory interviews with each of the final sample of 12 families. This level produced information of richness and depth but, as with all such clinical evaluations, was difficult to quantify. The rating scale approach (Chapter IV) was seen as a move in the direction of greater specificity with some sacrifice of clinical detail and depth.

The microanalytic level represented still greater precision and opportunity for quantification. A number of investigators, including Haley (4), Ferreira and Winter (3), Cheek (1,2), and Mishler and Waxler (6), have developed microanalytic techniques in an effort to find operational methods of assessing family interaction. We chose the method of Riskin and Faunce (7) because:

1) The population they studied was similar in social, economic, and ethnic backgrounds to our own.

2) Their methodology evolved from a theoretical approach to family systems that was compatible with and frequently overlapping our own.

3) The observational focus of their work was the family as a whole rather than dyads, triads, or other family subgroups.

4) Their instrument distinguished reasonably well between presumably normal families and a variety of disturbed ones.

The Riskin and Faunce methodology (7) focused primarily on the form of family communication rather than the specific content of the interaction. Its theoretical frame of reference, influenced by the work of Jackson (5) and Satir (8), emphasized the mutually interactive process involving all family members. The whole family was asked to "Plan something you could all do together as a family; all of you please participate in the planning." Six scales were constructed covering 68 categories. The scales made a close evaluation of literally every sound the family members made in 160 speech units. The microanalytic scales included:

1) *Clarity:* measured whether the family members spoke clearly to each other.

2) *Topic Continuity:* measured whether family members stayed on the same topic with each other and how they shifted topics.

3) *Commitment:* measured whether individual family members took direct stands on issues and feelings.

4) *Agreement/Disagreement:* measured whether family members explicitly agreed or disagreed with one another.

5) *Affective Intensity:* measured how family members showed variations in affect as they communicated with one another.

6) *Relationship:* measured whether family members were friendly or attacking toward one another.

In addition to those six scales, the patterns of who-speaks-to-whom and interruptions were scored. Most of the analysis was done using both a typescript and an audiotape of the family interaction. Both interrater and intrarater reliability studies demonstrated satisfactory levels of reliability. Data from a diverse group of 44 families revealed that many of the variables discriminated among the groups of families, although with wide differences in their ability to do so. In general, variables composed of ratios were more sensitive than simpler percentage variables. As even this brief summary of their methodology may suggest, the technique was very time-consuming, with a multiplicity of categories and many data that, at times, challenged interpretation.

Riskin and Faunce emphasized the enormous methodological complexities which result from the absence of a comprehensive family typology. They avoided either the simple dichotomized "normal-abnormal" system or a typology based upon individual psychopathology. Rather, they utilized an *ad hoc* grouping based upon degree of family dysfunction, the family focus of concern, and the general atmosphere of the family. Their normal group was comprised of nine families who were described as containing no individuals with diagnosable psychiatric syndromes. A second criterion involved the judgment of family interviewers that such families were functioning well.

The analysis of the microanalytic scale data from these nine families produced a composite of the Riskin and Faunce "normal" family. Such a family fell in the high-medium range on Clarity of speech, and the middle range on Unclarity of speech. The latter appeared related to their frequent use of sarcasm, irony, and laughter. The Clarity findings suggested the absence of a compulsive rationality.

These families tended to stay on the same Topic, resolve issues, and only then move on. They scored high on measures which suggested spontaneity. They were low on intrusiveness. Although high on Information—Asking and Giving—they were unexpectedly low on both Spontaneous Commitment and Requested Commitment. This suggested maximum interacting at a cognitive level with little expression of opinions or putting people on the spot. They were in the middle range on Disagree, which suggested that in such families it was not dangerous to disagree.

Normal families expressed a wide range of feelings with a major emphasis on friendly, supportive affects. Although anger was present, there was little attacking.

It appeared from the communication patterns that these families were not dominated by one family member, and that coalitions were intragenerational. Scapegoating was not seen. Differences were tolerated. Humor was common. Riskin and Faunce concluded that such families were able to provide the supportive atmosphere in which a child's self-esteem was able to develop adequately.

Our use of the Riskin and Faunce method took two forms. The first was to replicate a portion; that is, to analyze the data from our families using their method and variables that met three criteria: first, those variables that were simple, obtained by counting (rather than ratio variables derived from further manipulation of the data); second, we used only Whole Family variables; third, we restricted our analysis to those variables that distinguished one group of families from any other at a significant level (p <.05) in their work. Our approach of using a smaller number of Riskin and Faunce variables in the manner just described was due to their finding that the ability of these different variables to distinguish one family type from another varied greatly. Many of the scales, both simple and derived, were not discriminating in their study. In addition, we rejected the use of derived ratio variables from the Riskin data because of the difficulty in explaining the resulting correlations from a theoretical basis—either from the Riskin and Faunce theoretical orientation or our own. The simple frequencies of Riskin and Faunce, however, were developed from a coherent and explicitly stated theoretical base.

Originally Riskin and Faunce hypothesized that all of their variables would be curvilinear; that is, that the healthy families would be in the middle of a group with different kinds of disturbed families having either more or less of any quality measured. (This theoretical structure was based on the principle that moderation in all things would lead to optimal living conditions.) However, their empirical findings did not support this hypothesis. Of the total of 125 variables they reported, 48 reflected the whole family and, of these, 16 found the healthy families at one end or the other of a continuum, indicating a linear rather than a curvilinear ordering. Their empirical findings encouraged us to make theoretical room for linear family qualities (i.e., "the more the better" or "the less the better") in addition to variables in which a "golden mean" is optimal.

Since our own theoretical orientation (Chapter III) hypothesized that some variables would be linear—that is, healthy families were expected to be at one end of a continuum—we made a distinction between two kinds of interactional variables: *curvilinear* (with optimal families in the middle and different kinds of less functional families on either side), and *linear* variables (optimal families at one end of a continuum). A variable such as Relationship was thought to be linear because we could not conceptualize too much positive feeling. In contrast, a variable such as Clarity would be expected to be curvilinear since it was our own estimation (as well as that of Riskin and Faunce) that too much clarity would interfere with other valued qualities, such as spontaneity.

On the basis of the Riskin and Faunce findings from normal families, we further categorized the variables into three types: curvilinear, linear, and linear-reversed. Curvilinear variables included Clarity, Clarity Non-Scoreable, and High Intensity. Laughter, Total Non-Applicable, Non-Applicable Questions, and Agreement were categorized as linear variables. Linear-reversed variables included Total Commitment, Request Commitment, Requested Commitment and Negative Relationship.

Two raters were trained in the Riskin and Faunce technique. Following demonstration of exact agreement on 80% of ratings for each of the scales, they were considered reliable raters. Rater A, a psychiatric nurse, scored five of these families. Rater B, a psychology graduate student, scored the remaining seven.

Eleven* of the Riskin-Faunce variables met the criteria of simple frequencies rather than derived ratios, total family qualities, and distinguishing groups** of families at statistically significant

---

* Clarity, Laugher, Clarity Non-Scoreables, Total Commitment, Requested Commitment, Total Non-Applicable, Non-Applicable Questions, Agreement, Intensity, Negative Relationship.
** Their groups were: 1) multiproblem families, 2) constricted families, 3) child-labeled problem families, 4) families with no labels but significant problems, and 5) normal families.

levels. Each of these surviving variables was used to rank-order our group of 12 families from most to least healthy. These 11 rankings of the 12 families were compared to an independent ranking of the families by an experienced clinician-investigator following observing videotapes of six hours of exploratory family interviews for each family. This comparison is presented in Table 6-1.

Three facts emerged from this Table. First, all the correlations were positive in the anticipated direction. Second, the sum of the ranks of the 11 variables correlated significantly with the clinical ranking ($r = .52$, $p = .05$). Third, two individual variables, Clarity and High Intensity, resulted in rankings which correlated significantly with the clinical ranking.

We interpret these findings to suggest a correlation between two different levels of data analysis. We concur with Riskin and Faunce that carefully obtained information on a variety of family variables should be more useful in determining family capability than any one family interaction variable. Although the 11 variables used together produced a rank ordering significantly correlated with the clinical ranking of the families, two of the single variables, Clarity and High Intensity, were each more highly correlated with the clinical rank ordering than the sum of the variables. It is of interest to note that both of these significant variables were curvilinear and that, therefore, two of the three curvilinear variables were significantly correlated with the clinical rank ordering. Further, none of the eight linear variables correlated significantly. This may have been reflective of the nature of the variables chosen by the Riskin and Faunce group. Their theoretical structure delineated interactional functions with an expected golden mean; that is, the scales were constructed with the expectation that healthy families would fall in the center of the data range.

The significant correlations of rankings for the variables Clarity and High Intensity supported the observation that healthy families communicated clearly, but without obsessive clarity, and that

TABLE 6-1

Correlation of Rank Orders of Empirically Derived Riskin-Faunce Scales and Clinical Ranking

FAMILY Ranked Clinically	1 Clarity	2 Laughter	3 Clarity Non Score-able	4 Total Commitment	5 Request Commitment	6 Requested Commitment	7 Total Non-Applicable	8 Non-Applicable	9 Agree	10 High Intensity	11 Negative Relationship	Rank by Sum of 11 Ranks
	C	L	C	LR	LR	LR	L	L	L	C	LR	
Powers	1.5	2.5	7	5	9	9	5	8.5	6.5	2	2	2
Comfort	1.5	10	1.5	4	6	6.5	3	1	1	2	2	1
King	5.5	9	8	10.5	10	10.5	12	4.5	8.5	10	11	11
Ponder	3	4.5	9.5	8	2	1.5	6	4.5	4	2	8	4
Reasoner	5.5	11	1.5	1	1	1.5	1	6.5	12	7	5	3
Adams	12	1	12	12	7	6.5	11	12	5	4.5	7	10
Cooper	8	2.5	4	2	4.5	5	2	8.5	11	6	9	5
Prosper	5.5	7.5	6	6	12	10.5	7	2.5	8.5	9	4	9
Medders	9.5	7.5	9.5	3	3	3.5	4	2.5	6.5	12	2	6
Baker	9.5	12	11	9	11	12	8	10.5	3	8	12	12
Day	11	4.5	4	7	4.5	8	9	6.5	10	4.5	10	8
Abbott	5.5	6	4	10.5	8	3.5	10	10.5	2	11	6	7
r	.67	.06	.07	.20	.06	.00	.28	.32	.01	.59	.33	.52
p	.01	.42	.42	.25	.42	NS	.18	.15	NS	.03	.14	.05
Riskin Range *												
High	86.9	15.0	31.3	59.1	23.7	11.9	—	22.3	17.6	9.0	5.2	
Low	67.5	.6	11.9	19.5	.8	1.9	—	3.9	.8	.6	0	
Timberlawn Range												
High	83.1	11.3	20.6	48.1	12.5	11.9	70.0	13.1	18.1	35.0	21.9	
Low	63.8	2.5	8.1	16.3	1.9	1.9	36.3	3.8	.6	13.8	3.8	

* Personal communication. We cannot explain the finding that on some scales the range is wider on the presumably more circumscribed, non-clinical sample than for the broader distribution of the R-F sample.

in their communication they demonstrated variations in affective Intensity with few extremely high or extremely low statements.

A second approach to the use of the data gathered by the Riskin-Faunce methodology was also followed. Several Riskin-Faunce variables and combinations of variables which, according to the theoretical orientation in Chapter III, were thought most likely to be discriminating were selected by one of the investigators (WRB). The selection of each variable was made on the basis of the Riskin-Faunce definitions. Prior to data analysis, eight variables were selected which reflected the following theoretical premises regarding healthy families:

1) A tendency toward egalitarian structure.
2) High levels of individual autonomy of family members.
3) High levels of positive affect, warmth, and joy.

The following variables were selected:

1. Positive Relationship: A speech which is friendly, positive, or accepting. It carries an element of good will. This should be a highly significant variable and a linear one since the most Positive Relationship interactions would be found in the healthiest family systems.

2. Negative Relationship: A speech which is attacking, rejecting or complaining. It implies ill will, criticism of or annoyance with the person to whom it is addressed. This variable should reflect health in a linear-reversed fashion since the most Negative Relationships would be in the least healthy families.

3. A derived scale which included both Low or High Intensity remarks when they were associated with Negative Relationships. *High Intensity* is a speech which is intense, highly cathected, or empathic. *Low Intensity* is a speech which is flat, bland, mechanical, or subdued. This derived scale addressed itself to the emotional quality of the relationships in a family, with the view that extremes of intensity, when associated with Negative Relationships, would be inversely correlated with family health (linear-reversed).

4. Laughter associated with speeches which were also scored

Positive Relationships. Only Laughter which was Appropriate in tone and intensity to the conversation was counted. (Bizarre and Inappropriate Laughter were excluded.) Our assumption was that warm and positive laughter would be seen in the healthiest family systems.

5. Inappropriate Topic Change, a speech which shifts the topic from that of the previous speech in an inappropriate manner (that is, does not facilitate the task at hand) ; for example, questioning motives, making irrelevant statements, nonverbal interruptions, mind-reading and intrusive statements. This variable represents a measure of cognitive and perceptual sharing. It was our view that the least number of Inappropriate Topic Changes would be found in healthy family systems.

6. It was predicted that Clarity would be a curvilinear pheno- menon; i.e., that extreme clarity would be associated with undue rigidity on the part of the family system and too little clarity would indicate incoherence, hence difficulty in functioning as a family unit. In this regard, we agreed with Riskin and Faunce.

7. A combination of "Total Agree" and "Total Disagree" was predicted to be curvilinear. This was a measure of the number of explicit agreements and disagreements. Our view here was that the healthiest families are able to disagree and do not need to agree always; and that the families less effective in functioning would be at either end of this variable, having either a compulsive need for agreement or a very high number of disagreements in their interaction.

8. Total Commitment, whether family members take direct stands on issues and feelings, was expected to be curvilinear. That is, we predicted that less functional families would have either high levels of Total Commitment (reflecting severe conflict) or low levels of Total Commitment (reflecting amorphousness). Healthy families, with highly autonomous individuals and low levels of conflict, were hypothesized to fall between the extremes.

Table 6-2 presents the rank ordering of the 12 families for each of the Riskin-Faunce scales chosen for relevance to our theoretical

TABLE 6-2
Rank Orders Based on Theoretically Derived Scales

FAMILY Ranked Clinically	1 Positive Relationship	2 Negative Relationship	3 Low Intensity + High Intensity/Negative Relationship	4 Laughter/Positive Relationship	5 Inappropriate Topic Change	6 Clarity	7 Total Agree + Disagree	8 Total Commitment	Sum of Ranks
	L	LR	LR	L	LR	C	C	C	
Powers	2	2	8	5	6.5	1.5	4	3	1
Comfort	3	2	3	8.5	2	1.5	11	4.5	2
King	6	11	1	5	2	5.5	2	10.5	3
Ponder	9	8	11	3	8.5	3	2	4.5	5
Reasoner	4.5	5	6	10.5	4.5	5.5	8	8	7
Adams	7	7	4	7	8.5	12	9	12	10
Cooper	12	9	7	12	10.5	8	2	7	11
Prosper	1	4	12	5	10.5	5.5	6.5	1.5	4
Medders	10	2	2	8.5	6.5	9.5	6.5	6	6
Baker	11	12	5	10.5	2	9.5	12	9	12
Day	4.5	10	9	1.5	12	11	5	1.5	8
Abbott	8	6	10	1.5	4.5	5.5	10	10.5	9
r	.40	.33	.28	−.15	.29	.67	.33	.10	.71
p	.09	.14	.18	.31	.18	.01	.14	.37	.01
Riskin Range *									
High	6.3	5.2	—	—	6.5	86.9	—	59.1	
Low	0	0	—	—	0	67.5	—	19.5	
Timberlawn Range									
High	35	21.9	16.9	5.6	2.5	83.1	26.2	48.1	
Low	1.9	3.8	5	.6	0	63.8	7.5	16.3	

* Personal communications. We cannot explain the finding that on some scales the range is wider on the presumably more circumscribed, non-clinical sample than for the broader distribution of the R-F sample.

system as compared to a clinical level rank ordering from most to least healthy. The following can be noted:

1) The sum of ranks of the eight variables correlated significantly with the clinical level ranking.

2) One of the single theoretically selected variables, Clarity, correlated with the clinical level ranking.

3) With the exception of Laughter/Positive Relationship, the correlations for each variable were positive and in the predicted direction.

These results were similar to those using the Riskin-Faunce variables selected on empirical grounds. However, with the theoretically derived set, the sum of the variables had a higher correlation with the clinical rank ordering than did any of the individual variables. There was a relatively weak discriminatory power of any individual variables (save Clarity), but a pattern of positive correlations in the predicted direction with a significant correlation between sum of ranks and the clinical level. There was a somewhat stronger correlation ($r = .70$, $p = <.01$) with this group of variables derived from our theoretical set than there was with the empirically derived group ($r = .52$, $p = <.05$). This is supportive of the interrelationship between evaluation of family interaction at the clinical level and at the microanalytic level and, in addition, supports the view that there is no single thread which, by itself, predicts the upper levels of health.

It is our judgment that the pattern of correlations between the microanalytic and clinical levels of data analysis, and the rating scale data across a broad continuum of families (Chapter IV), provided support for the construct validity of the theory of family systems described in Chapter III.

In addition, there was a striking consistency to the correlations found between another source of independent ratings of family health and the Riskin-Faunce variables. Eleven raters independently ranked the 12 families in terms of Global Health-Pathology on the basis of observing from five to 60 minutes of videotaped interactional testing. The correlation of these rankings with the Riskin-Faunce variables was significant (Kendall-Smith Coefficient of Concordance, $W = .35$, $p = <.002$), and added emphasis to the relationship between the clinical, rating scale, and microanalytic levels of data analysis.

In summary, we found evidence that sets of microanalytic family interaction variables developed by another group of researchers using a different sample of families and a different theoretical orientation correlated significantly with a variety of independent assessments of family health in our sample of nonclinical families. Although few single variables correlated at statistically impressive levels, the consistent pattern of correlation of sums of variables, both empirically and theoretically derived, added weight to the concept that family system health is a result of a number of complex, interrelated family interaction characteristics. The fabric of a system's interaction was the important differentiating feature, rather than the individual functions; and the quality could be evaluated best by using a multiple variable approach. As information increases concerning varieties of populations of families, both healthy and disturbed, these variables can be weighted empirically for greater differentiation.

REFERENCES

1. CHEEK, F. E., "The schizophrenogenic mother in word and deed," *Family Process,* 3, 155, 1964.
2. CHEEK, F. E., "The father of the schizophrenic," *Arch. Gen. Psychiat.,* 13, 336, 1965.
3. FERREIRA, A. J., and WINTER, W. D., "Family Interaction and Decision-Making," *Arch. Gen. Psychiat.,* 13, 214, 223, 1965.
4. HALEY, J., "Critical overview of present status of family interaction research." In J. Framo (Ed.), *Family Interaction: A Dialogue Between Family Researchers and Family Therapists.* New York: Springer Publishing Co., 1972, p. 27.
5. JACKSON, D. D., and YALOM, I., "Family research on the problem of ulcerative colitis," *Arch. Gen. Psychiat.,* 15:410-418, 1966.
6. MISHLER, E., and WAXLER, N., *Interaction in Families.* New York: John Wiley and Sons, 1968.
7. RISKIN, J., and FAUNCE, E. F., "Family interactions scales," *Arch. Gen. Psychiat.,* Vol. 22 (6), 504-537, June, 1970.
8. SATIR, V., *Conjoint Family Therapy.* Palo Alto: Science and Behavior Books, 1964.

CHAPTER VII

INDIVIDUALLY BASED DATA

THE BASIC APPROACH of the research team was to examine family systems rather than to construct family composites based upon data derived from observations of individuals. Underlying this approach was the assumption that a family system is greater than the sum of its parts. While the results of this project do not constitute a crucial test of whether an analysis of a family system or a family composite derived from analyses of individuals produces deeper understanding of family dynamics and family health, they suggest the complementarity of the two approaches.

Two sets of individual data were obtained from the sample families: namely, individual interviews and psychological tests. The major focus of this investigation was through lengthy individual interviews and, accordingly, material from that source will be presented first. The remainder of the chapter will be devoted to a summary of the optimal and adequate families as seen from the individual interviews, and a comparison of the findings about the families obtained from individual interviews contrasted to interactional systems analysis. Following this presentation, the psychological testing information obtained from the optimal and adequate families will be summarized.

THE INDIVIDUAL INTERVIEW APPROACH

Each member of the 12 families was given a semi-structured, tape-recorded individual interview. The interview format included investigation of the subject's vocational or academic tasks and functioning, leisure time activities, and self-description.* Parents were also queried concerning their marital relationship and their perceptions of each of their children. The children were asked to discuss closeness between various family members and their perceptions of their parents. The interviews, conducted by experienced clinicians (JML and JTG), varied from 45 minutes to an hour-and-a-half in length and were most often conducted in the subjects' homes, although a few were conducted elsewhere. The purposes of the interview and procedures for de-identification and protection of confidentiality were explained and consent obtained from each subject. Thirty-three individuals from seven of the 12 families were interviewed by one investigator, and 22 from the remaining five families were interviewed by the other. To assess overall judgments of psychological health of the interviewees, verbatim transcripts of the interview tape recordings (de-identified except for the individual's age and sex) were presented in random order to the two interviewers, who were each then asked to make ratings of all 55 individuals on a Health-Illness Scale (1,2). As a check on the degree to which ratings might have been influenced by personal contact with a portion of the sample, the transcripts were also rated by an experienced psychiatric nurse (JS) who had not met any of the subjects. Interjudge reliability for these ratings are given in Table 7-1.

These results demonstrated excellent interrater reliability for such judgments. The two clinicians who had rated the individual interview transcripts were then given the transcripts again, grouped by families, and asked to make global ratings of psychological health on a one-to-ten continuum for each family. The interrater reliability coefficient between these two judges of the overall health composite based upon the individual interviews is .60 (p <.025), indicating acceptable interjudge reliability. When these family composite ratings were compared to the family systems ratings described in Chapter V, the following results were obtained.

---

* See Appendix G, p. 253.

TABLE 7-1

Interrater Reliability Between Judges Rating Individual
Family Members

Rater Pairs	Parents N = 24	Children N = 31	Total N = 55
JML-JTG	.56 *	.72 *	.68 *
JML-JS	.52 *	.63 *	.62 *
JTG-JS	.55 *	.55 *	.59 *

* P <.005 Significant Test for Rank Correlations Coefficient

TABLE 7-2

Relationship Between Family System Ratings of Health
and Family Composite Ratings of Health

	WRB Systems Ranks	JML Composite Ranks	JTG Composite Ranks
Optimal Families	A	B	H
	B	H	B
	C	D	K
	D	A	G
	E	G	D
	F	F	I
Adequate Families	G	E	A
	H	L	C
	I	K	F
	J	J	J
	K	I	E
	L	C	L

The family composite ratings of the junior clinician (JTG)
correlated .17 (non-significant) with the systems level judgments.
The senior clinician's ratings correlated .44 with the systems level
judgments (p <.10). The finding that the senior clinician's evaluation of overall family health derived from examining each individual's transcript related meaningfully to the systems level
analysis encouraged further examination of the interview trans-

cripts. This rater agreed with the systems judge on four of the six families in each of the optimal and adequate groups. In an attempt to pinpoint the specific areas in which the individual composites and systems approach produced similar or different findings, a detailed examination of the individual interviews of the family members in the optimal and adequate groups was conducted.

Description of the Six Optimally Functioning Families

The family descriptions will follow the format of the individual interviews. These interviews began with a discussion of vocational activities, followed by leisure pursuits, the marital relationship, children, self-descriptions, and style in the interview. Finally, a comparison will be made between the analysis based on the individual interviews and the systems analysis derived from observation of six hours of videotape of the family interaction (Chapter V). Within each category, the main themes of similarities and differences will be described.

Vocational Activities

All six men in this group were very successful vocationally, both in terms of economic rewards and status and influence within their chosen professions. Most of these men had essentially created their own jobs, did them well, and generally derived a great deal of satisfaction from their vocations. It was striking that five of the men tended, in general, to operate in a self-supervising fashion. They reported that they received very little, if any, supervision, being at the top level of responsibility for whatever they are doing. Only one of the six worked in a bureaucratic organization with strong supervision from above.

Each of the six men seemed to thrive on persuasion; that is, they described deriving a good deal of satisfaction from motivating others to excel, they were involved in "selling" or persuading their employees or clients on ideas, programs, and procedures of their own creation.

Five of the six wives in this group were primarily occupied in the traditional roles of wife, mother, and homemaker, and derived their greatest satisfaction from these pursuits. In this day of "liberated" women, it would not have been surprising to have seen several women in this group engaged in primary vocational pursuits outside the family, but that was not the case. Some engaged in volunteer work and enjoyed it, but this was clearly secondary to enjoyment of being wife-mother-homemaker during this phase of their lives with children still within the family circle.

While four of the men in this group reported (without apparent ambivalence) that, given the chance, they would do the same job over again, the other two indicated substantial ambivalence. One of the men related with a twinge of regret that if he had his life to live over, he probably would not have chosen his particular vocation, but instead would have pursued another one (for which he felt adequately skilled, and which he believed would have led to greater social status and larger economic rewards for less work). The sixth man indicated that he probably would choose the same work again because of the very substantial economic rewards. However, he was, after a number of years in his profession, becoming somewhat bored with it and at times yearned for a return to a very different job he held a number of years previously that had provided somewhat more stimulation and less routine, but that had been unrewarding economically.

Four of the women in this group engaged in many outside interests and pursuits, and obviously were receiving substantial pleasure from these outside activities without having given up any of what was important to them in their roles of wife, mother, and homemaker. This did not appear to be true, however, for the other two women. One of these impressed the interviewer as being a bit subservient to her husband, and perhaps so immersed in her homemaking duties that she had become rather cut off from the outside. However, she appeared to like what she was doing and did not complain about her position in life. The sixth woman impressed the interviewer as not only being somewhat cut off from outside interests, but also rather chronically exhausted and, to some degree, depressed by her multiple homemaker roles and a self-reported feeling of having had too many children. This woman did complain openly about being overstressed and under-stimulated in her chosen roles, but did not appear to be seriously contemplating changing her situation.

The one woman in this group involved in full-time employment outside the home seemed to thrive on it. She indicated she had never been very skilled as a homemaker, but was very skilled in her chosen vocation, and felt that she and her children were much happier as a result of her vocational activity. However, she also said that her husband seemed a bit threatened by this activity on her part, although, in general, he was supportive of her full-time employment.

Leisure Activities

It was striking that the leisure activities for ten of the 12 adults in this group were primarily family-centered. For example, there were many reports of primary leisure activities such as gardening, lawn care, reading, family-centered sports activities, and other similar functions. In most of these couples, the parents seemed at least as invested, and perhaps more invested, in these family-ori-ented leisure activities than they were in social pursuits involving other adult couples. However, at least one adult in three of the families complained mildly about having too few close adult friends.

Two of the families seemed somewhat different from the others in that the father in each of these families did have leisure pursuits that he conducted entirely on his own or with other adult men. In these families, the mother's leisure pursuits also removed her some of the time from the family, and the children's leisure ac-tivities also seemed mainly to involve peers and adults outside the family. However, even in these families the leisure activities were coordinated in such a way that the family members still had a good deal of time together in the home, and in various combina-tions of parents and children outside the home.

Marital Relationships

All six sets of marital partners were remarkable for the complementary nature of their relationships. Each husband and wife talked warmly and positively about the ways their skills and those of their spouses interlocked in a comfortable fashion. These comments were spontaneously offered and did suggest strongly that in these six families competition between parents was extremely rare. Rather, husbands and wives encouraged and admired each other for their competence. It appeared that there were almost no instances of major differences of opinion upon crucial issues involved in the marriage, child rearing, or other aspects of family life between these six sets of partners.

Long-term marital fidelity was reported by these six couples. The husbands and wives in each pair reported identically on frequency of intercourse, but there were marked differences between the couples, varying from several times a week to twice a month. All six wives reported experiencing orgasm, most since the early days of their marriage, but the frequency of orgasm varied widely. While 11 of the 12 marital partners reported a good deal of enjoyment in the sexual aspect of their marriage, the amount of importance placed upon the sexual relationship varied from central to peripheral. One of the 12 adults in this group did indicate some degree of frustration in the sexual area based upon its infrequency.

All six men in this group tended toward being reserved or slow to discuss their feelings with their wives. This was experienced as no problem at all for three of the women; however, the other three wives indicated more-or-less constant pushing to get their husbands to share more with them.

Children

In five of the six sets of children, there was a similar pattern of personality characteristics depending upon the birth order of the child. In each of these families, the oldest child (regardless of sex) was described by the parents (and perceived by the interviewer) to be somewhat overcontrolled, highly conscientious, driven to excel, and quite orderly and dependable. Impulse expression was somewhat inhibited in these oldest youngsters' life styles. In these families, the second child (regardless of sex) almost invariably demonstrated a good deal more openness of impulse expression. These second children were often described by the parents (and perceived by the interviewer) as being more emotional, more outgoing, more happy-go-lucky, and more entertaining. They were, upon occasion, seen as somewhat labile and impulsive, although these children also tended to be quite successful and well integrated. The third or youngest child of each of these families tended to be described by the parents (and perceived by the interviewers) as somewhat "immature" or overly dependent, or "spoiled," although, once again, generally not to a degree that seemed to be causing any clear-cut difficulties outside the family system—with two exceptions: two youngest children were experiencing some learning problems at school. This general pattern of some overcontrol in first children, more expressiveness in second children, and greater impulsivity in youngest children was strikingly consistent through five of the families.

While these personality characteristics were similar in the five sets of children, there was a general disinclination for these characteristics to follow the cultural stereotype of overcontrolled males and expressive or impulsive females. There were as many control-oriented females and expressive males among these children as vice versa. Thus, it would appear that the character typing was related much more to birth order than to sex of the child. The parents of these children consistently explained to the interviewer that they felt they had pushed their first child too hard, and then had been able to relax and enjoy their second child much more, and also felt that they were, to some degree, "hanging on to" or "spoiling" their youngest child.

In all six families the mother and father in their individual interviews gave almost identical descriptions of their children, and in all but one of these families the interviewer (after spending an hour with each child) came away with impressions essentially similar to those the parents had given. If one assumes that these similarities in observations between the parents and the interviewers are accurate ones, these parents might be described as rating very high in their ability to perceive their children accurately.

In one of the six families, all youngsters tended more toward the expressive, or impulsive, or mixed character formation; although, in this family as well, there seemed to be more of an expectation of excellence for the first child and more willingness to enjoy younger children, regardless of the degree of their impulse control or demonstrated competitive competence.

Self-Descriptions

All of the men in this group described themselves as very orderly, conscientious, hard-driving, and aggressive in their work and, in addition, impressed the interviewer as containing many of the assets and few of the liabilities of that characterological style. These men tended to be highly intelligent, extremely competent, and to form work-related friendships easily. They also described themselves as, and appeared to the interviewers to be, rather cautious and reserved in social relationships, and also to some degree with their wives.

The absence of traditional psychiatric symptomatology was impressive. This is not to say, however, that these men were free of conflict or of perceived psychological pain. They tended to experience and describe anxiety, depression, and stress-related somatic complaints, but such "symptoms" were transient and nondisabling. They tended to be non-smokers or light smokers and also light drinkers. The most frequent pattern of alcohol consumption, for example, was that of one or two drinks after work before dinner and perhaps two or three drinks at a party. None of them reported having used any kind of tranquilizers, stimulants, or sedatives. They did not report problems with sleeping, eating, or sexual functioning, and none of them had ever sought or received psychological counseling.

Five of the six women in this group gave essentially similar histories, while one did report anxiety, depression, and psychophysiological symptomatology.

Four of the wives in this group, like their husbands, tended to be controlled, orderly, mildly inhibited, and unusually conscientious; and in each of these marital pairs, the wife appeared to be more aggressive, gregarious, and energetic in family and social situations than was the husband. These characteristics, however, did not appear to bring them into competition with their husbands; but, rather, were integrated in a complementary fashion in these marriages. One had the sense of two strong partners pulling together rather than battling over control. It appeared in these families that the husband's energy was oriented a bit more in the work area and the wife's a bit more in the family area with a well integrated interface. In the other two couples, however, the wives tended more toward the impulsive, highly expressive, and somewhat labile; and, in these two marriages, the husband was also clearly the more aggressive or energetic in the family and social spheres as well as on the job.

An examination of the parents' personality styles and energy levels did not reveal any simple patterns or combinations that would suggest that the children had been forced or molded into any kind of conventional or stereotyped character styles. With the one exception of the influence of birth order, it appeared that the children in these families had been encouraged to develop along their individual lines with very little, if any, influence from either culturally stereotyped expectations of neurotic parental needs to mold. The parents in these families seemed much more to be "growers" of their children than "controllers" of them.

Style in the Interview Setting

Nine of the 12 adults in this group impressed the interviewer with their clarity, directness, openness, and spontaneity. The interviewers, accustomed to dealing with psychiatric patients, found these individuals remarkably easy and enjoyable to interview. The research subjects were very directly responsive to questions, and related with a degree of candor and genuineness that was refreshing.

Likewise, the children in these families appeared much more open, spontaneous, and comfortable than the youngsters seen in psychiatric interviews by these two examiners.

Three of the adults out of the group of 12 seemed somewhat vague, or rambling, in their styles. Although these two men and one woman were much easier to understand and were more clearly expressive than what the interviewers were accustomed to seeing in a psychiatric setting, they were noticeably less clear and direct than the other nine.

Comparison Between Individually
Derived and Systems Derived Data

In five of these families, a similar family picture was constructed from these two very different vantage points. In three of them, there were no areas of disagreement or differences between the two perspectives, while in two there were a few very mild differences that merely seemed to reflect variation in the interviewers' approach rather than any real disagreement in findings about the family. An impressionistic observation is that of a feeling of greater confidence in the systems approach, in that it tended to make manifest what might be described in individual interviews. This observation may be based in part upon the interviewers' greater experience in examining individual members from disturbed families. In this latter context, one becomes accustomed to interpreting verbal descriptions from each individual family member with caution because one so often sees the family functioning very differently when together due to the individual members' denials, projections, minimizations, and incongruent mythologies. However, in the optimal family group, the descriptions given by the individual members were played out congruently and clearly when the famly was seen functioning together.

One family in this group was seen very differently from the two points of analysis. In this particular family, the description based upon the videotape of the entire family functioning together referred several times to "complexity" and "ambiguity" in the family style of communication; in the individual interviews, sources of stress and difficulty within several family members surfaced that did not appear when the family was seen together. A tentative derivation from this observation is that when a generally healthy family system impresses an observer with particularly complicated or ambiguous communication styles, there may be material available in individual interviews that would give a somewhat different impression of family functioning than one sees when the family members are all together.

Description of the Six Adequately Functioning Families

The six adequate families will be described in the same format as were the optimally functioning families; that is, vocational activities, leisure pursuits, marital relationship, children, self-descriptions, style in the interview, and a comparison of the analysis based on the individual interviews with that of the systems approach.

Vocational Activities

All six of the men in this group were very aggressively work-oriented and had been quite successful in terms of vocational status, job accomplishment, and economic rewards.

Four of the six men functioned with very little supervision, while two were located in highly bureaucratic systems that involved a good deal of supervision from above. All six men were in leadership positions in their chosen vocations.

Four of the six men indicated that a major source of frustration or dissatisfaction in their work revolved around interpersonal frictions; that is, these men were extremely task-oriented and tended to view the complexities involved in relating to others at work as sources of frustration and irritation that divert them from specific job goals and accomplishments.

Of the six men, four indicated they would choose the same line of work again, with no qualifications. One replied that he would do the same work, but would change the management and financing of his work to be more independent. The sixth man indicated that he probably would do the same work again, but also dwelt at some length on a wistful fantasy of working entirely for himself, rather than having his work pay off for other people.

Only two of the women in this group reported any deep or abiding pleasure from their chosen roles as wife-mother-homemaker. The other four women complained of a great deal of stress in their role and appeared strained and worn out to the interviewer. They appeared, and spoke of being, tense and irritable, fatigued, and more-or-less chronically frustrated with what they were doing. However, only one of the six women had any significant amount of vocationally oriented activity outside this wife-mother-homemaker pattern.

Two of the six women seemed totally stuck in their wife-mother-homemaker situation. Two others had some outside interests that seemed to help a little, and the other two had substantial outside interests; but one of these seemed to derive little pleasure from these activities, considering them somewhat in the nature of "busy work," rather than genuine vocational accomplishments.

Leisure Activities

One was immediately struck by a sense of vacancy in the interviews regarding leisure activities. The general pattern seemed to be that the fathers worked long and hard and the mothers spent most or all of their time caring for the house or children, with very little true leisure pursuits for either parent, although many of the children in these families did have a variety of leisure activities. One family of the six was quite different in that all family members maintained an extremely high level of activity in both individual and shared leisure pursuits.

There was very little sign that these six married couples had very much going in the way of social activities with other adult couples.

In all six families, the parents did share substantial interest and investment in the leisure pursuits of their children, whether those might be athletic, creative, or whatever. In this area, the parents tended to come together as participants and observers in their children's activities, although most appeared to have very little sustained investment in either individual or shared adult leisure activities.

Three of the six fathers indicated they were avid "do-it-yourselfers" at home, spending much time with repair and construction activities, while the other three reported no such activities. One father was a competitor in a sports activity, and seemed to devote some time and interest to this leisure area without participation by his wife or children, and another father was involved in a wide range of avocational interests, some of which were conducted by himself, and some with various other members of the family.

Two of the women in the group had a wide variety of artistic, creative, and community volunteer leisure pursuits; however, all of these were conducted either alone or with other women, as neither their husbands nor their children participated in these activities.

Marital Relationships

While all 12 parents had some "nice" things to say about their marriage, it was striking that many had more negatives than positives to report. This was much more true for the wives than for the husbands. The men in this group tended to describe their marriages in rather bland and superficial terms without very much affect, either positive nor negative. Five of the six wives, on the other hand, came across with major complaints; for example, three of the six women stated that the qualities that had first attracted them to their husbands had long since disappeared. Five women complained, to varying degrees, about distance from their husbands and a lack of affective expression that gave a quality of deprivation or abandonment-depression to their descriptions of the marital relationship. Four of the six women complained about their sexual relations, although the complaints varied from "too much" to "too little" to descriptions of a variety of unpleasant experiences. It was striking that five of the six couples indicated they had sexual intercourse approximately twice a week, while one set stated an average of about once per week. While the men, in general, seemed mildly positive about this area, most of the women complained about it.

In the marital area, perhaps more strongly than in any other, one perceived a modal pattern of a work-enveloped, distant, and uncommunicative husband coupled with a needy, lonely woman who nevertheless came together strongly with substantial and consistent involvement and support concerning their children's day-to-day activities.

Two of the women in this group had clearly "married down" in socioeconomic status and remarked upon this to the interviewer. The other four had either selected mates from backgrounds more similar to their own, or "married up."

In terms of the style of interaction between husbands and wives, in one set the husband seemed very impulsive, while the wife provided a kind of settling, controlling influence over him. In three sets, the husbands and wives seemed to move almost entirely on parallel tracks, having little apparent interactional influence upon each other. In the fifth pair, a gamelike quality was apparent in which the husband played the role of "strong leader," while the wife played the role of "helpless child." At the same time the husband seemed noticeably insecure and uncertain about his "strength," and the wife was rather openly belittling of him and remarked frequently on the amount of conscious control and effort that it took on her part to play the "proper" role of subordinate helpmate. In the sixth pair, a very strong dominance-submission pattern was apparent, with the husband being quite autocratic and the wife quite subservient; however, both seemed comfortable with the marked power differential.

Children

Almost all of the 14 children in this group seemed to be doing well in terms of academics, peer relationships, athletic and extracurricular activities; and the absence of significant acting-out or other psychiatric disturbance was striking. However, three of the children did show some signs that they might be in the early stages of developing some difficulty. One was a mildly withdrawn and depressed girl with some suggestion of possible neurotic-level conflicts, and the other a similarly mildly withdrawn and depressed boy. The third child seemed to be showing some early difficulties in the areas of learning disability and impulse control.

As in the optimal families, a trend was noted for oldest children to be controlled, conscientious, and highly achievement oriented. Second children were noted to be more expressive, "happy-go-lucky," and sometimes mildly impulsive, while youngest children often appeared somewhat immature or "spoiled." These character styles seemed clearly related to birth order, rather than following cultural stereotypes of "masculine" or "feminine" traits.

In two of the families, the parents described their children in very similar terms, and the youngsters were seen along the same lines by the interviewer. However, in two other families, while the mother and father agreed very closely in their descriptions of the children in their separate interviews, the interviewer saw the children quite differently. In both these families, the interviewer noted areas of mild difficulty or problems not remarked upon by the parents. In the final two families, the parents disagreed sharply in their descriptions of one or more children; and in these families, the interviewer's perception agreed with the healthier description. This suggested that in the families where the parents were agreeing, there may have been some lack of awareness or glossing over of some child difficulties. In addition, in the families where the parents disagreed, these disagreements might have resulted from mild scapegoating, projection, or similar characteristics that would cause one parent to downgrade a given child. In any case, there was some lack of congruence of interpersonal perceptions between eight of these 12 parents and the interviewers when discussing the family offspring.

While sexual stereotyping did not seem to occur in these families to the degree that it does in families that produce clearly disturbed and dysfunctional children, there was one instance in which a father seemed to have cast his daughter in the role of "queen," or "great lady," somehow implying that his child must fit a rather rigid sex-role definition of a young lady. Interestingly enough, the girl so chosen seemed acutely aware of the restrictions placed around her by her father's fantasies, and while she showed some rebelliousness about this, the situation did not seem to have reached pathological proportions. One other family also tended to embody somewhat rigid sex-role distinctions for their children, but this did not seem to be creating any particular problems.

Self-Descriptions

All six of the men in this group were similar in that they were quite aggressive at work but generally less so at home. These were all highly intelligent and likeable men, but by and large they did not appear to be very close to anyone. All demonstrated some "compulsive" characteristics and, in several of the men, the liabilities of this style appeared to outweigh the assets.

With very few exceptions the men in this group seemed similar in that they reported some anxiety and depression related to work frustrations, but an absence of phobic problems, no clear-cut psychophysiological disorders, no apparent difficulty with sleeping or food, and a striking lack of reliance upon tobacco, alcohol, tranquilizers, stimulants, and sedatives. They demonstrated very little, if any, inclination to act out conflicts, and none of these men had had any prior contact with mental health professionals. Their anxieties and brief depressive episodes did not appear to have caused any significant interpersonal or vocational problems. One of the men in the group was on a special diet and medication for a stress-related medical disorder.

The women in this group seemed more troubled. Four of the six were openly dissatisfied with their roles in life, expressing disappointment in relation to their initial expectations about married life, and describing feeling cut off or isolated from their husbands and overworked by their children. Also, four of the six women in this group were mildly to moderately obese, and two of these seemed more-or-less constantly preoccupied with their overweight, but were unable to do anything effective about it.

In spite of a substantial amount of reported depression and dissatisfaction, these women did not seem at all inclined to rely upon alcohol or medication for relief. They reported very little alcohol consumption and typically no use of tranquilizers, stimulants, or sedatives. There were two women in this group who did report occasional use of a minor tranquilizer. Three of the six women reported overt depression of a more-or-less chronic nature, and five of the women appeared tired, mildly depressed, or harried to the interviewer.

Three of the men in this group seemed to be rather classical quiet, distant, introverted, compulsively oriented individuals. The other three, however, while sharing a variety of "compulsive" characteristics, seemed much more outgoing. Of these latter three men, one was jovial and warm, but also vague and distant, while the two others also showed a more excitable, outgoing, and, at times, mildly impulsive nature.

Of the six men, three were non-smokers, two were occasional users of pipes and cigars, while the remaining man was a one-and-a-half-packs-a-day smoker. Two of the men were total abstainers from alcohol, a third was a light drinker averaging one or two beers or drinks per day, and the remaining men were also typically light drinkers, but occasionally had periods of several days or weeks where their alcohol consumption might increase substantially. None of these men, however, had experienced any family, interpersonal, vocational, or legal difficulties with alcohol. One of the men apparently had had a very brief (one- or two-visit) psychiatric contact several years earlier relative to his wife's difficulties, although this information came from the wife rather than the husband.

Three of the women in this group seemed rigidly overcontrolled, while the other three demonstrated a variable pattern of heightened control and affective lability.

Three of the women in this group reported no psychophysiological disorders, while the other three did report some such difficulties. One of these had experienced rather chronic and severe somatic problems, which she (and her physician) had labeled as being due to tension and chronic dissatisfaction.

Four of the women in this group had received either an evaluation or treatment from a mental health professional in prior years. The fifth woman indicated that she might have been able to use some psychological help several years earlier during a period of great stress, while the sixth woman had never felt any need for contact with a mental health professional.

Style in the Interview Setting

All six of the men initially appeared very cooperative, willing, and open; however, after some reflection, and following a comparison of the information provided by the men, women, and children, it was the interviewer's judgment that three of the six men were, in fact, rather skillfully defensive, vague, or superficial, concealing as much as or more than they were revealing.

The women in this group seemed more genuinely open, in the sense that all six not only appeared to be trying to cooperate, but did in fact get into more affectively charged issues and more often were referred to by the interviewers as open and non-defensive.

Stylistically, as well as in their self-descriptions, three of the men in this group did seem to be rather introverted "compulsives." The fourth was more extroverted but quite vague, and the remaining two much more affectively expressive individuals.

The communication styles of two of the women in this group showed a marked tendency to state situations and then immediately disqualify them. An example was a woman who said several times during the interview that one of the things she liked best about her marriage was that her husband never set any limits or controls upon her. On each occasion, she also indicated, however, that she had to spend a great deal of time and effort to be careful not to violate the very strict limits placed upon her by her husband.

Reading the interviews of these two women, one comes away with a feeling of confusion and lack of clarity. A third woman tended to respond to almost every area of investigation by shifting rather quickly from the content being explored to a series of self-deprecatory statements. A fourth woman also tended to move from the goal of the interviewer's questions into more personal, affective statements, but her style was that of continually blaming her husband directly and indirectly for her pain. The other two women seemed much more clear, direct, open, and straightforwardly re sponsive to the interviewer's questions.

Comparison Between Individually
Derived and Systems Derived Data

While it was the interviewer's impression that the pictures of these six families were similar from the two approaches, the congruence seemed less striking than with the optimal families. Many minor differences did surface between the systems approach and the individual interview approach. The most frequent pattern (four of the six families) was for more problems, conflicts, and difficulties to emerge in the individual interviews, with fewer apparent strengths being detected. In the systems approach, problems and conflicts, although evident, seemed less severe, and strengths emerged more clearly in the family interactional patterns. The reverse was true for two of the six families. The general pattern may simply have been due to different sets or styles of the observers and judges, but it also might reflect a tendency for more interactional "glue" to be apparent when one observes families at this level of functioning working together than one sees in one-to-one interviews.

The one overriding exception to the characteristic noted above is that opposite sex, cross-generational coalitions seemed to emerge more clearly in the systems approach than in the individual interviews. These mildly oedipal patterns did emerge in all six families and, in general, seemed clearer in the systems analysis. It should be noted that these father-daughter or mother-son coalitions did not appear to be stronger than the husband-wife coalition in any family, but rather tended to exist in conjunction with the husband-wife power axis.

Comparison and Contrast Between the Optimally and Adequately Functioning Families Based on the Individual Interviews

Based upon the description of the six optimal and the six adequate families, the following similarities and differences between the two groups are noted.

Vocational Activities

All 12 men were noted to be aggressive and competent in their work, and all have achieved a high degree of status within their respective vocations. All were substantial achievers in an economic sense, and all had risen to leadership roles. Few received any direct supervision.

Most of the men in both groups indicated they would follow the same vocation again, if they could go back and start over; but also there were those in both groups who would do so only with some qualification, and wistful fantasies about what they "might have been" occurred in both groups. In neither group was there any strong sense of a man's being in the "wrong" job, or of having made job choices that were unsuited to his skills or vocational goals. All 12 men demonstrated stable job histories in roles that seemed generally suited to their talents.

Eleven of the 12 women appeared to have made the wife-mother-homemaker role the center of their vocational activities. None of these women had a primary, autonomous vocational pursuit separate from their status as homemakers. Some of the women in both groups maintained active interests outside the home, but these were of secondary importance to their central homemaking function.

The men in the adequate group seemed to focus more on the economic rewards of their work than on other aspects. In this group, there seemed to be a more general feeling of having struggled upward to much greater income than they knew as youngsters and, in fact, more than they had expected. The men in the optimal group also gave the impression of very hard work and high income, but one had a sense of more comfort and familiarity with an upper-middle-class lifestyle in these men; whereas in the adequate group, the men seemed more to be struggling above what they had previously experienced or expected.

Concurrent with this finding was the impression that the men in the adequate group seemed somewhat more focused on distant, perhaps unrealizable, vocational goals with less pleasure in the day-to-day process of their work, whereas the reverse seemed more true of the optimal group men.

In the optimal group, the men appeared to thrive on the interpersonal aspects of their work, frequently mentioning the pleasure derived from associating with peers, and saw persuasion or interpersonal relationships as a key element in both their success and in the pleasure they received from their work. By contrast, in the adequate group, the men seemed to thrive more on the technical or end products of objective job performance and were more often frustrated and irritated by the interpersonal friction and resistances they encountered.

In the optimal group, there seemed to be a good fit between the socially traditional demands of the wife-mother-homemaker role and the personal satisfactions of the women. Women's libbers they were not, but one sensed a good deal of comfort, satisfaction, and pleasure in their chosen roles. In the adequate group, however, the women seemed to experience more boredom, frustration, and irritation in the same chosen roles, coupled with an unwillingness or apparent inability to break out of these roles into other pursuits.

It appeared that 11 of the 12 women had chosen essentially a male-defined role (that of helpmate to a spouse). However, in the optimal group, the men, although very work-oriented, had helped this be a happy choice for their wives by more-or-less continual support and affective expression to them as well as to the children. In the adequate group, however, although the men said they valued their wives' supportive activities, they actually tended to be rather distant from them, offering much less interpersonal pay-off, leaving the wives feeling burdened, unappreciated, and unfulfilled.

Leisure Activities

In both groups, there seemed to be a low level of reaching out to other adults as friends or social companions. While all of these adults had some individual or couple-oriented social contacts, they were not a strikingly gregarious group of adults.

In both groups, the parents shared a deep and abiding interest in their children's leisure pursuits, and were frequently involved as observers, supporters, or participants in these child-oriented activities.

In the optimal group, the parents were very strongly invested in some kind of family-oriented pursuits—whether that might be gardening, sports activities, or whatever; whereas in the adequate group, there was a striking absence of shared adult leisure pursuits. When one of the adequate group adults did have a non-child-focused leisure activity, it was generally pursued apart from the mate and the children in a fashion that seemed to produce some isolation from the remainder of the family.

Marital Relationships

In all 12 couples, a major focus of the marital relationship was that of substantial interest and investment in the raising of the children. All couples apparently spent a good deal of time, energy, and hard work trying to do the best possible job for their youngsters.

When asked to discuss their marriage, partners in the optimal group offered almost entirely positively toned statements. In the adequate group, the statements offered by the husbands tended generally to be positive (although with less affective charge than noted by husbands of the optimal group) ; but the wives in the adequate group gave a preponderance of critical or negatively toned comments about their marriages.

While all 12 husbands were heavily work-oriented, with long hours and demanding tasks, the men in the optimal group managed, nevertheless, to give a great deal to their wives, whereas the men in the adequate group seemed generally much more distant from and/or demanding of their wives.

In the adequate group, two of the women had married down socioeconomically, and both remarked on this in a manner that suggested this was a chronic source of some dissatisfaction to them. One woman in the optimal group had also married down; and while she recalled the greater affluence of her childhood with some nostalgia or wistfulness, her current substantial basic respect for her husband's efforts and very real accomplishments appeared to modulate her discomfort substantially.

In the optimal group, 11 of the 12 marital partners described the sexual aspects of their marriage in very positive terms, although frequency of intercourse and the importance of sexuality in the marriage varied considerably from couple to couple. In the adequate group, the men seemed generally to feel positively about the sexual part of their marriage, but the wives complained about various sources of discomfort or displeasure in sexual functioning.

Children

All 12 families had two or more children, and in each family there tended to be a continuum of impulse management from older to younger offspring, with the first-born demonstrating greater impulse control and each younger child showing somewhat greater impulse expression. First children generally were referred to as studious, work-oriented, quiet, shy, very achievement-oriented, and somewhat less affectionate. Second children more often were referred to as bubbly, outgoing, gregarious, and somewhat less achievement-oriented, although in academic success second children seemed to do equally well. Third children, or youngest children, often were referred to as somewhat impulsive and disorganized, with a few parents in both groups referring to these children with some concern that they might "go hippie." Three instances of possible learning disability or academic underachievement occurred—two in optimal families and one in an adequate family, and in each case it was a youngest child.

Sex role stereotyping of the children seemed to be rare in both groups. While this may have been taking place at a rather subtle level, it certainly was not blatant, except for one girl in the adequate group who seemed to be struggling somewhat with her father's expectation that she should become a "great lady." In general, however, serious sex role stereotyping did not seem to take place in the children of these 12 families.

Of the 17 children in the optimal group, only one appeared to be having noticeable problems. This youngster, a male third child, had the appearance, history, and style of a hyperactive, immature boy with learning disability. Of the 14 children in the adequate group, three appeared to be having some psychological difficulty, with two (one boy and one girl) appearing to have primarily neurotic, withdrawn styles, and one (a girl) a more impulse-ridden, hyperactive, and possibly underachieving style.

In the optimal group, the two parents and the interviewer all tended to see the children very much alike in five of the six families. In the sixth family, the parents generally concurred about their children, although the interviewer noted some characteristics (problems) not described by the parents. In the adequate group, by contrast, there were many different perceptions between the parents and between the parents and the interviewer. The pictures of the children drawn from parental descriptions and individual interviews seemed less clear or more ambiguous in the adequate group. The interviewer's impressions were that various kinds of parental filtering (projection, oedipal ties, mild scapegoating) tended to obscure clear perception of the youngsters in the adequate group.

Self-Descriptions

All 12 men were very hard-working, successful breadwinners who pursued vocational activities in an aggressive manner. These were all intelligent, competent, and generally likeable men who shared a variety of more-or-less "compulsive" characteristics, usually demonstrating many of the strengths of that style with a relative absence of the liabilities.

There were no overt psychiatric disturbances in any of the 12 men, although several reported similarly that they had experienced occasional, work-related anxiety; only occasional and brief depressive episodes (also generally related to work-oriented frustrations); an absence of psychosomatic complaints; either no phobias or one or two rather mild, nonincapacitating ones; an absence of acting-out; and no tendency to rely on alcohol or medication for day-to-day functioning. Likewise, there was a general absence of sleeping disturbances, eating problems, or sexual dysfunction. Only one man out of the 12 had had a prior psychiatric contact, and this consisted of one or two visits to a psychiatrist in conjunction with his wife's psychotherapy.

None of the 12 women relied upon alcohol or medication for discomfort, and none of the women had shown patterns of acting-out of conflicts or difficulties.

While, as noted above, the men generally did not display diagnosible psychiatric difficulty, it was the interviewer's impression that the men in the adequate group had perhaps a higher ratio of the liabilities of the compulsive style than was true in the optimal group. In particular, the men in the adequate group seemed to experience less closeness to peers and to their wives, as compared to the men in the optimal group. Perhaps this is another way of saying that the men in the adequate group were slightly more compulsive, slightly more controlled, and somewhat less inclined to relate closely and openly to other adults.

The women in the adequate group clearly demonstrated more strain and pain than was apparent in the optimal group women. Only one of the women in the optimal group seemed overtly troubled, while almost all the women in the adequate group remarked upon substantial symptomatology, including obesity, psychosomatic distresss, frequent or chronic depression, and varieties of sexual dysfunction. These problems were most often attributed by these women to distance and stress in the marriage.

None of the women in the optimal group had sought or received any prior mental health contacts, while four of the six women in the adequate group had experienced some kind of previous contacts with a mental health professional.

None of the women in the optimal group were obese, while four of the women in the adequate group were, and two of these seemed more-or-less continually preoccupied with this problem.

Style in the Interview Setting

In the adequate group, as in the optimal, terms like "open" and "nondefensive" were frequently used by the interviewer, but nevertheless the interviews themselves seemed less clear and less internally congruent in the adequate group. In the optimal group, nine of the 12 adults seemed quite clear, open, and spontaneous, and their accounts of themselves and their children were generally in high agreement, both internally and between the interviews of husband and wife.

In the adequate group, however, only five of the 12 adults seemed equally clear, open, and spontaneous. By way of contrast, two of the four men seemed rather closed and detached, and the remaining man was jovial and apparently open, but superficial and vague. Two of the women in the adequate group created a degree of ambiguity in their interviews by a style of making statements and then immediately disqualifying them. A third woman seemed continually to distort in the direction of complaints about her husband. Frequently, major differences of fact, or affect around facts, occurred between the observations of the men, women, children, and interviewers in the adequate group interviews.

The adults in the adequate group, while generally more relaxed, clear, and open than the interviewers were accustomed to seeing in psychiatric patient populations, nevertheless seemed less so than the adults in the optimal group.

Comparison Between Individually
Derived and Systems Derived Data

In five of the six optimal families, very similar pictures emerged from the systems and individual interview vantage points. Minor differences from these two points of observation that were noted seemed due more to stylistic characteristics of the observers than to any basic disagreement between the different frames of reference.

However, congruence between the two observational vantage points was much less striking with the adequate families. In general, more problems, conflicts, and difficulties emerged from the individual interviews, while more signs of individual and family strengths were apparent from the systems point of view.

One clear exception to this general pattern was that opposite sex, cross-generational coalitions (which existed to some degree in all six adequate families) seemed more evident when the entire families were observed functioning together.

Psychological Testing Results

The mental health clinicians on the research team were accustomed to using data from standard psychological tests as one source of data in attempts to understand personality characteristics and levels of psychopathology in disturbed individuals and families. Familiarity with such data from the psychologically disturbed encouraged the view that some useful analysis might derive from similar personality testing of the presumed healthy as well. This was, of course, in the nature of a "fishing expedition," in that the research team was unaware of any published information that would strongly support this point of view.

The basic research question approached was that of the degree of agreement between ratings of families' psychological health based upon a skilled clinician's use of a standard personality test with the systems analysis findings concerning family functioning. Each member of the 12 families above the age of 13 was administered a Minnesota Multiphasic Personality Inventory. The MMPI profiles on these 43 individuals were identified only by age and sex, and were presented in a randomized order to a psychologist experienced in the use of this test but unfamiliar with the individuals tested. The psychologist rated each individual on a scale of one to ten, with one representing extreme health and ten representing extreme psychopathology. He relied entirely upon the MMPI profile for this evaluation.

The resulting ratings ranged from one to nine, with a median of three. These ratings of psychological health based upon analysis of the MMPIs correlated .19 (p <.10) and .26 (p <.05) with the individual ratings of the two clinical interviewers described earlier in this chapter. This finding suggests low, but not unusually low, reliability for judgments of this type.

A first approach in comparing the MMPI health ratings to systems analysis ratings tested the assumption that more of the 22 individuals from the optimal families should achieve healthier MMPI ratings than the 21 members of the adequate families. However, this hypothesis was not supported by the data. Of the 12 parents and ten children in the optimal families, only eight of the parents and four of the children were rated above the median by MMPI analysis. Likewise, of the 12 parents and nine children in the adequate group, only six parents and five of the children were rated below the median by the clinician using the MMPI.

As a second approach to the psychological testing data, the MMPI profiles were grouped by family units; that is, the profiles for each member of family A were stapled together, those for each member from family B were stapled together, and so on. The same clinician was then asked to rate each family unit on a one-to-ten-point Health-Pathology Scale, deriving his ratings from each family's MMPI profiles. Approached in this manner, the families received ratings from two to seven, with a median of 5.5. The rank order of family evaluation based on the MMPIs correlated with the clinician's rank orders of family health derived from the individual interviews (described above in this chapter), .53 and .54 (p=.03), once again demonstrating acceptable reliability for the ratings. However, the rank order correlation coefficient between the psychological testing-derived ratings of family health and the systems analysis was .01, which, of course, was not statistically significant.

Additional analyses of the MMPI data, including comparisons of the optimal and adequately functioning family members on the separate MMPI scales and on overall height of the MMPI profiles, were also unproductive.

These results suggest that a psychological test developed primarily for the evaluation of psychopathology did not produce ratings of psychological health that would relate significantly to the family systems approach for these well functioning individuals and families. While these results were not entirely unexpected, they should represent a data-based cautionary note to family researchers who attempt to construct family composites relying in part upon such individual psychological testing data. Future psychological testing of well functioning family members might more likely be productive if tests standardized on normal or healthy individuals were used.

REFERENCES

1. LUBORSKY, L., "Clinicians' judgments of mental health: A proposed scale," *Arch. Gen. Psychiat.*, 7 (6), 407-417, 1962.
2. LUBORSKY, L., and BACHRACH, H., "Factors influencing clinicians' judgments of mental health," *Arch. Gen. Psychiat.*, 31 (3), 292, 1974.

CHAPTER VIII

THE FAMILY SYSTEM AND PHYSICAL ILLNESS

DURING OUR CONTACT with the 33 research volunteer families, we obtained a traditional medical history dating from the parental marriage.* Striking differences were noted in their reports of family health and illness. Over the course of 20 years, some families experienced no life-threatening illness, no hospitalizations other than for the birth of children, no fractures, and minimal disability from minor illnesses. From the same cohort of research volunteer families, others had experienced multiple life-threatening illnesses, hospitalizations, fractures, and significant disability from minor illnesses. How are such differences to be understood? Do they result only from differences in genetic, constitutional, and other biologic variables, or do they reflect also something of what transpires among the members of each family? This chapter reports our initial work aimed at obtaining data which might be a step in the direction of answering that question.

DISEASE MODELS

In order to place this segment of our work in context, it is pertinent to review briefly some of the issues in any current consideration of physical health and disease. A primary, and in many ways overriding, factor is the model of disease which prevails at any given point in the history of a culture. Most of us are relatively culture-bound in thinking about health, illness, and disease, and

---

* See Appendix H, p. 255.

181

find it difficult to recognize the important role that cultural values and expectations may play in influencing our model of disease. What is of particular significance in this regard is that the model of disease which prevails in a given culture then influences very directly the characteristics of disease that are attended and those that are neglected. In this culture, the magnificent discoveries of the biologic sciences are basic to the development of a model of disease that is characterized by a focus on the individual patient, a dualism in which physical processes are considered as separate from and more "real" than psychological processes, a search for a single, specific cause for each disease and, all too frequently, an episode-oriented system for provision of health care.

Throughout history, a few individuals have attempted to conceptualize disease in a different manner. In recent decades, the movement called "psychosomatic medicine" has called attention to a specific group of diseases in which psychological processes are so obviously involved as to make their neglect difficult. This evolving model has attempted to stress the integrated nature of man's experience in health and illness. Fabrega and Manning (10) clearly demonstrated the impact of cultural processes upon one model of disease. In their study of a Spanish speaking people in the highland region of southeastern Mexico, they found evidence of a model of disease which includes aspects of emotions, interpersonal relations, naturalistic processes, and bodily change. The central construct was that altered processes we may term "disease" all have both emotional and bodily correlates. A definition of disease that emphasizes a discontinuity between these changes militates against effective treatment. In their terms, a theory of disease is like a map or blueprint that provides the outline of what members of a culture accept as real. Theories of disease not only explain, but also structure, the expectations and behaviors of persons in that culture during illness itself, thereby directly affecting the nature of the experiences and manifestations of disease. For the physician, the message is succinct: Our preconceptions of what disease "is" determines what we ask of, look for, and find in patients.

In the model of disease reported by Fabrega and Manning, the pathogenicity of the emotions is considered; that is, arguments, separations, envy, as well as intensely satisfying exchanges, all have relevance because they give rise to excessive feeling. The type of illness that develops, as well as its severity, is a function of the constitution and character of the person as well as the evolving interpersonal situation.

It is also worthwhile to note that illness conditions can affect families that participate in the interpersonal situations that are provoking. In this sense, the illness may be described as emotionally "contagious." In short, this "primitive" model of disease identifies a number of factors invariably held to be implicated in an occurrence of disease. These factors touch on aspects of personality, social relations, and strictly biological functioning, all of which are seen as linked in a homeostatic and feedback manner.

This fascinating description of another culture's model of disease highlights the fact that, despite the impact of psychosomatic theory upon medicine in this culture, much of the actual practice of medicine still appears to be influenced by a dualistic model of disease. The impact of this fractionalizing of the more holistic and integrated model significantly influences what people consider to be illness, as well as that for which physicians search in order to understand illness. In this way, illness behavior is not viewed, for the most part, as an inseparable part of the individual and his family and group.

Other writers have addressed themselves in a number of ways to the impact of the western model of disease upon health and illness. Cassell (6) points out that for the first time in history there is now the dream of curing disease, and hence of creating profound changes in age-old patterns of disease. This very welcome success in medicine has, however, created severe strains. Central to these strains is the fact that illness and disease have come to be separated—in Cassell's terms: "Patients now wander about disabled but without a culturally acceptable mantle of disease with which to clothe the nakedness of their pain, and doctors tend to define their role more narrowly, seeing themselves as curers of disease rather than as healers of the sick." He, too, stresses that with the discoveries of microbiology, an exactness of formulation was born—one cause, one disease—which is only now with our increasing awareness of the existence and significance of multiple causation beginning to weaken its hold on medicine. In talking about the impact of such a model on health care practice, Cassell makes the provocative point that curing the disease will be effective in resolving the illness to the degree that the illness is explained by the disease. In effect, he suggests that patients often take their feelings to the doctor and are reassured that they have no significant disease, but are given diagnoses which make their symptoms "honorable." As can be seen, Cassell adds his voice to those who feel that a non-integrated disease model increases the problems associated with health, illness, and health care.

Bakan (1) agrees that the doctrine of specific etiology impairs the development of a more useful concept of disease. He focuses on contemporary evolutionary theory that allows the possibility of individual survival-negative factors which are not mere anomalies. He prefers to regard any specific disease from which an individual suffers as the manifestation of a "deeper disorder" involving his total condition. In particular, he suggests that a loss of purpose (telic decentralization) may make him more vulnerable to illness.

Jourard (20) also focuses his theoretical model on a central construct that there is meaning, purpose, and value in existing. He is particularly concerned with interpersonal transactions which raise questions about the value of the participants' lives. At such a time an episode of illness can be seen as a protest, preventing further functioning until the individual's needs are met, thus saving the remnant of the system (the individual) from total destruction.

Balint (2) also questions the contemporary model of disease, suggesting that in order to understand disease one must consider man in his total context. He sees patients as going to physicians because of problems in living which he calls the "unorganized" phase of illness. The physician and the patient then negotiate a more "organized" phase in which the patient trades away the possibility of dealing directly with the problems which took him to the physician for a singular diagnosis which has the advantage of making him seem a victim.

STUDIES OF INDIVIDUALS

These recent writers who discuss the issue of the impact of disease models underscore the growing dissatisfaction with a model which emphasizes a separation of man's experiences and his biological processes at the level of organ systems or cells. Although general awareness of the concept of multiple causation has existed for some time, it appears to have had relatively slight impact on prevailing medical care. One segment of research in the area of multiple causation concerns the social and psychologic circumstances associated with episodes of disease in individual patients (13,14). Reports (16) suggest that in any given population a small percentage of the individuals experience a disproportionately high percentage of all the illness episodes. For many individuals, the episodes of apparently unrelated illnesses tend to cluster in time (39). These observations helped direct research efforts to the concept of general susceptibility to illness and those life circumstances associated with increased general susceptibility in individuals in addition to psychological factors involved in specific or so-called psychosomatic diseases.

Taken as a whole, this body of research suggests that man is predisposed to illness under a variety of circumstances:

1) When he perceives his social and interpersonal environment as highly unsatisfactory (5, 11, 13, 15, 17, 30, 32, 49). This group of studies focuses on the role of consciously experienced stress (much of which is interpersonal) and its role in disease etiology.

2) When he experiences a great number of life changes in a short time (19, 24, 28, 38, 39, 40, 41). This research emphasizes life change—theoretically, both positive and negative. Many of the heavily weighted items suggest loss, as such, and are interpersonal in nature.

3) When he experiences severe separation or object loss (7, 8, 23, 24, 33, 43, 45).

4) When he developes a prolonged affective state of hopelessness or helplessness (8, 9). This research, noting the universality
of separation and loss, focuses instead on the individual's affective
response to the real, threatened, or symbolic event.

Each of these studies is based upon data obtained from individuals; that is, the conceptual focus has been individual man as an
intrapsychic, psychologic entity unto himself. However, as noted,
many of the studies have implicit interpersonal considerations.
They describe individuals reacting within the context of significant
relationships.

If, indeed, man's interpersonal context plays a role in disease
etiology, then the question arises about what contextual factors
may be involved. Cultures with differing rates of various diseases
have caught the eye of some researchers. Levi (25) has suggested
that either deprivation or excess of total stimuli in a given social
system may be pathogenic. Lipowski (26), in a similar vein, notes
that affluent cultures may provide their participants with information overloads which have a deleterious effect on physiological
processes. Kiely (22), examining patterns of illness in occupational
groups, theorized that the stress of a social system which requires
sustained vigilance and provides little acceptance of error may increase susceptibility to disease. Moss (31) develops the concept of
biosocial reasonation, the relation between social behavior and
physical health. He examines social communication networks and
their processes of exchanging information, suggesting that a "person is involved in his communication networks to the degree he
perceives that the information of these networks is congruous
with his perceptions in the environment, and his susceptibility to
disease decreases to the degree that his information is congruous
with his perceptions of his milieu."

Consistent with this theory are the findings of Stout (47) and
co-workers who studied a small town, Roseto, Pennsylvania, known
to have an unusually low incidence of death from myocardial infarction, and hypothesized that the warm, supportive, insulated
social system may have been the contextual factor that was signifi-

cant in their apparent resistance to that specific, usually wide-spread, disease.

Those who have tried to find etiologic variables in the larger interpersonal contexts note the essentially speculative nature of the task. There is more substance, however, to the studies which explore the relationship between disease and man's most pervasive and enduring context, the family.

Family Studies

Studies representing a variety of conceptual viewpoints as well as different levels of data collection have focused upon the relationship of the family to the physical health of the family member. Many of them have been basically studies of the individuals in a family. Some, however, have been studies concerned more directly with the family as a unit. In a general way, these family studies have been of three types. The first might be described as "crisis-oriented," typically reporting the response of the family unit to either the illness or death of a significant member of the family. Parkes and Brown (33), for example, found in their study of young Boston widows and widowers that not only was there an increase in hospital admission rates for the surviving spouse, but that other members of the bereaved family were more frequently hospitalized during the ensuing year. Rees and Lutkins (43) found an increased death rate in bereaved families. Livsey (27) has discussed the reaction or response of the family as a unit to the illness of one of its members.

Secondly, there has been a search for those dimensions of family functioning which appear to be associated with specific psychosomatic illnesses. Most such studies have been clinical, although Jackson (18) applied the techniques of interactional testing to a small group of families containing a child with ulcerative colitis. There is a general consistency to the observations made about family functioning whether, however, the individual family member (most often a child) is suffering from ulcerative colitis, duodenal ulcer, asthma, or any of several other syndromes. Grolnick (12) recently reviewed the family factors in psychosomatic illness, finding that faulty family cohesiveness, overly rigid structure and rules, dominant depressive affect, limited capability for conflict resolution, and difficulty with object loss and/or separation anxiety have been noted by various writers.

Other observations of families with high rates of psychosomatic illnesses demonstrate a pattern of enmeshment in which individual ego boundaries are obscured and autonomy is rare.

Meissner (29) reviewed the literature and made a tentative formulation of the psychosomatic process as it takes shape in the family context. He emphasized that often the individual patient is immature and caught up in a family affective system which is undifferentiated. If emotionally significant events disturb the balance of interrelationships within the family system, subsequent disorganization within the affective subsystem troubles the individual patient on a deeply emotional level because his equilibrium is dependent on the family balance. Meissner points out that such a formulation raises more questions than it answers, but he emphasizes that the crucial variable in such a process may be the disruption of the family system rather than the external stress which precipitates the disequilibrium. He also notes that by focusing the family pathology the individual patient's illness may stabilize the family system.

One of the difficulties in interpreting this work is that the focus is on family factors associated with specific diseases. Additionally, the results do not appear to distinguish families which produce individuals with high rates of psychosomatic disorders from families which produce individuals with severe psychological disturbances.

The third approach to the study of family and physical illness has been at the level of the susceptibility of family members to all illnesses rather than to a few selected "psychosomatic" illnesses. Almost 30 years ago Richardson (44) wrote of general family susceptibility to illness; that is, the family as the unit of illness because the family is the unit of living. He delineated different types of family equilibria, seeing usually rigid family systems as having members who were particularly vulnerable. He saw the difficult decision of whether to focus on the individual or the family as related not so much to the kind of disease as to its duration and seriousness, suggesting that either chronic disease or repetitive acute illness may originate in the family.

Kellner (21) and Peachey (35) have also worked in this area, and presented evidence regarding family patterns of illness and the tendency in some families for illnesses to cluster in time. Bowen (4) noted a type of projection occurring at the level of physical illness. He hypothesized that the soma of one person reciprocates with the psyche of another person, and that this somatic reciprocation often includes definite physical pathology. Bowen felt this type of somatic reciprocation within emotionally disturbed families was most common in, but not limited to, the mother-identified patient relationship.

Recently, Weakland (48) enumerated ways in which family interactions may be related to disease. First, family interactions may be pertinent to the course and outcome of a given illness. In this regard the interactional viewpoint can lead to useful questioning of the usual distinction between the etiology and the course of a disease, changing focus from a search for single, linear causation to a greater concern with etiology involving feedback loops and reinforcements that maintain a given situation. This perspective suggests that the way a problem started (which in Weakland's terms may involve rather ordinary matters) is often less important than why the problem develops and persists.

A second possible relationship between personal interactions and disease is that a certain sort of interaction, presumably over time, might itself constitute sufficient condition for the onset of a specific disease.

Third, there may be disease to which certain sorts of family interactions (while neither necessary nor sufficient) would contribute a sensitizing or predisposing influence.

Weakland then moves from a framework which focuses on specific disease to a more general framework in which he suggests that some form or forms of family interaction may increase susceptibility to illness, generally with the particular disease developing being dependent upon factors other than the family interaction.

The complexity of such a framework is suggested by the report of Polak and co-workers (37). They found that a family's response (including physical illness) to the sudden death of a family member could be predicted best by a consideration of the circumstances of the death (role of deceased family member, suddenness and violence of death, direct observation of the death, etc.) ; the more-or-less enduring characteristics of the family (communication, flexibility, problem-solving, etc.) ; and the individual's capacity to cope and deal with despair. Although their data analysis does not report on physical health specifically, their work emphasizes the need to attend a variety of interrelated systems.

Another recent circumstance relevant to research exploring the relationship of family interactions to physical illness has been the development of family medicine. Ransom and Vandervoort (42) underscored the concept of family medicine as an emerging discipline concerned with the relationship of life in small groups to health, illness, and care. These clinicians attend the ecology of relations among individuals and families and between families and their surrounding environment and, therefore, view disease in one member as one symptom of a pathological family process. They hope that by focusing systematically on the ecology of relationships within which their patients exist, they will be able to understand and bring together all elements related to an individual's well-being that most current medical practice divides up and parcels out to subspecialists.

The researchers and writers from many disciplines who emphasize the importance of studying the relationship of illness to family interactions, whether it is the response of families to external events or the search for specific patterns of family interaction associated with general susceptibility to all illnesses, form a growing movement to which we hope to add our own research efforts.

RESEARCH EXPLORATIONS INTO FAMILY INTERACTIONS AND PHYSICAL ILLNESS

Our study of the relationship between families' interaction and their physical health was based on the study of a family interactional task and the subsequent daily health logs of 33 families. In light of the literature regarding the relationship between disease and loss or separation, we wished to measure the openness with which families could deal with this theme.

Becker (3) surveyed the literature regarding the denial of death. He views the fear of death and the need to deny it as basic and fundamental to the human condition. He summarizes Perls' (36) concept of a four-layered personality structure with the innermost layer having to do with fear of death. To have emerged from nothing, to have a name, to have consciousness, to have feelings, to yearn for life and self-expression, and yet to die is a terror which most men evade by keeping their minds on the small problems of their lives. Each society maps out these problems for its participants, but to avoid the realization of one's own death is to constrict what life offers. From Becker's viewpoint, the capacity of an individual (and by extrapolation, a family) to deal honestly and openly with the fact of personal death suggests a very high level of overall functioning.

Searles (46) has interpreted the psychodynamics of schizophrenic illness as a strong defense against the fear of death. Paul and Grosser (34) have studied families containing a severely disturbed member and suggest that the family's inability to deal with prior losses is related to the persistence of symbiotic relationships within the family. They report also a relationship between such symbiotic ties and psychosomatic disturbances.

In this exploratory stage of our work, we searched for correlates between families' responses to a death or dying stimulus and the amount of physical illness recorded during the ensuing six-month period.

We prepared a brief audiotaped vignette of a hospital scene in which a family is visiting a gravely ill family member (referred to as "he"—silent but with stertorous breathing). They are joined by the physician who, in response to the family's question of whether "he" will live or die, responds that he doesn't know but that there is damage. At this point the taped vignette ends and instructions ask the family to construct an ending to the story. They are told that there is no right or wrong ending and that they have ten minutes for the task.

The research staff studied the videotaped "loss" segments of three families and developed rating scales based on the premise that death and dying were the explicit themes involved in the vignette. Five-point scales were constructed for the following variables:

a. *Cognitive Involvement.* The degree to which the family system allowed human death to be discussed.

b. *Empathy to Loss.* The degree to which a family was able to project itself, at a feeling level, into the situation in the vignette.

c. *Personalization.* The degree to which the family system discussed death, or the threat of loss, of a member of the nuclear family or extended family.

d. *Task Efficiency.* The degree to which the family discussed alternatives and agreed on an ending.

e. *Overall Coping.* The rater's impression of the capacity of the family to face the death of the oldest child.

Six members of the research staff independently scored three additional family videotape segments to insure that the scales could be used reliably.

Following the videotaping, each family kept a daily log for a minimum period of six months.* A recorder (usually the mother) noted each day any physical symptoms of any member of the family, a description of the symptoms, the degree of disability associated with the symptoms, the duration of the symptoms and disability, treatment of the symptoms, and whether or not any unusual life circumstances occurred before or during the period of symptomatology. Illustrations were included in the loose-leaf health log, and the recorder was asked to write "all well" for those days in which no one in the family manifested symptoms.

---

* See Appendix I, p. 259.

The families were not aware of the use of these records in relation to their videotaped interaction.

Thirty-one families maintained health records for the six-month period. The daily notations were detailed and revealed that most illnesses reported were minor—respiratory, gastrointestinal, and musculoskeletal. There were only three hospitalizations totaling 18 days of disability for the entire group. There were 184 days in the six-month period and the 144 individuals had a total of 160 office visits to their physicians and averaged only 3.43 days of disability.

The 31 videotaped "loss" segments were scored independently by two raters, one of whom had participated in the evolution of the rating scales used for this purpose (see Appendix E: Loss Scales—Ability to Discuss the Concept of Loss Scales). The Spearman Rank Correlation Coefficient between these two raters' scores for the five scales range from .35 to .84 (p <.05 to <.001).

The families were then ranked according to the number of "all well" days. The Personalization Scale correlated significantly (r_s= .35, p <.05) with this rank order of global family physical health, while the other four scales did not.

The Personalization Scale is a continuum measuring whether family members responded to the taped vignette with a serious discussion of the threat of loss (a) within their *nuclear* family group, or (b) the *extended* family group, or (c) in terms of people known but *not related* to them, or (d) in terms of people *not personally known* to them, or (e) if they discussed the threat of loss in an *abstract, diffuse,* manner, or in terms of *fictional characters or animals,* or simply *avoided* the task.

The 31 ten-minute videotaped segments were reviewed again, focusing selectively on the personalization process. Responses ranged in quality from giggling, artificial references to taking a dog to the veterinarian; to a terse, "he got well and lived happily ever after"; to serious explorations of how the members of that particular family would feel and act if specific members of their family died. In 20 of the families, one family member introduced the subject of death, but was ignored by the other family members. These families will be referred to as "death-mentioned." In the

TABLE 8-1

Relationship Between Family Discussion of Death
and Average Number of "All Well" Days

	N	Average Number "All Well" Days
Death Discussed in Personalized Way	7	131.9
Death Discussed Impersonally	4	95.8
Death Mentioned But Not Discussed	20	96.8
Total Sample	31	104.6

other 11 families, seven discussed death in highly personalized terms; that is, death in terms of either the nuclear or extended family. Table 8-1 compares the average number of "all well" days for these groups.

The difference of 36 "all well" days between those families who personalized the loss vignette and those families who either mentioned death and did not discuss it, or discussed it impersonally is significant at the .025 level.* Small sample means are difficult to evaluate; however, it should be noted that only one family which personalized the loss vignette fell below the overall average number of "all well" days. The median of those families who personalized the segment was 137 well days.

Reviewing other data regarding these groupings of families, we found no significant differences in family size or average age of the children. Also, there were no significant differences depending upon whether a parent or child introduced the subject of loss. The differences between these groups remained when they were compared after dropping out data about the individual member in each family who had the most sick days, revealing that the rank order of physical health in a family by "all well" days was not dependent on the presence of the least well member.

---

* Student's t distribution, one-tailed test. t = 13.85

DISCUSSION

The correlation between the ability of a family to discuss death as it relates to the nuclear or extended family, and subsequently reporting significantly more "all well" days in the following six months substantiates our exploratory hypothesis, but requires more rigorous testing. In future research we hope to improve our methodology by including a larger sample of families drawn from a broader ethnic and socioeconomic pool, and families with more severe degrees of psychological dysfunction. We also wish to distinguish between illness and illness reporting; that is, to be able to monitor the family's health by direct observations.

There are other issues to be considered. We need to clarify, for example, how current events influence a family's response to the loss stimulus. There were no differences in the frequency of recent loss among the groups of families which responded differently to this loss stimulus, but this variable needs greater attention in future studies.

This sample of families was limited socioeconomically and ethnically and represented a relatively narrow range of family psychological health—i.e., the absence of severe psychological dysfunctioning. During the six months they reported their physical health, the family members experienced little in the way of serious illness or disability.

Also, this exploratory research does not clarify the relationship between the families' physical health as measured by "all well" days and their psychological health as measured by the Global Health Pathology ratings of four independent raters. The correlation (Spearman r = .32) between these two measures, although positive, did not reach statistical significance.

It appears that prior research foci may have been too narrow in several respects. The study of individuals separate from their primary context may not only restrict our understanding of etiological variables, but also may focus prevention efforts selectively on the individual rather than on young families who, like an infant in terms of responsivity, may be less entrenched in a long pathological chronology of developmental events.

Second, preoccupation with specificity may result in premature closure. Specific vectors may best be considered *after* exploration of psychosocial factors involved in general susceptibility to disease.

We wish to suggest that an adequate illness model must include specific *and* general psychosocial variables, as well as attending to the individual and his interacting family system, extra-family social systems (i.e., religious or corporate affiliations), and wider cultural factors as both potential etiologic or mitigating forces in a complex field. Ultimately it may be possible to understand cultural, institutional, family, individual, organ, and cellular systems in a truly integrated model of disease upon which to base not only effective treatment, but useful preventive efforts.

REFERENCES

1. BAKAN, DAVID, *Disease, Pain and Sacrifice: Toward a Psychology of Suffering.* Chicago: U. of Chicago Press, 1968.
2. BALINT, MICHAEL, *The Doctor, His Patient and the Illness.* New York: International Universities Press, Inc., 1972.
3. BECKER, E., *The Denial of Death.* New York: Free Press, 1973.
4. BOWEN, M., "Family psychotherapy with schizophrenia in the hospital and in private practice." In I. Boszormenyi-Nagy and J. L. Framo, Ch. V, *Intensive Family Therapy.* New York: Hoeber Medical Division, Harper and Row, 1965.
5. CANTER, A., IMBODEN, J. F., and CLUFF, L. E., "The frequency of physical illness as a function of prior psychological vulnerability and contemporary stress," *Psychosom. Med.,* 28:344, 1966.
6. CASSELL, J. T., "Social science theory as a source of hypotheses in epidemiological research," *Am. J. Public Health,* 54:1482-1488, 1964.
7. ENGEL, G. L., "A life setting conducive to illness," *Bull. of the Menninger Clinic,* 32:355-366, 1968.
8. ENGEL, G. L., "A psychological setting of somatic disease: The 'giving-up, given-up' complex," *Proceedings of the Royal Society of Medicine,* 60:553, 1967.
9. ENGEL, G. L., and SCHMALE, A. H., "Psychoanalytic theory of somatic disorder," *J. Am. Psycho-Anal. Assn.,* 15:344-365, 1967.
10. FABREGA, H., and MANNING, K., "An integrated theory of disease: Ladino-Mestizo views of disease in the Chiapas Highlands," *Psychosom. Med.,* 35 (3), 223-299, 1973.
11. GREENE, W. A., YOUNG, L. E., and SWISHER, S. N., "Psychological factors and reticuloendothelial disease," *Psychosom. Med.,* 18:234-303, 1956.
12. GROLNICK, L., "A family perspective of psychosomatics factors in illness: A review of the literature," *Fam. Proc.,* 11 (4), 457-486, 1972.
13. HINKLE, L. E., JR., "The distribution of sickness in homogeneously healthy men," *Am. J. Hygiene,* 64:220, 1956.

14. HINKLE, L. E., CHRISTENSON, W. N., KANE, F. D., OSTFELD, A., THETFORD, W. N., and WOLFF, H. G., "An investigation between life experiences, personality characteristics, and general susceptibility to illness," *Psychosom. Med.*, 20:278-295, 1958.
15. HINKLE, L. E., and WOLFF, H. G., "The nature of man's adaptation to his total environment and the relation of this to illness," *Arch. of Internal Med.*, 99:442-460, 1957.
16. HOPKINS, P., "Health, happiness and the family," *The British J. of Clinical Psychiat.*, 13:311-313, 1959.
17. JACKSON, D. D., "Family homeostasis and the physician," *Calif. Med.*, 239-242, Oct., 1965.
18. JACKSON, D. D., and YALOM, I., "Family research on the problem of ulcerative colitis," *Arch. Gen. Psychiat.*, 15:410-418, 1966.
19. JACOBS, M. A., SPILKEN, A., and NORMAN, M., "Relationship of life change, maladaptive aggression, and upper respiratory infection in male college students," *Psychosom. Med.*, 31:31-44, 1969.
20. JOURARD, S. M., *The Transparent Self*, Van Nostrand Reinhold Co., 1971.
21. KELLNER, R., *Family Ill Health*, Springfield, Ill., C. C Thomas, 1963.
22. KIELY, W. F., "Editorial: Stress and somatic disease," *JAMA*, Vol. 224 (4), 521, April 23, 1973.
23. LEMKAU, P. V., "Discussion," *Psychosom. Med.*, 23:296-297, 1961.
24. LESHAN, L., and WORTHINGTON, R. E., "Loss of cathexis as a common psychodynamic characteristic of cancer patients: An attempt at statistical validation of a clinical hypothesis," *Psychological Reports*, 2:183-193, 1956.
25. LEVI, L., "A synopsis of ecology and psychiatry: Some theoretical psychosomatic considerations, review of some studies and discussion of preventive aspects," *Reports from the Laboratory for Clinical Stress Research*, No. 30, Nov., 1972.
26. LIPOWSKI, Z. J., "Affluence, information inputs and health," *Soc. Science and Med.*, Vol. 7, 517-529, 1973.
27. LIVSEY, G. G., "Physical illness and family dynamics," *Advances in Psychosomatic Medicine*, 8:237-251 (Karger-Basel, 1972).
28. MASUDA, M., and HOLMES, J. H., "Magnitude estimation of social readjustments," *J. of Psychosom. Research*, 11:219-255, 1967.
29. MEISSNER, W. W., "Family dynamics and psychosomatic processes," *Fam. Process*, 5 (2), 142-161, 1966.
30. MEYER, R. J., and HAGGERTY, R. J., "Streptococcal infections in families," *Pediatrics*, 539-549, April, 1962.
31. MOSS, GORDON E., *Illness, Immunity and Social Interaction*. New York: Wiley-Interscience, 194-197, 1973.
32. MUTTER, A. Z., and SCHLEIFER, M. J., "The role of psychological and social factors in the onset of somatic illness in children," *Psychosom. Med.*, 28:333-343, 1966.
33. PARKES, C. M., and BROWN, J., JR., "Health after bereavement," *Psychosom. Med.*, 34 (5), 449-461, 1972.
34. PAUL, N., and GROSSER, G. H., "Operational mourning and its role in conjoint family therapy," *Community Mental Health Journal*, 1:339-345, 1965.
35. PEACHEY, R., "Family patterns of stress," *General Practitioner*, 27:82, 1963.
36. PERLS, F., *Gestalt Therapy Verbatim*, Lafayette, California: Real People Press, 1969.
37. POLAK, PAUL R., EGAN, D. J., VANDEN, BERGH, R., and VAIL, W. W., "Prevention

in mental health: A controlled study," *Am. J. Psychiat.*, Vol. 132 (2), 146-149, Feb., 1975.

38. RAHE, R. H., "Life change measurement as a predictor of illness," *Proceedings of the Royal Society of Medicine*, 61:1124-1126, 1968.

39. RAHE, R. H., McKEAN, J. D., and ARTHUR, R. J., "A longitudinal study of life change and illness patterns," *J. of Psychosom. Research*, 10:355-366, 1967.

40. RAHE, R. H., McPUGH, N. M., ERIKSON, J., GUNDERSON, E. K. E., and RUBIN, R. T., "Cluster analysis of life changes," *Arch. of Gen. Psychiat.*, 25:330-339, 1971.

41. RAHE, R. H., MEYER, M., SMITH, M., KJAER, G., and HOLMES, T. H., "Social stress and illness onset," *J. of Psychosom. Research*, 8:35, 1964.

42. RANSOM, D. C., and VANDERVOORT, H. E., "The development of family medicine," *JAMA*, 225 (9), 1098-1102, 1973.

43. REES, W. D., and LUTKINS, S. G., "Mortality of bereavement," *British Med. Journal*, 7:13-16, 1967.

44. RICHARDSON, H. B., *Patients Have Families*. New York: Commonwealth Fund, 1945.

45. SCHMALE, A., "Relationship of separation and depression to disease," *Psychosom. Med.*, 20:259-277, 1958.

46. SEARLES, H. F., "Schizophrenia and the inevitability of death," *Psychiat. Quart.*, 35:631-664, 1961.

47. STOUT, C., MORROW, J., BRANDT, E. N., and WOLF, S., "Unusally low incidence of death from myocardial infarction," *JAMA*, Vol. 18 (10) June 8, 1964.

48. WEAKLAND, JOHN H., "Family somatics—a neglected edge," Prepared for the Nathan W. Ackerman Memorial Conference, Feb., 1974.

49. WOLFF, STEWART, "Life stress and patterns of disease," in Lief, et al. (Eds), *The Psychological Basis of Medical Practice*. New York: Harper & Row, 1963.

Chapter IX

AN OVERVIEW

OUR INITIAL WORK involved a number of issues related to judgments regarding the competence of family systems. The demonstration that raters agreed with excellent reliability about the relative health of a broad range of families was a critical early finding. The evidence also suggested that observing ten minutes of video-taped family interaction was adequate to make the judgment. Such evaluations appeared to rely primarily upon cues which reflected total family system variables, and judgments regarding family competence were to a considerable degree independent of the nature of the interactional task provided the family. Although raters of widely differing family expertise did agree, those raters with greatest clinical experience demonstrated higher degrees of agreement.

The raters' judgments about the competence of family systems correlated significantly with the average of the individual family members' estimates of their family's competence. This suggested that, by and large, individuals within a variety of families have rather accurate perceptions of their family's competence. Although on the surface this result appears to contradict the findings regarding family mythology, it should be emphasized that at this point we are discussing individual perceptions of family competency whereas the concept of family mythology is a total family variable —i.e., it attempts to measure the "reality" of a family's self-appraisal rather than individual family member's percepts. We would not necessarily anticipate agreement from these two quite different sources of data.

The ratings distinguished patient-containing and control families and, in the former group, demonstrated a significant correlation between the degree of family dysfunctioning and the severity of individual adolescent patient psychopathology. Also, independent judgments of the parental marital relationship correlated with the total family competence.

These findings led us to focus research efforts on healthy or competent families. Before doing so, however, it was necessary to demonstrate that raters could agree about the relative health of families which did not contain an identified psychiatric patient, and in which all could be presumed to share the same "set" about the family testing. This step was accomplished with a second group of research volunteer families, and satisfactory rater reliability was demonstrated under severe circumstances; i.e., the use of only five minutes of videotaped family interaction as the basis for rater judgments.

Having dealt with those basic methodological issues, we moved to a more intensive study of this sample of families with the primary aim of identifying interactional variables which characterize psychologically healthy functioning. Our theoretical base (articulated in Chapter III) was the entropy model of family systems. From this base a series of family system rating scales were constructed. After establishing satisfactory interrater reliability, we found that the 13 scales each correlated with independent ratings of Global Family Health-Pathology, or overall competence. The scale correlations ranged from .30 to .79 across a spectrum of 103 families ranging from high levels of competence to severe dysfunction. These correlations were significant (p < .005) .

Also bearing on the same issue was the ability of mean scale values to discriminate between four groups of families: healthy and those containing a neurotic, behavior disorder, or psychotic adolescent. This finding added substantial support to the usefulness of the Beavers-Timberlawn Family Evaluation Scales. Although the group of 33 healthy families was found to represent a range of functioning, mean scale values distinguished this group from families containing a neurotic adolescent for 9 of the 13 scales; from families containing an adolescent with the diagnosis of behavior disorder for 12 of the 13 scales; and from families containing a psychotic youngster with all 13 scales. The individual scale means distinguished the three groups of patient-containing families from each other on ten of 39 scale comparisons.

The fact that the mean scale values reflected more competent functioning for the healthy families, midrange levels for the families containing neurotic and behavior disorder patients, and most pathological levels for the families containing a psychotic youngster was impressive evidence for the usefulness of the Scales and provided construct validity for the theoretical system from which they were derived.

It is important to emphasize that the sum of the 13 Scales correlated at a very high level with independent judgments of family system competence. We interpret this finding to mean that assessments of family system competence involved a large number of variables rather than a few very important ones.

The demonstration that both the sum of the 13 Scales, and independent global judgments of family functioning correlated with independent, quantified ratings of adolescent psychopathology in patient-containing families suggested the role of ongoing family functioning upon the severity of individual psychopathology.

The findings obtained by a microanalytic technique and based upon a different theoretical orientation provided additional evidence for the validity of our findings. It is important to note that the rank order of the final sample of 12 families based on the Riskin-Faunce technique correlated significantly with a rank order based upon Global Health-Pathology ratings ($r = .85$, $p = .002$); with a rank order based upon the sum of the Beavers-Timberlawn

Family Evaluation Scales (r =.78, p =.005) ; and with a rank order based upon the clinical observation of the exploratory family interviews (r =.66, p =.01).

The third level of data analysis involved the clinical observations of six hours of family interviews of each of the selected sample of 12 families. This research procedure yielded two important clusters of data: eight descriptive characteristics at a different level of complexity than the rating scale variables, and the further verification of the separation of the 12 families into two groups, one designated as "optimal" and the other as "adequate." This separation allowed us to focus on the optimal families.

The eight descriptive characteristics represented various combinations of the more focused rating-scale variables at another level of abstraction. These characteristics were: 1) an affiliative versus an oppositional attitude about human encounter; 2) a respect for one's own and the subjective world view of others; 3) openness in communication versus distancing, obscuring, and confusing mechanisms; 4) a firm parental coalition without evidence of competing parent-child coalitions; 5) an understanding of varied and complex human motivations versus a simplistic, linear, or controlling, orientation; 6) spontaneity versus rigid stereotyped interactions; 7) high levels of initiative versus passivity; and 8) the encouragement of the unique versus bland human characteristics.

Seven of these variables clearly distinguished optimal from adequate families. The exception was that both of the subgroups appeared to be high in initiative. The adequate families resembled patently dysfunctional or midrange families in their oppositional attitudes, only modest respect for subjective world views, use of distancing communication mechanisms, less than firm parental coalitions, reliance upon simple explanations of human behavior, reduced spontaneity, and a tendency toward blandness in individual characteristics. The strengths of these adequate families which have militated against the development of individual symptomatology or family system dissolution included high initiative resulting in multiple family involvements with neighborhood and community, predictability of structure and function, high levels of self esteem (often based upon favorable contrast of one's family to less fortunate others) and a firm belief in the value of family.

Rank ordering of these 12 families on the basis of this clinical observation correlated significantly with independent assessments of global family competence; with a rank order based upon the sum of the 13 family evaluation scales; and with the rank order based upon Riskin-Faunce microanalytic technique, both the empirical and theoretical.

The individually based studies focused also on the selected sample of 12 families and further distinguished the optimal and adequate families. The differences between these two groups at the level of individual interviews were impressive. The fathers from the families rated as optimal were more inclined to focus on interpersonal vocational satisfactions, and to be more directly supportive of their wives. Fathers from families rated as adequate were equally successful in providing for the family's economic needs, but appeared to focus less on interpersonal satisfactions. They were less supportive of their wives and although complementary, their comments suggested greater interpersonal distance.

Although almost all the wives were involved primarily in the home, those from families designated as optimal expressed far greater degrees of marital and family satisfaction. The wives from adequate families were the most pained of any individuals in this sample. They clearly verbalized disappointment and frustration in their roles; had frequent psychophysiologic symptoms; were more often obese; and, in general, appeared to fulfill the stereotype of the disappointed, depressed, upper-middle-class housewife.

The children from these two groups of families were more alike than different. With rare exception, they appeared psychologically healthy; i.e., they were mastering age-appropriate developmental tasks, developing significant interpersonal skills, accomplishing academic goals. They demonstrated little in the way of psychiatric symptomatology. The MMPI data did not distinguish between the children from the optimal and those from adequate families. Although our sample was small, the data revealed that even with considerable pain and struggle families could and did produce healthy children.

In comparing a family appraisal based on a total family system approach and the more traditional, individually-based appraisal, for the most part these two approaches were complementary. The data suggested, however, that the systems approach was more apt to reveal the strengths of a family. The individual, "composite" approach to family appraisal more often highlighted the family problems.* The exception to this impression was in the area of potentially pathological parent-child coalitions which were more readily detectable in the family system testing than in the individual data.

Other substantive findings involved the area of family physical health. Here the work was preliminary and caution must be exercised in interpreting the data. We did find, however, that families differed grossly in the amount and seriousness of physical illness. The way a family organizes itself may influence the resistance and vulnerability of family members to specific pathogens. The correlation between family psychological health and family physical health was positive, but not statistically significant. Our work suggested that a focused area for subsequent investigation involves the family's capacity to deal openly and personally with death and dying. It may be that families who deal openly and personally with profound loss teach their children to grieve, and in so doing influence vulnerability and resistance to disease.

HEALTHY FAMILIES

In this review of the variables which characterize healthy families, we focus specifically on the group of families we designated as optimal. We have no epidemiologic data with which to estimate the prevalence of such families in the general population. In the two groups of screened, research volunteer families (N = 44),

---

* Impressionistic observations from the study of patient-containing families suggest the reverse may hold for this clearly dysfunctional group. That is, indicators of psychopathology appear more strongly in family interactions, while strengths emerge more clearly from individual interviews.

there were ten or twelve such families, but we caution against generalizations regarding frequency of occurrence. The families we came to term "adequate" were more often encountered in this population, and may be closer to the modal, middle- to upper-middle-class family. We simply do not know the relative proportions of optimal, adequate, or various degrees of dysfunctional families in a general population. In addition, our sample included no lower-socioeconomic-class families and no representatives of other ethnic groups. Studies of such groups of families remain to be accomplished. What we wish to emphasize, however, is the fact that families seen by our methods as optimal in functioning were not fictitious nor even rare. That which these families reflect as possible in human interaction is available within the community for study. Researchers do not have an opportunity to know or appreciate this fact if their entire professional energies involve interventions with families containing schizophrenics or individuals with other individual symptomatology.

The variables to be described are of different degrees of complexity and have been appraised at several levels of quantification. We bring them together at this point in order to provide the reader with a gestalt. It may be that the future will reveal more cogent ways to order and classify them. For now, however, we present them as they appeared to us—there is some degree of significance to the order: those presented first seem more important but the order may change often before our studies are completed.

1. *The Role of Many Variables*

We found no single quality that optimally functioning families demonstrated and that less fortunate families somehow missed. On the contrary, optimally functioning or competent families appeared to be so because of the presence and interrelationship of a number of variables. It was this mixture that accounted for the impressive differences in style and patterning among the optimal families. At this level, they were dissimilar—there was no "one way." It was only upon analysis of structure and function that the commonalities emerged, and even at this level there were significant differences in the relative contributions made by discrete variables.

This observation paralleled that of some students of pathological family processes. During the very early stages of family systems research, there was a search for etiological factors or family processes which were specific for schizophrenia, ulcerative colitis, or other symptomatic states. In more recent years, however, there has been a growing appreciation that if such specific family processes were operative at all, it was within the context of family dysfunction across many important parameters. Lidz (12), for example, in discussing the origin of schizophrenic disorders, indicated that whatever aspects of the families were examined were found seriously amiss. Whatever specific vectors could be distinguished had to be considered within the context of a detrimental family setting as a totality. Meissner (13) suggested that interaction patterns within the family were not specific to any type of pathology. Levinger (11) put it succinctly, "Is it a difference of kind or degree? If we are to progress in terms of moving away from discrete typologies and towards variables and continuous formulations, we would want to focus on the *degree* of difference and the dimensions along which these kinds of relationships differ."

Our data suggest that health at the level of family was not a single thread, and that competence must be considered as a tapestry, reflecting differences in degrees along many dimensions.

2. An Affiliative Attitude About Human Encounter

Optimally functioning families demonstrated strikingly affiliative attitudes about human encounter. This appeared to be a global, complex characteristic that overlapped and encompassed a number of simpler variables. Its presence within a family was suggestive of high levels of health. The expectation that human encounters were apt to be caring encouraged reaching out to others. The converse, a pervasively oppositional attitude, encouraged the maintenance of distance. Either expectation can provide others with a variety of messages that encourage self-fulfilling prophecies. Families with strong affiliative attitudes demonstrated this expectation in all their communicative and behavioral acts. There was little of the guarded, distant, or hostile responses seen in dysfunctional families. Indeed, the presence of an affiliative attitude was one of the variables that distinguished optimal from adequate families.

Blum (4) approached this concept in his description of the "excellent" families he studied when he stated that such families love and respect those around them, old and young. It seems that this concept is related also to Erikson's (8) *basic trust*. Although his focus was developmental and applied to the individual, one would anticipate that strong affiliative attitudes serve as powerful, ongoing reinforcers throughout the lives of the family members. At this stage of our knowledge, the relative significance of early developmental phases within the individual and the potentially reinforcing or extinguishing family processes that go on daily, year after year, is not known.

3. Respect for Subjective Views

This is another complex family variable that involves respect for one's own world view as well as that of others. It appears that simpler family variables such as expressiveness and empathy are part of its foundation. Families which reflected this characteristic seemed free to be open and honest in agreement or disagreement, and they did not speak for each other. A minimum of absolutes or core superego beliefs were shared, but they did not rely on a pervasive family referee. It was apparent that basic respect for one's own subjective world view and that of others was a family characteristic intimately related to the family's use of power. Authoritarianism, or patterns of dominance and submission were incompatible with the pervasive respect that we describe here as a family characteristic.

A number of workers have discussed this or closely related concepts. Laing (10) indicated that in order to recognize persons rather than objects, one must realize that another human being is another center of orientation in the objective world. He indicated that the issue of person perception was a central concept in their family studies. Blum (4) discussed the capacity of an excellent family to tolerate individual differences and teach respect for the values of others.

4. A Belief in Complex Motivations

This, another rather abstract variable, shares the greater level of inference found in the preceding two variables. In our experience, it was rarely verbalized directly, but was suggested by the behavior of healthy families. In approaching problems within the family, they explored numerous options; if one approach did not work, they backed off and tried another. This was in contrast to many dysfunctional families in which a dogged perseverance with a single approach was noted. This latter style suggested an allegiance to the concept of linear causality.

A belief in complexity or multiplicity of motives and causes appeared to be related to the use of power within the family. Families which demonstrated the belief in complex motivations did not demonstrate a reliance upon the raw power of one family member nor the absolute authority of an external referee. Although, as noted earlier, each of the optimal families appeared to have a core of absolute beliefs, this core was small and did not interfere with the creative exploration of a number of explanatory concepts in problem solving.

This variable appears related to what Moss (16) called "homeomaistre." This refers to a complex system's active resonation with the environment in the attempt to improve information congruities and reduce uncertainty. Moss contrasted this characteristic with passive responsivity or adaptation. It implied the capacity of such a system to test, modify, insulate, explore, and to change form and structure. It is this capacity to utilize many options that suggested a family was open to the concept of complex motivations.

5. High Levels of Initiative

This variable appeared to be less complex and more directly observable than those discussed above. There was little that was passive about healthy families. The family as a unit demonstrated high levels of initiative in responding to input. Although such families differ in the degree of energy displayed, they all demonstrated more constructive reaching out than did patently dysfunctional families. This family characteristic was seen also in families who were less competent and have been designated as adequate families. This characteristic was seen rarely in dysfunctional families who were more likely to reveal a passive, controlled, contained type of responsivity. These differences in level of family activity were seen with some individual variation in the individual members of famlies. At the present time, understanding of this complex variable is incomplete. There may be biological or temperamental factors involved. It appeared that initiative was closely related to an affiliative attitude about human encounter.

As a consequence of this characteristic, optimal families were very much involved in the community. The focus of this involvement varied from family to family. Most had many interests: recreational, athletic, artistic, educational. As a consequence, such families received a tremendous variety of stimuli. In this regard they were not at all like the families studied by Westley and Epstein (23) who were described as much more isolated.

6. The Structure of the Healthy Family

This group of family characteristics and those which follow were more easily measurable and required less inference. For the most part, the findings which support their centrality in optimal families were seen at all three levels of data analysis: the clinical, the rating scale, and the microanalytic.

Structure, as we use the term, involved the enduring patterns which characterized family systems and ordered families across a spectrum of functioning. In accord with the entropy concept, the most severely dysfunctional families presented chaotic structures; midrange families presented rigid structures; and the most competent families presented flexible structures. The most direct measures of structure concerned the distribution of power or influence within the family.

In healthy families the parental coalition played a crucial role in the determination of overall family competence. Starting with the pilot study's demonstration of significant correlations between independent assessments of marital and total family function, this finding persisted through the rating scale data, the clinical observations, and the information on individuals. Health, in terms of optimal family functioning, was characterized by a parental marriage which was effective in meeting the needs of both parents.

Leadership was provided by the parental coalition as was a model of relating which appeared to be of great learning value to the children. Leadership was shared by the parents, and although more often than not father was seen as more powerful, this was not inevitable as contextual factors played a major role in determining who was in charge of what. This trend toward an egalitarian marriage was in striking contrast to both the more distant (and disappointing) marriages of the adequate families and the marital pattern of dominance and submission that so often was seen in dysfunctional families.

The power of the parental coalition was not exercised in an authoritarian way. The children had opinions which were considered and negotiation was common. Nevertheless, power was clear; there were generation boundaries; and we did not see competing parent-child coalitions in optimal families.

The strong affectional bond between the parents was not always accompanied by high levels of sexual activity. Different couples reported considerable variation in frequency of intercourse, although consistently high levels of satisfaction.

These marriages revealed a high degree of complementarity. There was a "fit" between the parents' varying individual skills, pride in each other's assets, and no strong competitive pulls. As a consequence, there appeared to be little need for emotionally charged alliances with opposite sexed others, either from outside the family or with one of the children. This characteristic was one which distinguished the optimal from the adequate families. In the latter group there was a less effective parental coalition, occasional competing coalitions, in or out of the nuclear family, and considerable verbalized frustration and dissatisfaction on the part of the wife.

These findings paralleled a number of observations made by other workers. Westley and Epstein (23) described similar marriages in their most healthy families. Mishler and Waxler (15) described normal families in which the distribution of power was like that described for our sample. They pointed out that the dependency of the children was temporary; that is, it was not needed nor considered permanent. Caputo (7) emphasized that it was not as important with whom the power rested, but whether it could be shared without conflict. Spiegel (21), Ackerman (1), and Meissner (14) emphasized the complementarity found in normal families. They focused on high levels of mutual need fulfillment. Tyler (22) described reciprocity as cooperative behavior involving two individuals whose final accomplishment depends on their mutual participation because of their dissimilarities. He contrasted this to competitive relationships. These processes of complementarity and reciprocity were seen to a high degree in the parental marriages of optimal families.

Another striking structural characteristic of healthy families was closeness. Healthy families showed no evidence of blurred boundaries (amorphous ego mass (6), mystification (9), fusion or symbiosis (5)) which characterize severely dysfunctional families. The individual family members had clear ego boundaries and as a consequence demonstrated closeness to each other. In this way, such families were distinguished from the pattern of clear boundaries or separateness associated, however, with considerable distancing which characterizes midrange families.

Related to the high degrees of closeness apparent in optimal families was the structural characteristic of respectful negotiation. Because separateness with closeness was the family norm, differences were tolerated and conflicts were approached through negotiation which respected the rights of others to feel, perceive, and respond differently. There was no tidal pull toward a family oneness which obliterates individual distinctions.

7. The Healthy Family and Personal Autonomy

As can be noted, healthy families contained individuals who demonstrated high levels of personal autonomy. This capacity of a family to encourage personal autonomy was, of course, crucial to the central task of the family. Beavers (2) has termed this the family's ability to "self-destruct." Much of what has been discussed in the way of variables characteristic of healthy families impinges upon the construct of personal autonomy. In attempts to study total family system characteristics which promoted this individual attribute we focused particularly upon a group of family communication variables. These were the clarity of communication; the permeability of the family; and a measure of responsibility within the family.

Children raised in families in which there is a strong pull for the clear definition of what each individual feels and thinks are exposed thereby to a powerful, day-to-day training program in defining where "one's skin ends and another's begins." This clarity of boundaries is not autonomy, but is the basic foundation from which autonomy evolves. Healthy families communicate clearly. In watching family videotapes, the observer had no difficulty knowing what each family member felt and thought. There was not, however, the obsessive clarity of some midrange families in which every statement was complete and well punctuated. The spontaneity of healthy families licensed much in the way of interruptions.

There was evidence of high degrees of permeability in healthy families. What each member felt or thought was acknowledged by others. Each was treated as present and, therefore, real.

There was strong encouragement to accept responsibility for each individual's own feelings, thoughts, and actions in such families. Projective mechanisms were rarely seen, and when they did appear, were dealt with most often by respectful confrontation.

A major consideration underlying these three communication variables related to autonomy was the belief that man's basic needs and drives are not evil. There was, therefore, no compelling need to confuse, distort, hide, or experience overwhelming shame. Sexuality and ambivalence were accepted as natural emotions.

As one might anticipate, there was little in the way of invasiveness or "mind reading" in healthy families. Our data suggested, for that matter, that this particularly destructive characteristic was rarely seen except in the most severely dysfunctional families.

These communication variables thought to be essential in the family production of personal autonomy have been noted by others. Their absence in severely disturbed families is reflected in the overlapping concepts of mystification (9), amorphous ego mass (6), and pseudomutuality (24). Their presence in normal families has been noted by Blum (4), Mishler and Waxler (15) and Riskin (19).

8. A Congruent Mythology

We think of the congruence of family mythology as an assessment of the manner in which the family perceives itself compared to the way the family is seen by others. A family with a congruent mythology perceives itself much as they are seen by a competent observer. It is important to emphasize that we are stressing the total family's shared percept of its own functioning. This is not the same as individual family members' perceptions of the family. We found families at all levels of competence which seemed, as a whole, to appraise the "reality" of the family's competence accurately. Healthy families were much more apt, however, to perceive themselves as others did. Dysfunctional families, although not rarely demonstrating some individual and family "realistic" assessments, were much more likely, as a group, to appraise their function at levels far higher than others did. These striking incongruities appeared to involve a semi-conscious, shared denial of painful realities—i.e., the presence of severe conflict, the flagrant psychosis, a family member's drug abuse problems, or other family difficulties.

9. *The Healthy Family and Feelings*

A central aspect of all human interaction is how affect is communicated. A significant human need is that of sensing that one's feelings are understood, that one may deal openly with all that one feels. There is a fundamental reciprocity to affective relationships—the capacity to communicate, and also the ability to encourage others to do so. The family system rating scales measured the degree to which each family system encouraged the open expression of feelings, the prevailing mood or tone of the family, and the capacity of the family for empathic responsiveness.

Healthy families were open in the expression of affect. The prevailing mood was one of warmth, affection, and caring. There was a well developed capacity for empathy. The children who had spent formative years in such a family had learned that it was safe and acceptable to talk about feelings. Although conflicts and anger were felt and expressed, there were many affectionate, loving messages. The freedom to be expressive was coupled with a sense of worth and value. They had learned the basic interpersonal skill of empathy, i.e., the capacity to understand what another was feeling and to communicate it.

These fundamental characteristics having to do with feelings appeared to minimize the amount and intensity of conflict within a family. Although not without conflict, healthy families did demonstrate less conflict than other families, and almost none which appeared unresolvable. Healthy families did not have long-term, ongoing conflicts that the family did not or could not resolve. There did not, therefore, appear to be lingering, chronic resentment in such families.

A large number of family researchers have reported on the expression of affect in normal families. Blum (4) reported that the freedom to be oneself and to express innermost feelings characterized superior families. The prevailing family attitude was one of caring. Mishler and Waxler (15) described the normal family's expressiveness as pervasive. In their terms, it made little difference who was expressing what feeling. In a similar vein, the object of the affect can be anyone in the family. Bell (3) indicated that the conflicts of normal families were open, and occurred upon the foundation of a basic family integration. They did not appear to limit the range of interaction in the future.

Our data suggested that the high levels of empathy demonstrated by healthy families must be considered in the context of the generally warm, caring feeling tone of such families. (It may be, however, that reduced empathy or a certain degree of obliviousness may be a necessary or even desirable characteristic in dysfunctional families experiencing high levels of pain.)

Children growing up in these healthy families learned that all feelings are human, and that to be expressive is normal. Facing conflict openly, having high levels of empathy, and tenderness were family characteristics which may best prepare individuals for future human intimacy beyond the family or origin.

10. And Yet More

The variables described above do not exhaust the characteristics of healthy or optimally functioning families. We noted also the high degrees of spontaneity in such families; there was little of the dreary, stereotyped sameness to such family interactions. Humor and wit were frequent. What was important to note, however, was that each member of the family contributed to the free-flowing spontaneity.

In earlier sections we described the high levels of involvement of healthy families with those about them. Scapegoating was at an absolute minimum in such families. There was no evidence of internal scapegoating, but occasionally there was a degree of external scapegoating. Although families described as adequate appeared to maintain esteem in part by frequent comparisons to less fortunate others, optimal families also occasionally scapegoated outsiders. Esteem in optimal families did not appear as dependent upon this process but, nevertheless, some was noted.

Our studies did not directly assess the family's capacity to deal with loss. Theoretically we anticipate that optimal families are more clearly attuned to the passage of time, but our cross-sectional design did not approach the issue directly. The data suggested a correlation between family competence and the capacity to deal personally with a death or dying stimulus. The correlation did not reach statistical significance and we consider the issue undecided. Paul (18) has suggested that dysfunctional families avoid dealing with loss.

Our tentative impression was that family strengths may be understood better through the study of the total family system than a study of the individual. Specific family problems (with the notable exception of pathological family coalitions) were more readily apparent from interviewing individual family members. Basically, however, individual exploratory interviews with the members of optimal families reinforced the significance of the variables which characterized their family systems.

At this point, it is well to emphasize the limitations of this study. The sample was a narrow one—white, middle- to upper-middle-class, Protestant, urban, biologically intact families. Although follow-up studies are in process, the findings reported here were cross-sectional in nature. Despite these limitations, the focus on family health illuminated a level of psychological function infrequently studied. They did appear to be a special group of families. A recent study by Oatis (17), added emphasis to this specialness. He studied the values of a subgroup of this sample utilizing the Rokeach Value Survey (20). They reported values having to do with family functioning and self-realization, and their ranking of values did not correspond with any group tested by Rokeach. Optimal families supported their choice of values by reference to rational and emotive, but not authoritarian, statements. These families also were found, in general, to score low on other measures of reliance upon external authority.

We saw this group of healthy families as an unusual, but not necessarily rare, group of families. Perhaps most of all, these optimal families did us the service of revealing a model of what is possible in family relationships. For this, we are in their debt.

REFERENCES

1. ACKERMAN, N. W., *The Psychodynamics of Family Life*. New York: Basic Books, 1958.
2. BEAVERS, W. R., "Family variables related to the development of a self," *Timberlawn Foundation Reports*, Dallas, 1973.
3. BELL, NORMAN W., "Extended family relations of disturbed and well families." In N. W. Ackerman (Ed.), *Family Process*. New York: Basic Books, 1970.
4. BLUM, R. H., et al. *Horatio Alger's Children*. San Francisco: Jossey-Bass, 1972.
5. BOWEN, M., "Family psychotherapy with schizophrenia in the hospital and in private practice." In I. Boszormenyi-Nagy, and J. L. Framo, Ch. V, *Intensive Family Therapy*. New York: Hoeber Medical Division, Harper and Row, 1965, p. 213-243.
6. BOWEN, M. A., "Family concept of schizophrenia." In D. D. Jackson (Ed.), *The Etiology of Schizophrenia*. New York: Basic Books, 1960.
7. CAPUTO, D. V., "Parents of the schizophrenic," *Family Process*, 2:336-356, 1963.
8. ERIKSON, E., "Identity and the lifecycle," *Psychological Issues*, Vol. 1 (1). New York: International Universities Press, 1959.
9. LAING, R. D., "Mystification, confusion, and conflict." In Nagy and Framo (Eds.), *Intensive Family Therapy*. New York: Hoeber, 1965.
10. LAING, R. D., *Politics of Experience*. New York: Pantheon Books, 1967.
11. LEVINGER, G., "Basic issues in interaction research." In J. L. Framo (Ed.), *Family Interaction*. New York: Springer Publishing Co., 1972.
12. LIDZ, T., *The Origin and Treatment of Schizophrenic Disorders*. New York: Basic Books, 1973.
13. MEISSNER, W. W., "Thinking about the family—psychiatric aspects." In N. W. Ackerman (Ed.), *Family Process*. New York: Basic Books, 1970.
14. MEISSNER, W. W., "Family dynamics and psychosomatic processes," *Fam. Process*, 5 (2), 142-161, 1966.
15. MISHLER, E., and WAXLER, N., *Interaction in Families*. New York: John Wiley and Sons, 1968.
16. MOSS, GORDON E., *Illness, Immunity and Social Interaction*. New York: Wiley-Interscience, 194-197, 1973.
17. OATIS, STEPHEN J., *An Inquiry into the Values and Beliefs of Twelve Healthy Families*, Th. D. Thesis, Perkins School of Theology, SMU, 1975.
18. PAUL, N., and GROSSER, G. H., "Operational mourning and its role in conjoint family therapy," *Community Mental Health Journal*, 1:339-345, 1965.
19. RISKIN, J., and FAUNCE, E. F., "Family interactional scales," *Arch. Gen. Psychiat.*, Vol. 22 (6), 504-537, June, 1970.
20. ROKEACH, M., *The Nature of Human Values*. New York: The Free Press, 1973.
21. SPIEGEL, J. P., "The resolution of role conflict within the family," *Psychiat.*, 20:1-16, 1957.
22. TYLER, E. A., "The Process of Humanizing Physiological Man." In N. W. Ackerman (Ed.), *Family Process*. New York: Basic Books, 1970.
23. WESTLEY, W. A., and EPSTEIN, N. B., *The Silent Majority*. San Francisco: Jossey-Bass, Inc., 1969.
24. WYNNE, L. C., RYCKOFF, I. M., DAY, J., and HIRSCH, S. L., "Pseudomutuality in the family relations of schizophrenics," *Psychiat.*, 21:205-220, 1958.

CHAPTER X

IMPLICATIONS FOR THE CLINICIAN

IN THIS FINAL CHAPTER we focus on the findings of this project that we feel to be most relevant for the clinician. Much of what follows affirms that which is already a part of clinical practice; some of what is suggested is either new or emphasizes that which appears incompletely appreciated. The implications for the clinician are organized in three parts: findings of general or broad concern; findings involving the family as man's crucial interpersonal system; and findings which have relevance for therapeutic interventions whether at the level of the individual, the marital system, or the family system.

FINDINGS OF GENERAL CONCERN

Perhaps the primary finding of general concern was the affirmation of the clinician's need to be pluralistic in his conceptual bases, and in his resulting observational methods and techniques of intervention. This premise, so central to the concept of a systems approach, has recently been emphasized by Havens (6) regarding individual psychotherapy. The need for the clinician to be flexible

218

—to have a capacity to move from individual to marital to family levels (and for some, to social network, community and culture) according to the potential for helpfulness at each level, in each clinical situation, poses considerable challenge for the clinician. First, it involves familiarity with multiple conceptual levels of human behavior—a task of considerable cognitive dimensions. It involves the acquisition of therapeutic expertise at several levels of intervention or, failing that, the capacity for thoughtful referral to others with different expertise. Of major consequence, however, is that this type of flexibility means giving up a rigidly held, or evangelical, attitude that one's approach to intervention is the best or only approach. Whether the clinician's primary base is psychoanalysis, family therapy, transactional analysis or whatever, the application of a constricted set of methodologies to every clinical situation suggests that the therapist's needs, rather than those of the patient, couple, or family, are being served. The importance of the clinician's flexibility is highlighted by the contemporary development of a variety of new interventions, each of which appears to attract a group of advocates of clinicians, many of whom may become avid proponents. The need for a careful diagnostic exploration at multiple levels is lost because the presumed potency of the new technique transcends any consideration of the nature and source of the dysfunction.

Our findings have implication for the treatment of the individual, the marital couple, and the family system. Observational methodologies at each of these levels frequently produce complementary findings. There is, however, the suggestion that reliance upon a single observational level may result in significant clinical error. Despite the development of group, marital, and family techniques, the individual level of observation remains, for most, the keystone of clinical practice. The concern, therefore, is how to augment the modal clinician's ability to move beyond the individual level of observation and intervention. The significance of levels is illustrated in Lewis Thomas's essay *On Societies as Organisms* (17). He describes a solitary ant as a few neurons strung together by fibers, an organism that can't be imagined to have a mind, much less a thought. Six ants together, however, encircling a dead moth on a path begin to look like an idea. Observation of the solitary ant, separate from its social context, would result in incomplete understanding of ant behavior. Analogously, the clinician who restricts his input to but one of man's crucial systems is apt to misunderstand his patient's behavior.

A second conclusion of general concern was an affirmation of the importance of observations focusing on process as well as on content. In studying family systems, we found that a focus on family process not only distinguished the functional from the dysfunctional, but made the differences in style, interests, and goals of families that share high levels of competence comprehensible. What was common had much more to do with the processes of family life than with the content.

FINDINGS REGARDING THE FAMILY

The central finding from our study was that the family is alive and well. If one takes a sample of middle- and upper-middle-class families, a by-no-means rare number will demonstrate high levels of ability in what Parsons (12) has called the primary tasks of family: raising competent children and stabilizing the adults' mental health. For the clinician this may come as a surprise. There is much in the professional and lay literature to suggest that the nuclear family has about "had it." Our study did not approach the issue of how common family health may be, and the need to study the impact of socioeconomic and ethnic vectors upon family health is urgent. Despite the narrowness of our sample, the demonstration that high levels of family health are possible (and not rare) is considered a significant finding.

In this way we re-emphasize what is known but may be forgotten: The clinician's usual sample of human behavior is not representative and extrapolations, therefore, should be cautious. At the level of family, a professional concern with families containing an identified patient may lead to a growing conviction that all, or most, families are in serious trouble. In addition, what

data we have on the families created by mental health professionals themselves and on their families of origin suggest that many or
even most of us have had little intimate exposure to optimal family
functioning (3). We are all, to various degrees, captives of our
own experiences; and if one has been raised in a severely dysfunctional family (or perhaps more likely, a midrange or adequate
one), has participated in the creation of a new and similar nuclear
family, associates primarily with peers of similar experience, and
is involved in treating the products of midrange and severely
disturbed family systems, the idea that much more is possible in
family life may seem at best a wistful fantasy. Our findings did not
confirm such a bleak outlook.

*Accordingly, our findings also give the family clinician or re-
searcher a data-based standard against which to measure dysfunction and toward which intervention efforts may be aimed.* More
specifically, for the family researcher, the data revealed that a
more-or-less typical control group of families may reflect a continuum of competence. A group loaded toward what we have
arbitrarily designated as adequately functioning rather than optimally functioning families will minimize the differences between
the controls and the patient-containing families. A control group
weighted toward the optimal end of the continuum will emphasize such differences. Not to recognize such composition of a
control group is to invite erroneous conclusions.

Two well established constructs about families were validated
by this study. *The first has to do with the primary importance of
communication variables in conceptualizing and assessing family
function.* While not replacing insights derived from observations
of the individual, this movement away from a *sole* focus on individual, intrapsychic psychodynamics has enriched understanding
of a variety of individual symptomatic pathologics. Our rcscarch
indicated that the information about family communications also
added to the understanding of health or competence. The capacity
of families we termed optimal to communicate thoughts and feelings was greater than any group of families studied.   ·

This broadening of the focus to the interactional, communication framework followed the work of a larger number of investigators who have focused on the dysfunctional. Jackson (7), Reusch (14), Wynne and Singer (19), Lidz and Fleck (8), Mishler and Waxler (11), and Satir (15) are but a few in a long line of significant contributors.

A second construct which our study validated was the cardinal role of the parental coalition in establishing the level of function of the total family. This finding confirmed the early work of Bowen (2) and Lidz and Lidz (9), the clinical insights of Ackermann (1), Zuk (20), and Minuchin (10), and the research of Westley and Epstein (18). The extension of the earlier work regarding the role of marital dysfunctioning upon the quality of total family life to competent, functional families not only affirmed the importance of the construct, but extended the range of observations. Indeed, it was tempting to make the marital coalition the central construct. Crucial differences in the quality of the parental coalition distinguished the optimal from the adequate families. Although we did not see the "total marriage" described by Cuber and Harroff (4), we found evidence that the parental coalition in optimal families was one of unusual complementarity and reciprocity. Westley and Epstein found "a direct relationship between the degree of emotional health found in the children and the degree to which the relationship between the parents was positive. . . . The success of the relationship seemed to rest on the attitude of the wife toward her husband. . . . The most positive were those in which the wife demonstrated the 'adoration pattern' in which she literally felt that her husband was the perfect man for her and had been responsible for most of the good things that had happened in her life."

In our own sample of healthy families, both optimal and adequate husbands and wives appeared to have married with high expectations of their partners. In the optimals, at the time they were studied, both husbands and wives spoke highly of each other and seemed to have had their expectations met or surpassed. In the adequates, the husbands spoke well of their wives and their own satisfaction in the marriage. The wives, however, while functioning well in their parental roles, appeared disappointed to a degree, and expressed some pain and lack of gratification in their relationships with their husbands. Although the marital styles differed, these couples shared profound affectional bonds, significant opportunities for intimacy, and major reliance upon truly respectful negotiation as hallmarks of their relationship.

The implications of this concept for the clinician are numerous. Perhaps the most common clinical situation the mental health professional meets is the woman who presents with dissatisfaction, depression and frequent physical symptoms. Often the major therapeutic thrust is either the attempt to clarify the historical determinants of her disturbance or the encouragement of growth experiences to be found outside the family. Both may be useful or necessary. Our data suggested additionally that assessment and intervention at the level of the marital system has considerable potential. Again, multiple-level assessment and intervention would appear to offer the greatest leverage, regardless of which member of the family presents as the patient. If circumstances dictated that only one level could be approached, and if there was question in the clinician's mind about which level to direct his attention to (individual, marital, or family), these findings urge strong consideration of the marital level as having potentially greatest impact upon both the individual and the total family.

Our work demonstrated the advantages to the clinician of a systems model of family function. We found it meaningful to conceptualize a broad continuum of family functioning. Locating a family on this continuum involved the appraisal of many variables. Some of the variables were relatively easy to measure (e.g., clarity of communication) while others involved significant inference (e.g., an orientation of affiliative or oppositional expectation of human encounter). Our systems model attended many variables, each conceptualized as a continuum measuring the degree of entropy in that component. For example, if the family's structure is taken as a starting point in the appraisal of family system competence, it is useful to think of three labeled points on the structure continuum. When the structure is clear in the sense that power or influence is not murky—if it is shared, responds differently to differing contexts and in that sense appears flexible, the initial presumption can be one of considerable health in the system. If the impression, however, is one of a structure characterized by rigidity, patterns of dominance and submission, and suggestions of unresolvable conflict, the implication is that the system is midrange in functioning with considerable likelihood of pathology. If the initial observations suggest a chaotic power structure with boundaries difficult to ascertain, the initial premise is one of severe dysfunctioning associated with significant pathology. These initial observations may be thought of as providing the clinician with a springboard from which to explore. The importance of retaining a tentative, easily modifiable set until sufficient data are on hand is axiomatic.

We found family interactional testing, i.e., asking the family (or marital couple) to approach a task (without the clinician present) to be a particularly useful initial evaluation procedure. Often it appeared that the clinician interfered with a family's characteristic processes. Both his presence and his activity can become the focus of family attention. We found the specific task did not alter a family's interactional processes, but the presence of the children appeared to do so in some families.

Several of the findings deserve additional emphasis; for one, in optimal families the degree of impulse control in the children was related to birth order rather than sex. Older children demonstrated greater order, deliberateness and emphasis upon control. Younger children revealed increasing spontaneity and freedom with affect. In less functional families these characteristics were more likely to be sex-linked. *This suggests that less than optimally functioning families may have more narrow definitions of sexual role functioning.* In healthier families there was less of "you're a girl, therefore, you ought to be this or that" or "you're a boy and, therefore, you cannot do this or that." In the absence of narrow sexual role family prescriptions it appeared that children were exposed to different developmental contingencies. Older children were more apt to be exposed to greater structure than younger children in many well-functioning families.

Another finding deserving repeated emphasis was that psychological pain in families was not invariably associated with disability. The optimal families experienced pain, and did so openly and without apparent disability. In addition, the presence of considerable pain (not so openly expressed) in families designated as adequate did not preclude the evolution of competent children. The implication for the clinician is that a sole focus on the pain may lead to an underestimation of the system competence.

The data also suggested that in less than optimal families the mother was the first to suffer from the system's inadequacy. She was most often the first to become dissatisfied, distressed, or symptomatic. At increased levels of family system dysfunctioning, a child may also begin to experience distress and becomes symptomatic. Frequently, then he will become an identified patient. The father, with more in the way of outside sources of esteem, is often the last family member to become symptomatic. This scheme is oversimplified and there are many exceptions, but our data did suggest this general trend.

The research reported suggested that the clinician should attend the family's pattern of physical illness. High levels of physical illness should encourage the clinician to be particularly attentive to the family's systematic ways of dealing with separation, loss, and death. Although our work in this area is at an early stage, the sensitive clinician will utilize the family's pattern of physical illness as another way of better understanding that may lead to more effective intervention.

FINDINGS REGARDING THE PROCESS OF THERAPY

The research reported in this volume had no direct relationship to the process of any variety of psychotherapy. As one part of our research regarding family systems, it presents findings from a group of families called healthy, with subgroups we designated as optimal and adequate. It is our impression, however, that apart from the clinical implications which bear directly upon the goals and processes of family therapy (and to which we have made brief reference) our findings may have relevance for the broader field of psychotherapy. If one agrees that psychotherapy is based upon an intense relationship and is, in its essence, communication, can the study of optimal families—their relationships and communication patterns—speak to the nature of the psychotherapeutic relationship? We think so and offer, therefore, the following tentative premises as potentially isomorphic processes.

The goals of family and therapy share a commitment to the evolving autonomy and health of those who present as most needful, namely children and patients. The therapist, like the parent, has expertise and power. Our findings suggested, however, that in optimal families power was shared and not used in authoritarian ways. The translation to psychotherapy entails the concept of the therapist as collaborator. The essence of collaborative therapeutic work is a respect for the subjective world view of others; a basically affiliative rather than oppositional attitude towards others; and a commitment to negotiation as a basis of effective treatment.

Optimal families acted as if human behavior resulted from complex motivations. Linear causality as an explanatory scheme has a limited place in such families. Therapists, for the most part, appear to believe in complex causation. *In dealing with psychotherapeutic interactions perhaps the crucial issue is how aware the therapist is of the essentially reciprocal nature of any human relationship.* It is crucial for the therapist to be aware of his impact upon the patient-therapist interaction. Just as optimal families did not rely upon projective devices, therapists do not assume that all the transactions in the therapeutic encounter spring unaided from the patient.

At a different level, the communication processes of optimal families were clear as well as spontaneous. They were rarely intrusive or invasive. Expressions of all kinds of affect were acceptable; empathic responses were frequent; individuals were "heard" and acknowledged. The feeling tone was predominantly caring. We suggest (along with students of psychotherapy as diverse in theoretical position as Greenson (5), Strupp (16), and Rogers (13)) that these communication processes may characterize also much that is effective about psychotherapy.

The extrapolation from processes which characterize optimal families to process underlying effective psychotherapy appears to have a degree of surface validity. What does not fit, however, is psychotherapy in which therapists, unlike optimal families, appear to experience themselves as powerful agents capable of quickly formulating the "underlying" problem, intervening aggressively and often with exquisite invasiveness and, in general, coming across as ruthless, omnipotent rulers. Such observations are difficult to integrate with the concept of parallel processes in therapy and optimal families. If one assumes that such therapists do help some people (the commonsense of the market place does suggest this), how is it to be understood? First, of course, is the idea that our search for parallel process applies only under certain circumstances. The possibility is that if one is dealing with a chaotic system (i.e., a process schizophrenic family) therapeutic techniques may need to be "powerful" in order to assist the family to reach a more organized state, what we call midrange functioning—i.e., functioning characterized by rigid structure and patterns of dominance and submission. For chaotic families such movement would represent considerable improvement. We would doubt (on theoretical grounds) that such an approach (i.e., authoritarian) to therapy would be capable of taking a family beyond midrange functioning. The process of improvement is blocked unless, of course, the therapist can then switch styles and become a collaborative helper— and, in so doing, provide a model of optimal functioning. In our understanding, one cannot move from rigidity to flexibility if one's guide is rigid.

This attempt to find parallel processes in the psychotherapeutic encounter to those our data reveal in the optimal families is at an early stage. We share it with the reader because we find it both promising and exciting.

Conclusion

As we close this report of our work in progress, we wish to emphasize the hope that we, as clinician-researchers, experienced in studying this group of families:

. . . that the skills in relating and communicating which the optimal families demonstrated are teachable and learnable;

. . . that mastery of such skills can enable helpers, whether parents, teachers or therapists, to enrich the fabric of life for those who are growing;

. . . that, indeed, the threads of competence can be woven in many and varied patterns.

REFERENCES

1. ACKERMAN, N. W., *The Psychodynamics of Family Life*. New York: Basic Books, 1958.
2. BOWEN, M. A., "Family concept of schizophrenia." In D. D. Jackson (Ed.), *The Etiology of Schizophrenia*. New York: Basic Books, 1960.
3. BURTON, ARTHUR et al., *Twelve Therapists*. San Francisco: Jossey-Bass, Inc., 1972.
4. CUBER, J. F., and HARROFF, P. B., *The Significant Americans*. New York: Appleton Century, 1965.
5. GREENSON, R. R., *The Technique and Practice of Psychoanalysis*. New York: International Universities Press, 1967.
6. HAVENS, L. L., *Approaches to the Mind*. Boston: Little, Brown & Co., 1973.
7. JACKSON, D. D., "Family practice: A comprehensive medical approach," *Comp. Psychiat.*, Vol. 7 (5), 338-344, 1966.
8. LIDZ, T., FLECK, S., and CORNELISON, A. R., *Schizophrenia and the Family*. New York: International Universities Press, 1965.
9. LIDZ, R. W., and LIDZ, T., "The family environment of schizophrenic patients," *Am. J. Psychiat.*, 106:332-345, 1949.
10. MINUCHIN, S., *Families and Family Therapy*. Cambridge, Mass.: Harvard Univ. Press, 1974.
11. MISHLER, E., and WAXLER, N., *Interaction in Families*. New York: John Wiley and Sons, 1968.
12. PARSONS, T., and BALES, R., *Family, Socialization and Interaction Process*. Glencoe, Ill.: Free Press, 1955.
13. ROGERS, C. C., *The Therapeutic Relationship and Its Impact*. Madison: The University of Wisconsin Press, 1967.
14. RUESCH, J., *Disturbed Communication*. New York: Norton, 1957.
15. SATIR, V., *Conjoint Family Therapy*. Palo Alto: Science and Behavior Books, 1964.
16. STRUPP, H. H., *Psychotherapy: Clinical Research and Theoretical Issues*. New York: Jason Aronson, Inc., 1973.

17. THOMAS, LEWIS, *The Lives of a Cell.* New York: Viking Press, 1974.
18. WESTLEY, W. A., and EPSTEIN, N. B., *The Silent Majority.* San Francisco: Jossey-Bass, Inc., 1969.
19. WYNNE, L. C., and SINGER, M. T., "Thought disorder and family relations of schizophrenics," *Arch. Gen. Psychiat.,* 9:191-206, 1963.
20. ZUK, G. H., and BOSZORMENYI, NAGY (Eds.), *Family Therapy and Disturbed Families.* Palo Alto: Science and Behavior Books, 1967.

Appendix A

FAMILY CHARACTERISTICS INVENTORY

Name ....

Date ....

The following statements fit some families better than others. Please circle the number that best describes how well each statement fits your family.

	Does Not Fit Our Family At All		Fits Our Family Some		Fits Our Family Very Well
1. We live in a good neighborhood.	1	2	3	4	5
2. Our family talks things out.	1	2	3	4	5
3. We have a sense of humor.	1	2	3	4	5
4. There is an opportunity for each member to express himself in his own way.	1	2	3	4	5
5. There are activities which we all enjoy doing together.	1	2	3	4	5
6. We respect each other's feelings.	1	2	3	4	5
7. In our home, we feel loved.	1	2	3	4	5
8. We have the right kinds of friends.	1	2	3	4	5
9. Discipline is moderate and consistent.	1	2	3	4	5
10. Educational goals are important to us.	1	2	3	4	5
11. There is a sense of belonging in our family.	1	2	3	4	5
12. Our family is a reliable, dependable family.	1	2	3	4	5
13. We establish reasonable goals for ourselves.	1	2	3	4	5
14. We encourage development of potential in all members of our family.	1	2	3	4	5
15. We express appreciation for what we do for one another.	1	2	3	4	5
16. We plan ahead.	1	2	3	4	5
17. We share experiences.	1	2	3	4	5
18. We live in a good school district.	1	2	3	4	5
19. Father is a good provider.	1	2	3	4	5
20. There is enough money for special things.	1	2	3	4	5

231

Appendix B

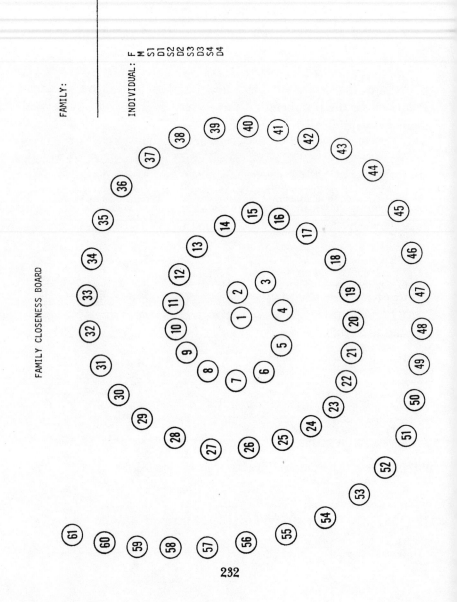

FAMILY:

INDIVIDUAL: F
M
S1
D1
S2
D2
S3
D3
S4
D4

FAMILY CLOSENESS BOARD

232

Appendix C
CONSENT TO INVESTIGATIONAL PROCEDURE

I/we, the undersigned, do hereby consent to participate in interviews or therapeutic sessions in certain research and educational projects to be undertaken by the Director of Research and Training and the staff of Timberlawn Foundation, Inc., and other researchers, which will involve the making or production of pictures or videotapes, including closed circuit television and/or voice recordings of said interviews, with the definite understanding that said pictures or videotapes and voice recordings, or interviews may be viewed, imparted to and/or heard by others in the usual and normal course of events in the furtherance of educational and research training.

Executed this .... day of ...., 19....

WITNESS: ....

WITNESS: ....

WITNESS: ....

WITNESS: ....

Appendix D
FAMILY HISTORY

1. Name .... 2. Telephone ....
3. Address ....
4. Husband's occupation .... 5. Company ....
6. Title .... 7. Years employed ....
8. Telephone ....
9. Wife's occcupation .... 10. Company ....
11. Title .... 12. Years employed ....
13. Telephone ....
14. Number of marriages: Husband .... Wife ....
15. Year of current marriage ....
16. Children

	AGE	SEX
....	....	....
....	....	....
....	....	....
....	....	....
....	....	....
....	....	....
....	....	....

17. Any deaths in the immediate family? ....
....
18. Do you own or rent your home? ....
19. How many rooms? ....
20. Does any one outside immediate family live in the home? ....
....
21. Husband's birth place .... 22. Education level...............
23. Religious affiliation ....
24. Wife's birth place ....
25. Educational level .... 26. Religious affiliation ....

234

Appendix E

BEAVERS-TIMBERLAWN
FAMILY EVALUATION SCALE

Family Name.................. Rater..........
Segment................... Date..........

Instructions: The following scales were designed to assess the family functioning on continua representing interactional aspects of being a family. Therefore, it is important that you consider the entire range of each scale when you make your ratings. Please try to *respond on the basis of the videotape data alone,* scoring according to what you see and hear, rather than what you imagine might occur elsewhere.

I. Structure of the Family

A. Overt Power: Based on the entire tape, check the term that best describes your general impression of the power structure of this family.

1	1.5	2	2.5	3	3.5	4	4.5	5
Chaos		Marked dominance		Moderate dominance		Led		Egalitarian
Leaderless; no one has enough power to structure the interaction.		Control is close to absolute. No negotiation; dominance and submission are the rule.		Control is close to absolute. Some negotiation, but dominance and submission are the rule.		Tendency toward dominance and submission, but most of the interaction is through respectful negotiation.		Leadership is shared between parents, changing with the nature of the interaction.

If 2 to 4, indicate:

Who is #1 in power: Father .... Mother .... Child (specify) ....

Who is #2 in power: Father .... Mother .... Child (specify) ....

B. Parental Coalitions: Check the terms that best describe the relationship structure in this family.

1	1.5	2	2.5	3	3.5	4	4.5	5
Parent-child coalition				Weak parental coalition				Strong parental coalition

C. Closeness

1	1.5	2	2.5	3	3.5	4	4.5	5
Amorphous, vague and indistinct boundaries among members				Isolation, distancing				Closeness, with distinct boundaries among members

D. The power structure, or "pecking order," in this family is:

1	1.5	2	2.5	3	3.5	4	4.5	5
Hard to determine		Relatively hard to determine				Relatively easy to determine		Quite easy to determine

II. Mythology: Every family has a mythology; that is, a concept of how it functions as a group. Rate the degree to which this family's mythology seems congruent with reality.

1	1.5	2	2.5	3	3.5	4	4.5	5
Very congruent		Mostly congruent				Somewhat incongruent		Very incongruent

III. Goal-Directed Negotiation: Rate this family's overall efficiency in negotiation and problem solving.

1	1.5	2	2.5	3	3.5	4	4.5	5
Extremely efficient		Good				Poor		Extremely inefficient

IV. *Autonomy*

A. Communication of Self-Concept: Rate this family as to the clarity of disclosure of feelings and thoughts. This is not a rating of the intensity of feelings, but rather of clarity of expression of individual thoughts and feelings.

1	1.5	2	2.5	3	3.5	4	4.5	5
Very clear				Somewhat vague and hidden				Hardly anyone is ever clear

B. Responsibility: Rate the degree to which the family members take responsibility for their own past, present, and future actions.

1	1.5	2	2.5	3	3.5	4	4.5	5
Members regularly are able to voice responsibility for individual actions				Members sometimes voice responsibility for individual actions, but tactics also include sometimes blaming others, speaking in 3rd person or plural				Members rarely, if ever, voice responsibility for individual actions

C. Invasiveness: Rate the degree to which the members speak for one another, or make "mind reading" statements.

1	1.5	2	2.5	3	3.5	4	4.5	5
Many invasions				Occasional invasions				No evidence of invasions

D. Permeability: Rate the degree to which members are open, receptive and permeable to the statements of other family members.

1	1.5	2	2.5	3	3.5	4	4.5	5
Very open		Moderately open				Members frequently unreceptive		Members unreceptive

V. Family Affect

A. Expressiveness: Rate the degree to which this family system is characterized by open expression of feelings.

1	1.5	2	2.5	3	3.5	4	4.5	5
Open, direct expression of feelings		Direct expression of feelings despite some discomfort		Obvious restriction in the expressions of some feelings		Although some feelings are expressed, there is masking of most feelings		No expression of feelings

B. Mood and Tone: Rate the feeling tone of this family's interaction.

1	1.5	2	2.5	3	3.5	4	4.5	5
Usually warm, affectionate, humorous and optimistic		Polite, without impressive warmth or affection; or frequently hostile with times of pleasure		Overtly hostile		Depressed		Cynical, hopeless and pessimistic

C. Conflict: Rate the degree of seemingly unresolvable conflict.

1	1.5	2	2.5	3	3.5	4	4.5	5
Severe conflict, with severe impairment of group functioning		Definite conflict, with moderate impairment of group functioning		Definite conflict, with slight impairment of group functioning		Some evidence of conflict, without impairment of group functioning		Little, or no, conflict

D. Empathy: Rate the degree of sensitivity to, and understanding of, each other's feelings within this family.

1	1.5	2	2.5	3	3.5	4	4.5	5
Consistent empathic responsiveness		For the most part, an empathic responsiveness with one another, despite obvious resistance		Attempted empathic involvement, but failed to maintain it		Absence of any empathic responsiveness		Grossly inappropriate responses to feelings

VI. *Global Health-Pathology Scale: Circle the number* of the point on the following scale which best describes this family's health or pathology.

Healthiest
1 — 2 — 3 — 4 — 5 — 6 — 7 — 8 — 9 — 10
Most Pathological

LOSS SCALES. *Ability to Discuss Concept of Death*: Make your ratings on the following scales immediately after the second ten-minute (loss) section.

A. Cognitive Involvement with Loss

1	1.5	2	2.5	3	3.5	4	4.5	5
Human death discussed without any specific resistance		Human death discussed openly despite obvious resistance		Attempted, but failed to discuss human death openly at any time. Death in general, as an abstraction, or non-human death, discussed with apparent freedom		Brief, cursory efforts to discuss death in general, as an abstraction, or non-human death		No discussion of death

B. Empathy to Loss

1	1.5	2	2.5	3	3.5	4	4.5	5
Consistent empathic response at a feeling level with one another and/or people in the story		For the most part, an empathic response at a feeling level with one another and/or people in the story, despite obvious resistance		Attempted empathic involvement, but failed to maintain it		Absence of any observable empathic response		Grossly inappropriate response

C. Personalization of response to threat-of-loss stimulus.

1	1.5	2	2.5	3	3.5	4	4.5	5
	Discuss seriously the threat of loss within their nuclear family	Discuss seriously the threat of loss in terms of extended family		Discuss seriously the threat of loss in terms of people known, but not related to them		Discuss the threat of loss in terms of real people not personally known to them		Discuss the threat of loss in an abstract, diffuse manner, or in terms of fictional characters, animals, etc., or do not deal with loss

D. Task Efficiency

1	1.5	2	2.5	3	3.5	4	4.5	5
	Discuss alternatives and agree on a single ending	Discuss alternatives, but don't agree on a single ending		Several alternatives briefly attended, without a single ending		Settle on first solution offered		Make little, if any, effort to accomplish the task

E. Overall Coping Ability: Rate your impression of this family's ability to adapt to a major loss, such as the death of a nuclear family member.

1	1.5	2	2.5	3	3.5	4	4.5	5
Good coping ability				Fair coping ability				Poor coping ability

Appendix F

GOSSETT-TIMBERLAWN ADOLESCENT PSYCHOPATHOLOGY SCALE

Total Score . . . .

Patient . . . .

Date . . . .

Rater . . . .

Psychiatric Hospital Admission Form: Based on everything you know about this patient, evaluate his or her level of functioning during the most characteristic weeks or months just prior to hospital admission.

HOW WELL DO YOU KNOW THIS PATIENT?

DISCUSSION: The knowledge scale is an opportunity for you to indicate the confidence you have concerning rating the adolescent. We are not referring to the confidence of choosing alternative 16 over 14, but rather your ability to substantiate your choice based on personal observation of the adolescent. Choosing alternative 1 on this scale would mean that you could substantiate most, if not all, of your ratings based on personal observation.

. . . . 1. I know this adolescent extremely well.
. . . . 2.
. . . . 3. I know this adolescent fairly well.
. . . . 4.
. . . . 5. I do not know this adolescent well.
. . . . 6.
. . . . 7. I do not know this adolescent.

NOTE: Please do not add your responses to this scale
to total psychopathology score

I. *AUTONOMY: The person's ability to function independently versus need to be protected and/or supported by a therapist or hospital.*

. . . . 1. Productive autonomy; superior adaptation at an independent level.
. . . . 2.
. . . . 3. Normal, average, healthy level of genuine autonomy.
. . . . 4.

242

.... 5. Still within the "normal" range, but occasional or mild reliance on alcohol, tranquilizers (or other prescribed or self-medication), or other basically normal regulatory devices to maintain functioning.

.... 6.

.... 7. Need for outpatient psychotherapy (or equivalent) in order to function.

.... 8.

.... 9. Possible need for inpatient management; need a more extended period of evaluation to determine whether needs outpatient or inpatient management.

.... 10.

.... 11. Clear need for inpatient management but expect this person to have little difficulty in rapidly earning or maintaining grounds privilege status.

.... 12.

.... 13. Clear need for inpatient management and expect this person to have moderate difficulty in earning or maintaining grounds privilege status.

.... 14.

.... 15. Clear need for inpatient management and expect this person to be unable to leave a locked unit, unless accompanied, for an extended period of time.

.... 16.

.... 17. Clear need for inpatient management and expect this person to be unable to leave a locked unit for an extended period of time.

.... 18.

.... 19. Need for constant inpatient supervision and control such as special duty nursing care or physical restraint.

II. *DIAGNOSTIC SEVERITY: The degree of personality integration or disorganization in psychodiagnostic terms.*

.... 1. Superior level of personality integration and organization.

.... 2.

.... 3. Average, everyday, healthy level of personality integration and organization.

.... 4.

.... 5. While still essentially normal, slight but definite disturbance of organization; slight, but definite impairment of smooth adaptive control—"nervousness."

.... 6.

.... 7. More than everyday discomfort resulting from a substantial amount of energy being harnessed by mildly neurotic tension-reducing and compensating living devices. No characterological or psychotic symptoms noted.

.... 8.

.... 9. Clear mild neurotic symptoms, inhibitions, or mechanisms are noted, but, in addition, there is a suggestion of some possible characterological defects or disturbances.

.... 10.

.... 11. Moderate neurotic disorder *or* a clear mild characterological dis-order; behaviors may include (but are not limited to) fainting spells, phobias, psychosomatic reactions, drug abuse, suicide gestures, ritu-als, sexual deviances, generalized inadequacy, exaggerated passivity or aggressiveness, and so forth.

.... 12.

.... 13. Severe neurotic disorder, *or* moderate characterological disorder, *or* hints of mild compensated or underlying psychosis; behaviors here may be similar to #11 above, but are seen as more frequent, more constant, or more severe.

.... 14.

.... 15. Profound neurotic disorder, *or* severe character disorder, *or* clear borderline and mild to moderate overt psychotic disorder; behaviors here may include (but are not limited to) chronic repetitive violent aggression, expansive and excited syndromes, episodic violence, near total dysfunction due to extreme withdrawal, or phobic or severely passive life style, etc.

.... 16.

.... 17. Profound character disorder *or* severe overt psychosis; behaviors here may include (but are not limited to) severe addictive states, extreme states of disorganization, regression, and reality repudiation as in delirium, severe paranoid or depressed psychoses, confusion, cata-tonia, etc.

.... 18.

.... 19. Malignant anxiety and depression which, if not immediately con-trolled by external devices will eventuate in death; psychogenic death, psychotic depressive suicide; total despair, ego disintegration and exhaustion.

III. *SUBJECTIVE DISCOMFORT: The degree of distress con-sciously experienced by the individual while engaged in age-appropriate scholastic, vocational, and interpersonal situations. If a person generally avoids such situations through running away, passivity, or other avoidance style defenses (denial, re-pression, etc.), rate the degree of discomfort you judge the person would feel in age-appropriate school, work, or interper-sonal situations if the avoidance mechanisms were suddenly removed.*

.... 1. Unusual degree of serenity based on superior personality organiza-tion.

.... 2.

.... 3. Average, everyday, healthy level of experienced comfort.

.... 4.

.... 5. Vague or occasional discomfort; mild anxiety, worry, restlessness, or somatic dysfunction.

.... 6.

.... 7. Clear occasional discomfort of a mild degree; anxiety, depression, or somatization; this degree of discomfort will sometimes motivate the person to seek religious, medical, psychotherapeutic, self-medicated, or other tension-reducing aid.

.... 8.

.... 9. Clear frequent discomfort of a mild degree; anxiety, depression, somatization, loneliness, or negative feedback elicited by one's behavior; this degree of discomfort will sometimes motivate the person to seek religious, medical, psychotherapeutic, self-medicated, or other tension-reducing aid.

.... 10.

.... 11. Occasional discomfort of a moderate degree from symptoms or environmental feedback; may be some brief episodes of extreme discomfort; this degree of discomfort will usually motivate the person to seek religious, medical, psychotherapeutic, self-medicated, or other tension-reducing aid.

.... 12.

.... 13. Frequent or continuous moderate discomfort from symptoms or environmental feedback; may be some brief episodes of extreme discomfort; this degree of discomfort will usually motivate the person to seek religious, medical, psychotherapeutic, self-medicated, or other tension-reducing aid.

.... 14.

.... 15. Severe symptom discomfort; frequent intense discomfort from extreme anxiety attacks, depressions, psychophysiological symptoms or negative environmental feedback; this degree of discomfort will almost invariably motivate the person to seek religious, medical, psychotherapeutic, self-medicated, or other tension-reducing aid.

.... 16.

.... 17. Severe symptom discomfort; continuous intense discomfort from extreme anxiety attacks, depressions, psychophysiological symptoms or negative environmental feedback; this degree of discomfort will almost invariably motivate the person to seek religious, medical, psychotherapeutic, self-medicated, or other tension-reducing aid.

.... 18.

.... 19. Profound symptom discomfort; continuous and extreme discomfort as in panic, delirium, utter helpless hopelessness; person may seek some kind of tension-reducing aid or may be unable to do so.

IV. *ENVIRONMENTAL EFFECT: The manner in which the person's behavior influences those around him; rate according to how an "average man" would judge the situation.*

.... 1. Superior positive effect on family, peers, school or community through unusual productivity, leadership, or participation.

.... 2.

.... 3. Average, everyday, healthy effect on others; not remarkably constructive or destructive with family, peers, school or community.

.... 4.

.... 5. Occasional or mild inconvenience to family, peers, school or community but still within the normal range; rarely, if ever, enough of a problem to cause any authority (parents, school, law) to intervene strenuously.

.... 6.

.... 7. Clear occasional, mild discomfort to family, peers, school or community; may be one or two instances of intervention by parents or other authorities.

.... 8.

.... 9. Frequent, mild discomfort to family, peers, school or community; may be several instances of intervention by parents or other authorities.

.... 10.

.... 11. Moderate discomfort to family, peers, school or community through physical aggressiveness or destructiveness, legal violations, alcohol or drug involvement, sexual promiscuity, or unusual passivity, apathy, or withdrawal, etc.; likely to have been one or more instances of strenuous interventions by parents or other authorities.

.... 12.

.... 13. Severe discomfort or mild danger to family, peers, school or community through behaviors such as those listed in #11 above; likely to have been several instances of strenuous intervention by parents or other authorities.

.... 14.

.... 15. Moderate danger to family, peers, school or community; enough to warrant one or two legal or psychiatric incarcerations through behaviors such as those listed in #11 above, at least in part to protect society from the person's actions.

.... 16.

.... 17. Severe danger to family, peers, school or community through behaviors such as those listed in #11 above; enough to warrant several brief, or one or two lengthy legal or psychiatric incarcerations, at least in part to protect society from the person's actions.

.... 18.

.... 19. Profound danger to family, peers, school or community through accomplishment or genuine threat of actions such as homicide, rape, arson, bombing.

V. *SCHOOL PERFORMANCE: Level of academic achievement in relation to actual ability level; rate on the basis of the current semester's performance level.*

.... 1. Superior level of school performance in relationship to intelligence or ability level; performs above measured IQ or ability level; "overachiever."

.... 2.

.... 3. Average level of school performance for IQ or ability level; performs at measured IQ or ability level.

.... 4.

.... 5. Level of school performance seems somewhat below ability level, but not extreme enough to be clear underachievement.

.... 6.

.... 7. Mild underachievement in one or two courses; that is, person may have one or two courses in which he is performing one or two letter grades below his ability level.

.... 8.

.... 9. Mild underachievement in most or all courses; that is, person is functioning one or two letter grades below ability level in most or all courses.

.... 10.

.... 11. Moderate school underachievement; assuming average or above average intelligence, person is failing one or two core courses.

.... 12.

.... 13. Moderate school underachievement; assuming average or above average intelligence, person is failing three core courses.

.... 14.

.... 15. Severe school underachievement; assuming average or above average intelligence, person is failing all core courses.

.... 16.

.... 17. Severe school underachievement; assuming average or above average intelligence, person is failing all courses.

.... 18.

.... 19. Profound school underachievement; person is totally unable to function in the area of academic achievement at this time; or person is out of school at this time.

VI. INTERESTS: Breadth and depth of interests.

.... 1. Unusual range and depth of productive interests.

.... 2.

.... 3. Average breadth and depth of interests.

.... 4.

.... 5. Some slight restriction in breadth or depth of interests.

.... 6.

.... 7. Mild but clearly greater than normal restriction in breadth or depth of interests; enough restriction to be noted by parents, peers, or teachers.

.... 8.

.... 9. Mild but clearly greater than normal restriction in breadth and depth of interests; enough restriction to be noted by parents, peers, or teachers.

.... 10.

.... 11. Enough restriction in breadth or depth of interests to stimulate clear reaction by parents or teachers; interests may not only be restricted but may also tend to be in unrealistic or pathological topics more than healthy ones; for example, person may be interested in activities in the clear absence of relevant skills (grossly unattractive girl wanting to be teenage fashion model; brain-damaged boy inter-

.... 12.

.... 13. Enough restriction in breadth *and* depth of interests to stimulate clear reaction by parents or teachers; interests may not only be restricted, but may also tend to be in unrealistic or pathological topics more than healthy ones; for example, person may be interested in activities in the clear absence of relevant skills (grossly unattractive girl wanting to be teenage fashion model; brain-damaged boy interested in flying airplanes) or may focus on drugs, violence, or self-mutilation more than productive hobbies, athletics, academics, or other positive activities.

.... 14.

.... 15. No genuine interests can be noted; person seems uninterested in anything.

.... 16.

.... 17. Of the interests that can be noted, all are clearly bizarre, or severely pathological.

.... 18.

.... 19. The only interests that can be noted are lethally destructive (e.g., murder, suicide).

ested in flying airplanes) or may focus on drugs, violence, or self-mutilation more than productive hobbies, athletics, academics, or other positive activities.

VII. *INTIMACY OF RELATIONSHIPS: Qualities of interpersonal warmth, intimacy, genuineness, closeness; need to distort perceptions of significant others; stereotypy of relationship style.*

.... 1. Able to form unusually warm, intimate, undistorted and flexible relationships with a variety of persons.

.... 2.

.... 3. Average ability to relate, has several close, meaningful relationships.

.... 4.

.... 5. Slight, but definite distance from or dependency on significant others; has several close, meaningful relationships at present.

.... 6.

.... 7. Mild stereotypy in relationship style; some restriction in choices of relationship objects to persons who fit limited neurotic needs, but still has several close, meaningful and largely non-neurotic relationships.

.... 8.

.... 9. Mild stereotypy in relationship style, restriction in choices of relationship objects to persons who fit limited neurotic needs so that no more than one or two can be considered primarily non-neurotic.

.... 10.

.... 11. Noticeable lack of genuinely close, warm, intimate relationships; clear distortions in perceptions of others; moderate stereotypy in relationship style, but still has one or two somewhat non-neurotic relationships.

.... 12.

.... 13. Noticeable lack of genuinely close, warm, intimate relationships; clear distortions in perceptions of others; moderate stereotypy in relationship style, with all meaningful relationships being dominated by neurotic elements.

.... 14.

.... 15. Severe stereotypy, restrictedness, or distortion in the several relationships noted.

.... 16.

.... 17. Only one or two clear relationships can be found and these are severely distorted, stereotyped and/or pathological.

.... 18.

.... 19. The only relationship that can be noted is profoundly pathological; or the person appears to have no meaningful relationships of any kind at this time.

VIII. *MATURITY OF OBJECT RELATIONSHIPS: The direction and nature of the person's most meaningful relationship ties.*

.... 1. Primary relationships are with relatively healthy peers and are quite lasting and stable.

.... 2.

.... 3. Primary relationships are with peers of variable psychological health and are of variable duration and stability.

.... 4.

.... 5. Primary relationships are with peers of variable psychological health and tend to be relatively brief or stormy.

.... 6.

.... 7. Primary relationships seem more or less evenly split between peers and parents (or parent surrogates).

.... 8.

.... 9. Primary relationships are with parents (or parent surrogates); the relationships may contain elements of unrealistic idealization.

.... 10.

.... 11. Primary relationships are with parents (or parent surrogates); the relationships may contain distorted elements of hostility and rebelliousness.

.... 12.

.... 13. Extreme tenuousness or apparent absence of significant relationships with peers, parents, or parent surrogates; may relate to animals or inanimate obects; may be shy, lonely, withdrawn or isolated and may, in addition, be grandiose, narcissistic and fragile.

.... 14.

.... 15. Clear absence of significant relationships to people, animals, or inanimate objects; is shy, lonely, withdrawn, or isolated and, in addition, is grandiose, narcissistic and fragile.

.... 16.

.... 17. Any relationships noted are clearly regressed and psychotic, and characterized by primitive identification and ego diffusion; interpersonal affect noted is likely to be extremely aggressive and/or clinging.

.... 18.

.... 19. Any relationships noted are clearly regressed and psychotic, and characterized by primitive identification and ego diffusion; interpersonal affect noted (if any) is likely to be silly, infantile, incoherent.

IX. *INSIGHT: The degree to which the person's perception of his disturbances corresponds to realistic assessment made by others; acceptance of inner responsibility; rate on the basis of the person's full conscious awareness, whether or not he will verbally acknowledge his awareness to you.*

.... 1. The person has an unusually deep level of functional understanding of the connections between his past experiences, current feelings, and on-going behaviors, and typically accepts full personal responsibility for his behaviors.

.... 2.

.... 3. The person has an average, healthy level of functional understanding of the connections between his past experiences, current feelings, and on-going behaviors, and typically accepts full responsibility for his behaviors.

.... 4.

.... 5. The person has a slightly below average but still basically healthy level of functional understanding of the connections between his past experiences, current feelings, and on-going behaviors, and usually accepts full responsibility for his behaviors.

.... 6.

.... 7. Many (but not all) significant areas of disturbance are recognized, and the person is usually aware of crucial connections between the past experiences, current feelings and behaviors; inner responsibility for behavior is usually accepted and insights are often used to modify behaviors.

.... 8.

.... 9. Many (but not all) significant areas of disturbance are recognized, and the person is usually aware of at least some connections between past experiences, current feelings and behaviors; inner responsibility for behavior is usually accepted and insights are often used to modify behaviors.

.... 10.

.... 11. Some significant areas of disturbance are recognized, and the person is sometimes aware of the crucial connections between past experiences, current feelings and behaviors; inner responsibility for behavior is sometimes accepted and insights are sometimes used to modify behaviors.

.... 12.

.... 13. Some significant areas of disturbance are recognized and the person is sometimes aware of at least some connections between past experiences, current feelings and behaviors; inner responsibility for behavior is sometimes accepted and insights are sometimes used to modify behaviors.

.... 14.

.... 15. Few significant areas of disturbance are recognized, and the person rarely is aware of the crucial connections between past experiences, current feelings and behaviors; inner responsibility rarely is accepted; instead, there is a heavy reliance on rationalization or minimization; insights rarely are used to modify behaviors.

.... 16.

.... 17. Few (if any) significant areas of disturbance are recognized; and the person is rarely (if ever) aware of any connections between past experiences, current feelings and behaviors; inner responsibility is rarely accepted; instead, there is heavy reliance on projection of blame; insights are rarely used to modify behaviors.

.... 18.

.... 19. No significant areas of disturbance are recognized and the person never seems aware of any connections between past experience, current feelings and behaviors; there is no acceptance of inner responsibility, with blanket denial and gross distortion the primary means of avoiding responsibility.

X. MOTIVATION: The amount of goal-directed energy the person can expend toward realistic self-exploration and productive personality change.

.... 1. Unusually strongly motivated toward personally and socially productive goals, and very effective in combining realistic goal selection, self-analysis, and consistent high energy output, and persistent productive response to frustration.

.... 2.

.... 3. Strongly motivated toward personally and socially productive goals and very effective in combining realistic goal selection, self-analysis, consistent high energy output and persistent productive response to frustration.

.... 4.

.... 5. Slightly below average but still basically healthy amount of motivation toward personally and socially productive goals, and usually effective in combining realistic goal selection, self-analysis, consistent high energy output and persistent productive response to frustration.

.... 6.

.... 7. Clear occasional, mild impairment in motivation; may be due to passivity, inability to persevere when frustrated, unwillingness to endure discomfort, inability to risk exposure with therapist and others, or overly restricted goals such as superficial symptom relief, magical "cure," or change in persons other than self.

.... 8.

.... 9. Clear continuous, mild impairment; may be for reasons similar to those in #7 above.

.... 10.

.... 11. Continuous mild impairment in motivation with occasional periods of moderate impairment; may be for reasons similar to those in #7 above, but with heavier stress on desire for superficial (or effortless) symptom relief, magical "cures," or changes in persons other than self.

.... 12.

.... 13. Continuous moderate impairment in motivation, reasons similar to those in #7 above, but with heavier stress on desire for superficial (and effortless) symptom relief, magical "cures," or changes in persons other than self.

.... 14.

.... 15. Occasional severe impairment in motivation with chronic mild to moderate impairment; some desire for personal change, but only if it does not involve any appreciable energy, frustration, anxiety, depression or risk; tends to persistently demand magic "cures," or change by others rather than self.

.... 16.

.... 17. Continuous severe impairment in motivation; may refuse to participate in any treatment in absence of magical changes in others; may perceive treatment as a means of coercing significant people to change their "noxious" manner of dealing with him (or her).

.... 18.

.... 19. No apparent motivation to change anything concerning self, significant others, or the environment; person may or may not suffer, have secondary gain, or possess insight, but in any case, person cannot or will not expend any energy in involvement in treatment at any level.

Appendix G

PROTOCOL FOR INDIVIDUAL INTERVIEWS

1. *Vocational Activities:* "Describe the type of work you do"; interrupting this description from time to time, determine the individual's specific job activities, how long he/she had been in this type of work, why he had chosen it, his degree of success, the amount of supervision he received, the number of people and type of supervision he directed, and his level of satisfaction and/or dissatisfaction with various aspects of his work. For the woman the questions are somewhat different, but focus on exactly what she does and how she feels about it. For those who have activities outside the home, ask that they be discussed in the same terms.

2. *Leisure:* Attempt to determine what each individual does during non-working hours, individually, as a couple, and as a family. Explore each adult's social relationships to peers.

3. *Marital Relationship:* "Out of all the people in the world, how did you happen to choose your wife (husband)?" Encourage each to discuss in detail his/her perception of the strengths and weaknesses of the marital relationship. Specifically, obtain the frequency of sexual intercourse, and feelings of satisfaction or dissatisfaction with this aspect of the marriage. Ask if there have been any extramarital sexual relationships, and explore the context.

4. *Perception of Children:* Although information obtained previously may provide leads, consider each child from the oldest to the youngest with "Tell me about Jane." Determine the parent's affective involvement with the child, expectations of the child, disciplinary practices, and any problems encountered in rearing each youngster.

5. *Self-Description:* Ask each husband and wife to state what kind of person he/she is, determining self-perceived assets and liabilities, and direct questions toward ascertaining character forma-

tion and psychiatric symptoms (hysterical or obsessional traits, anxiety, depression, conflicts, phobias, self-esteem). Inquire specifically about use of tobacco, alcohol, and medications in terms of frequency of use and reasons. Ask each adult if he has ever talked to a psychiatrist, psychologist, social worker, marital counselor or other mental health professional. If so, determine the context of the discussions.

6. *Style in Interview:* Immediately following each interview, dictate observations about the individual's style in terms of degree of comfort or anxiety, openness, clarity, and any other characteristics noted.

FOR CHILDREN:

1. *School Activities:* Determine academic function in terms of grades and other achievements. Explore school-related athletic activities, extracurricular activities, and feelings about school. Also, particularly with older adolescents, ask academic and vocational plans for the future.

2. *Leisure:* Ask each child to describe out-of-school activities and determine how much time is spent with peers and how much time at home, the degree to which leisure pursuits involve other youngsters, or are family-centered activities. Determine not only the "facts," but also the feelings about these activities.

3. *Sibling and Peer Relationships:* Ask each child to describe other children in the family and clarify the relationship to and feelings about each. Ask about friendships; what is liked about each friend, what kinds of things they do together, and how the child feels about this area.

4. *Perception of Parents:* Ask each child to describe Mother and Father in as much detail as possible, and determine closeness to his parents, and disciplinary practices. Ask how the child sees himself/herself as similar to or different from each parent.

5. *Self-Description:* Ask each child to describe himself/herself as fully as possible, trying to elicit information concerning self-esteem, anxiety, depression, phobias, strengths, and character-trait formation.

6. *Style in the Interview:* Immediately following the interview, dictate observations about the child's style in the interview.

Appendix H

FAMILY MEDICAL HISTORY

We are interested in the past medical history of the family. As such, we need to obtain as much information as possible in order to develop an estimate of family medical health. For these purposes, date the onset of the family medical history to the parental marriage.

1. *Serious Illness*—Has any member of the family experienced a serious (life-threatening) illness? If so, please give details.

2. *Hospitalization*—Please list all hospitalizations for each member of the family. (Exclude childbirth.) We are interested in the cause of hospitalization, month and year in which it occurred, and approximate length of hospitalization.

3. *Serious Accidents*—Has any member of the family experienced a serious accident? If so, please give details.

4. Have there been any *miscarriages, stillbirths or neonatal deaths?* If so, please give approximate date and brief description of the circumstances.

5. *Presence of Medical Conditions*—We are interested in all chronic medical conditions which either require medical supervision or medication, or interfere with family members' productivity or efficiency. Please include the full spectrum of conditions from those more serious ailments like heart disease or peptic ulcer to those less serious like sinusitis or indigestion for each family member.

Father—

Mother—

Child 1—

Child 2—

Child 3—

Child 4—

6. *Interference with Usual Pursuits*—We are interested in your estimate of the number of days each member of the family was unable to work, go to school, or tend to usual responsibilities because of illness or accidents *during the past year*. Please check the number of days which most closely describes the total time lost for each family member.

	None	Less than 5 days	5-10 days	More than 10 days
Father	....	....	....	....
Mother	....	....	....	....
Child 1	....	....	....	....
Child 2	....	....	....	....
Child 3	....	....	....	....
Child 4	....	....	....	....

7. *Nature of Health Care*—Here we are interested in a number of issues. Please check the box which most closely describes your family.

	True	False
a. We have a family doctor.	....	....
b. We have periodic checkups.	....	....
c. We consult physicians only when ill.	....	....
d. We have a pediatrician.	....	....
e. We are exacting about inoculations, boosters, etc.	....	....
f. We have periodic dental examinations.	....	....

8. *Medications*—Here we are interested in the medicine each family member takes. These would run the range from aspirin to antacids to tranquilizers to digitalis. Please record all medication use *during the past month* for each family member.

	Medication	Symptoms	Frequency
Father	. . . .	. . . .	. . . .
Mother	. . . .	. . . .	. . . .
Child 1	. . . .	. . . .	. . . .
Child 2	. . . .	. . . .	. . . .
Child 3	. . . .	. . . .	. . . .
Child 4	. . . .	. . . .	. . . .

9. *Estimate of Family Health*—Please check the statement which most closely describes each family member's general health status.

	Unusually Healthy	Average Health	Slightly Unhealthy	Distinctly Unhealthy
Father	. . . . . .	. . . . . .	. . . . . .	. . . . . .
Mother	. . . . . .	. . . . . .	. . . . . .	. . . . . .
Child 1	. . . . . .	. . . . . .	. . . . . .	. . . . . .
Child 2	. . . . . .	. . . . . .	. . . . . .	. . . . . .
Child 3	. . . . . .	. . . . . .	. . . . . .	. . . . . .
Child 4	. . . . . .	. . . . . .	. . . . . .	. . . . . .

10. *Response to Illness*—Some individuals respond to medical illness with a type of refusal to "give in" to the symptoms while others do not respond in that manner. Please indicate by number your estimate of each family member's typical response to an illness.

1. Tends to deny illness and pushes on.

2. Reacts with appropriate responses of bed rest, medicine, etc.

3. Is somewhat quick to call the doctor, go to bed, etc.

4. Obviously capitalizes on symptoms with exaggerated responses.

Father...... •Mother......

Child 1...... Child 2...... Child 3...... Child 4......

11. *Family's Recent Emotional Losses*—We are interested in an estimate of the important or significant losses experienced by the family *during the past two years*. Here include family members, friends, and relatives who have died, moved away, or in some way become alienated from the family during that two year period. For each loss, we would like the family's estimate of who in the family experienced the loss most intensely or "took it the hardest." (Use back of page if necessary.)

Appendix I

FAMILY HEALTH LOG

It is necessary to record the following items:

1. *The member of the family developing the symptom or symptoms.*

2. *A description of the symptoms or illness.*

3. *The degree of disability associated with the illness.* Here we are interested in the concept of interference in normal functioning. This may range from slight interference in efficiency to staying home from work or school to staying in bed to actual hospitalization.

4. *The duration of the symptoms.* Although "beginnings" and "ends" of symptoms or illnesses often are not felt with precision, we need the recorder's evaluation of the length of a "sick" period —even though the degree of disability may change from day to day.

5. *What was done about the symptoms.* Here information regarding specific medicines taken (prescription or non-prescription), whether or not a physician or other health care person was consulted, and other treatment efforts should be recorded.

6. *The presence or absence of unusual circumstances before or during the illness.* Some illnesses develop in the context of unusual worry, stress or strain, and sometimes accompany happy or exciting events. We need to have recorded brief notes regarding such if they exist for a given episode of illness.

The following examples may be helpful:

MONTH   March   FAMILY   John Doe

---

(1)
— Sunday

Everyone well.

---

(2)
— Monday

Everyone well.

---

(3)
— Tuesday

Father—migraine headache; algoson and phena-phen taken; doctor not called; stayed home from work (one day).

Unusual circumstances: Father received official notification of promotion yesterday.
